FLOWERS
AT HOME

FLOWERS AT HOME

Sandra Kaminski
Photography by Geoff Hedley

CONTENTS

FOREWORD BY TRELISE COOPER
14

INTRODUCTION
16

SPRING
20

SUMMER
112

AUTUMN
142

WINTER
196

HOLIDAYS
262

CARING FOR FRESH CUT FLOWERS
330

NEW ZEALAND FLOWER GROWERS
332

SUPPLIERS
334

ACKNOWLEDGEMENTS
335

To my mother, who taught me that dreams are important, and to Andrew, for adding the sparkle and making them come true.

FOREWORD

Sandra Kaminski is a stylist with an 'eye'. She expresses her love of flowers in a passionate and imaginative way through this most gorgeous and inspiring book, taking us through the seasons and occasions that are important in our lives.

In *Flowers at Home*, her very refreshing take combines infectious enthusiasm, the diversity of colours that nature happily puts together and even a harmonising energy to create an overall style or mood that celebrates life – from small everyday pleasures to familiar rites of passage. We can be inspired through her stylish yet uncomplicated designs and replicate them in our own homes.

My work as a designer has been hugely influenced and inspired by my passionate and almost evangelical love of flowers. I love flowers! The partnership that exists between my 'muse' (ie, the flower) and my unconscious creativity plays a vital role in all of my collections and designs, be they garments, fabrics, fragrance, interiors or homewares. It began as a small child when my father planted a garden for me and filled it with freesias, boronia and daphne. He then went on to grow roses – but only the perfumed varieties. My darling father never visited me without a bouquet of freshly cut flowers from his garden. My husband Jack now makes sure I always have flowers at my bedside. Their gentle beauty and fragrance as I'm falling asleep and waking up is love, grown and expressed every day.

Sandra's spectacular book feeds that inspiration in dynamic, creative and beautiful ways, and will be a classic in my reference collections.

I can't wait to recreate her ideas in my home and when I next entertain.

Trelise Cooper

INTRODUCTION

This book has come about through my love of flowers. I find it amazing how they can change the energy in any room and I love the way a floral offering – whether a sumptuous bouquet or a modest posy – can lift the spirits of those lucky enough to receive such a gift. It's my belief that flowers can bring joy through the simple act of just gazing at them and because so many of us live such busy city-based lifestyles, it's too easy to overlook the serenity and fragrance that a thoughtful arrangement can bring to a home or workspace.

It feels like a lifetime ago since my love affair with flowers began. One of my earliest memories of this grand passion of mine is of picking flowers for my mother out of other people's gardens on the way home from school. While she always expressed great delight with my offerings, it was clear to me even then that she hoped no one had seen me.

In our own garden, especially in early spring when so much was in bloom, I could often be found out there with my nose in everything. I loved creating tiny posies to bring inside, particularly any that included my father's beloved freesias – I would ask myself time and time again how it was possible for anything to smell so good. Another favourite was the viburnum, or snowball tree, which would only flower for a very short time but for that period the petals scattered over the lawn looked to my child's eyes just like snow.

Mum's roses also attracted my attention. The sheer enormity of them along with their fragrance made them uncrowned royalty for my family. Because I loved them so much and wanted to bring their magnificence indoors to enjoy I learned at a very early age how to cut them correctly.

Then there were the magically scented sweet peas, which I looked after along with my sister Lucinda. Each evening we would take turns to cut them to ensure their constant flowering. The volcanic soil in our garden resulted in my growing the skyscraping sunflowers – the biggest I have ever seen to this day with flower heads the size of charger plates. And when we cut them down the

ground literally shook with their weight! But I wasn't finished with them yet; the next stage involved drying them in my father's shed, carpeting the floor with all the seeds that later on my pet budgie, Tweety, got to eat. Not surprisingly perhaps, he was the biggest budgie I have ever seen . . . but that's another story.

The rest of my childhood memories are also connected to the family garden and members of my family still laugh when they recall my reaction to my first boyfriend's Christmas gift. When he presented me with a bracelet and then gave my mother a bunch of long-stemmed red roses I couldn't help myself. Why hadn't he given me those stunning beauties? Many years later he told me he'd wanted so much to make a good impression on my mother and I guess he achieved this. But I would have happily swapped the bracelet for those roses in a heartbeat.

Over the years many glorious flowers have arrived at my door to mark a variety of occasions, some celebratory, some otherwise, but the most memorable was the huge bunch of pale pink peonies that my father showed up with one day. These flowers make me go weak at the knees and my love for them has only grown stronger over the years.

Although I was lucky enough to grow up surrounded by flowers, I'm well aware that in this day and age few people have the time – or the space – to cultivate a large garden. However, we're fortunate that here in New Zealand there is a huge variety of beautiful fresh cut flowers and foliage available at any time of the year from our local florists and flower sellers.

Please note that templates for the labels, gift tags and related personalised stationery that appear throughout this book can be downloaded at www.sandrakaminski.com

SPRING

I must have flowers, always,
and always.

Claude Monet

When it comes to flowers, spring could well be described as a frenzy of growing activity in the natural world; it's a time when flowers are at their most prolific. And in terms of colour, variety and scent this season is probably the most rewarding of them all. It's as if the world has suddenly woken up and decided to celebrate the end of the cold weather with as much colour, variety, texture and fragrance as possible.

Little wonder, then, that so many people choose this time of year to get married or mark a particular occasion in a special way. Whether it's a wedding, an anniversary, a house-warming or perhaps a birthday, flowers are a stunning way to enhance an occasion.

However, you don't need to wait for a special occasion to enjoy spring offerings such as these St Patricks roses and white freesias seen here on the right.

For me, making up a floral arrangement is always about the flowers themselves. It's about simplifying the colours used so you can see what you're looking at, rather than trying to show off a whole host of different flowers in varying colours.

If you do choose to show off more than one variety, then perhaps pick a unifying colour and arrange the blooms by variety in a number of different vases so that each can be recognised and admired for its unique properties.

Select vases or vessels that will show off the flowers. These don't have to be expensive items; so many of the containers that I use on a regular basis can be found around the home – everything from jam jars through to take-away food containers and even cans.

While your own garden may not yield very much in the way of sophisticated blooms, don't overlook flowering herbs such as the chive flowers seen on the left that provide such an attractive contrast against the cool green of the table linen. Against the same colour palette, these sweet peas and simple cosmos (right) need little if no embellishment.

Spring 27

Mix snowball viburnum, white freesias, Fresh Moment roses and pale yellow stock to create a fresh and fragrant table setting.

The vibrant hued violas topping the cupcakes on the left look especially effective as does the simple arrangements of pink stock, freesias and roses (below) and the spray rosebuds adorning the wine glasses.

This combination of Gold Strike roses and green snowball viburnum looks stunning (above), while the same yellow roses paired with small jars of striped parrot tulips look equally effective in this plain metal tiered stand.

Pink is the perfect colour for any festive occasion and spring is celebrated in an endless number of glorious shades of pink. The fabulous blooms used in the different table settings over the next few pages are a combination of commercially grown roses together with a few picked from my garden. The opened roses are complemented by the perfect pink peonies I've added for texture and softness.

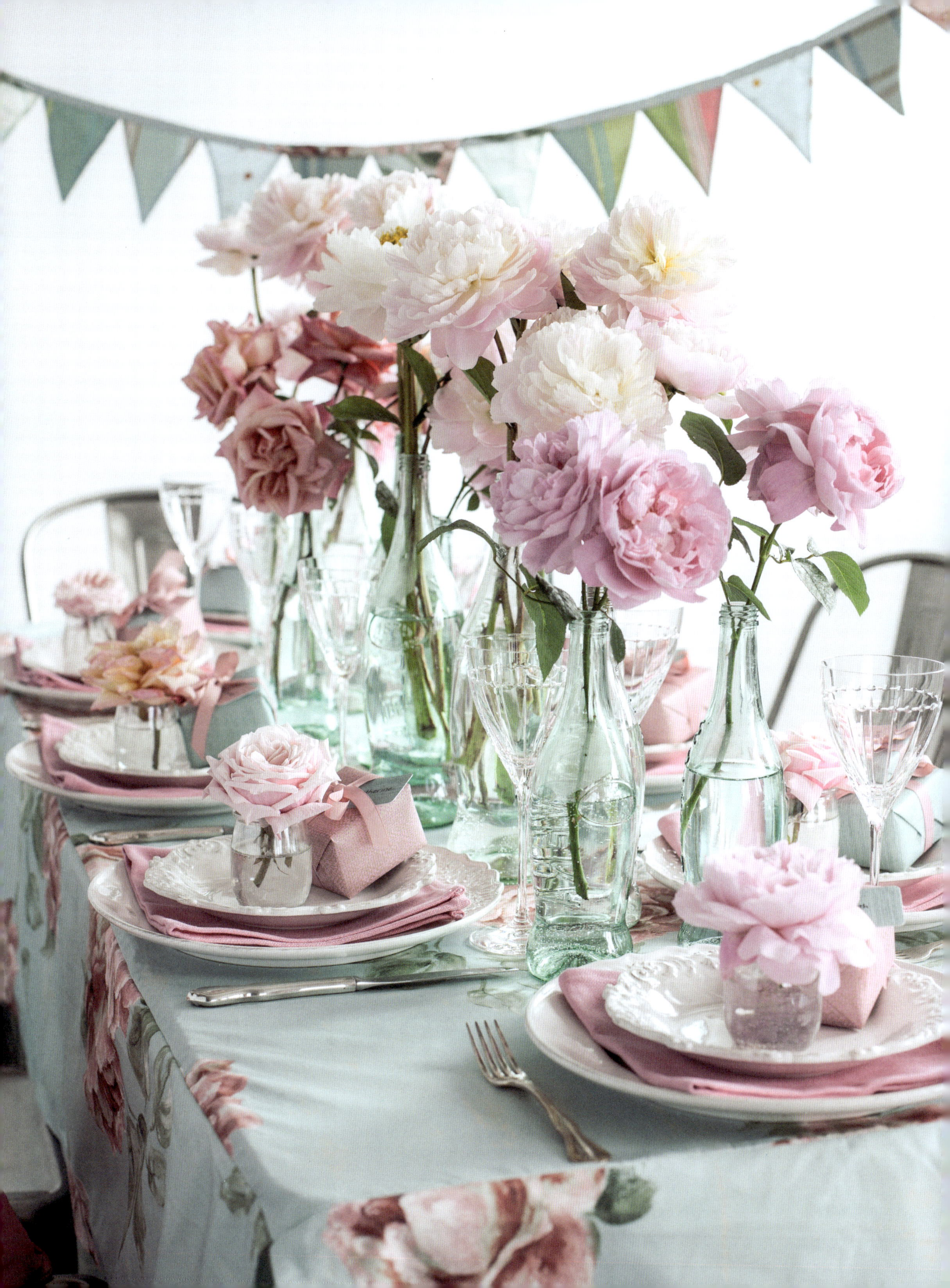

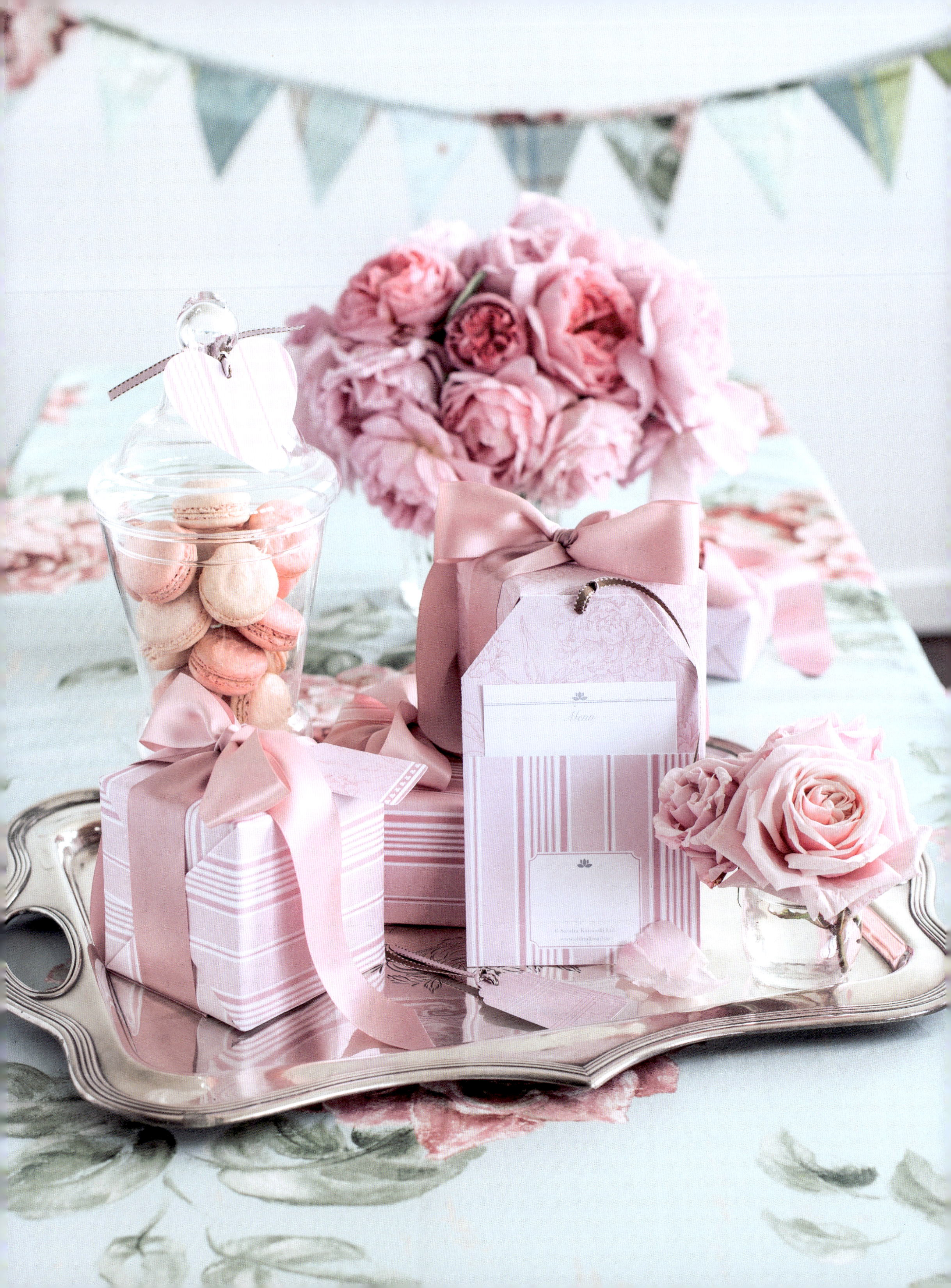
Menu

Life is the flower for which love is the honey.

Victor Hugo

Spring

Rachael

Whenever a special event takes place, chances are that roses will feature somewhere in there. It's not surprising given the glorious choices available – both modern and old-fashioned – as seen here. The close-up image on the right is of a peony.

Spring

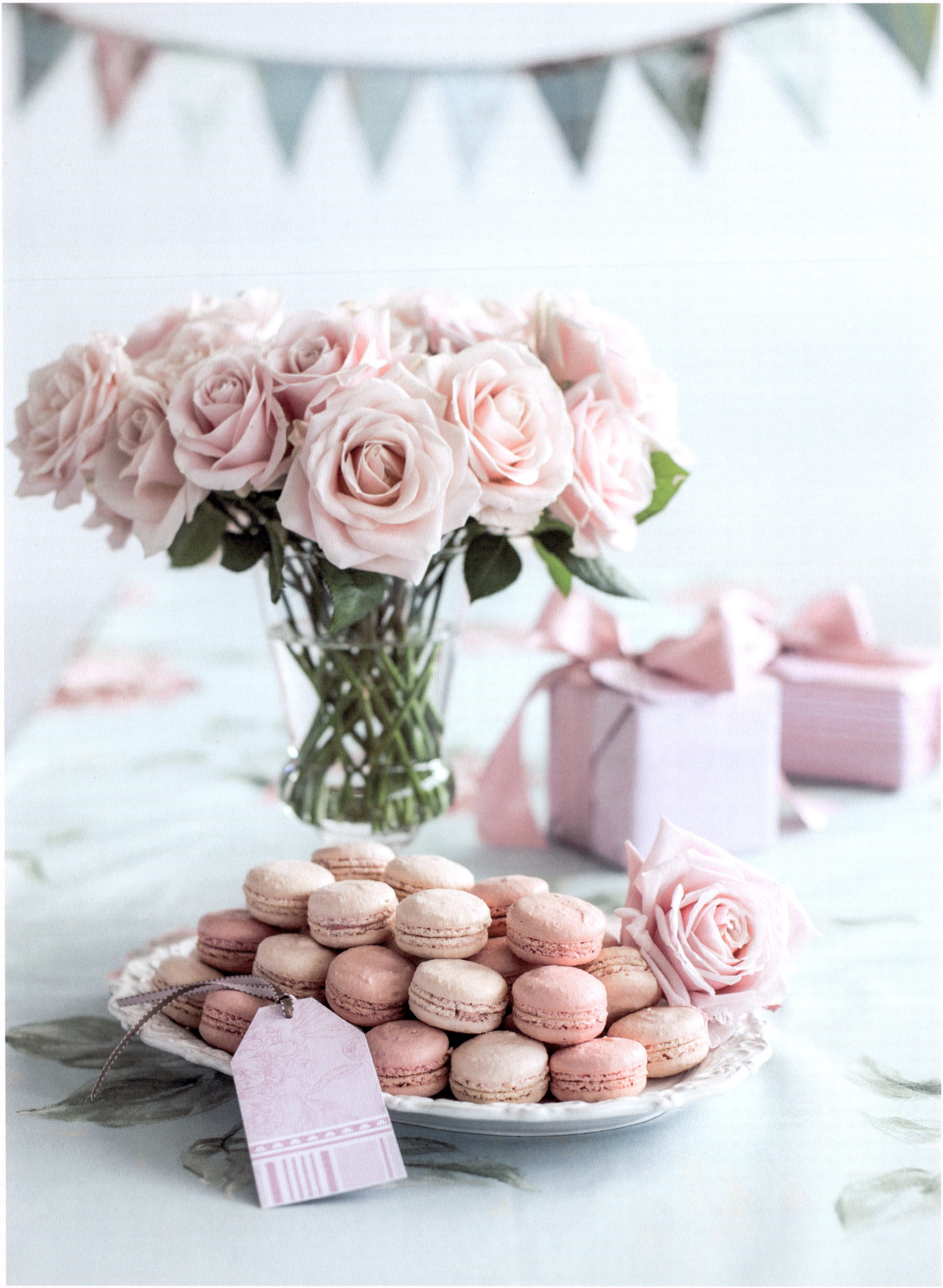

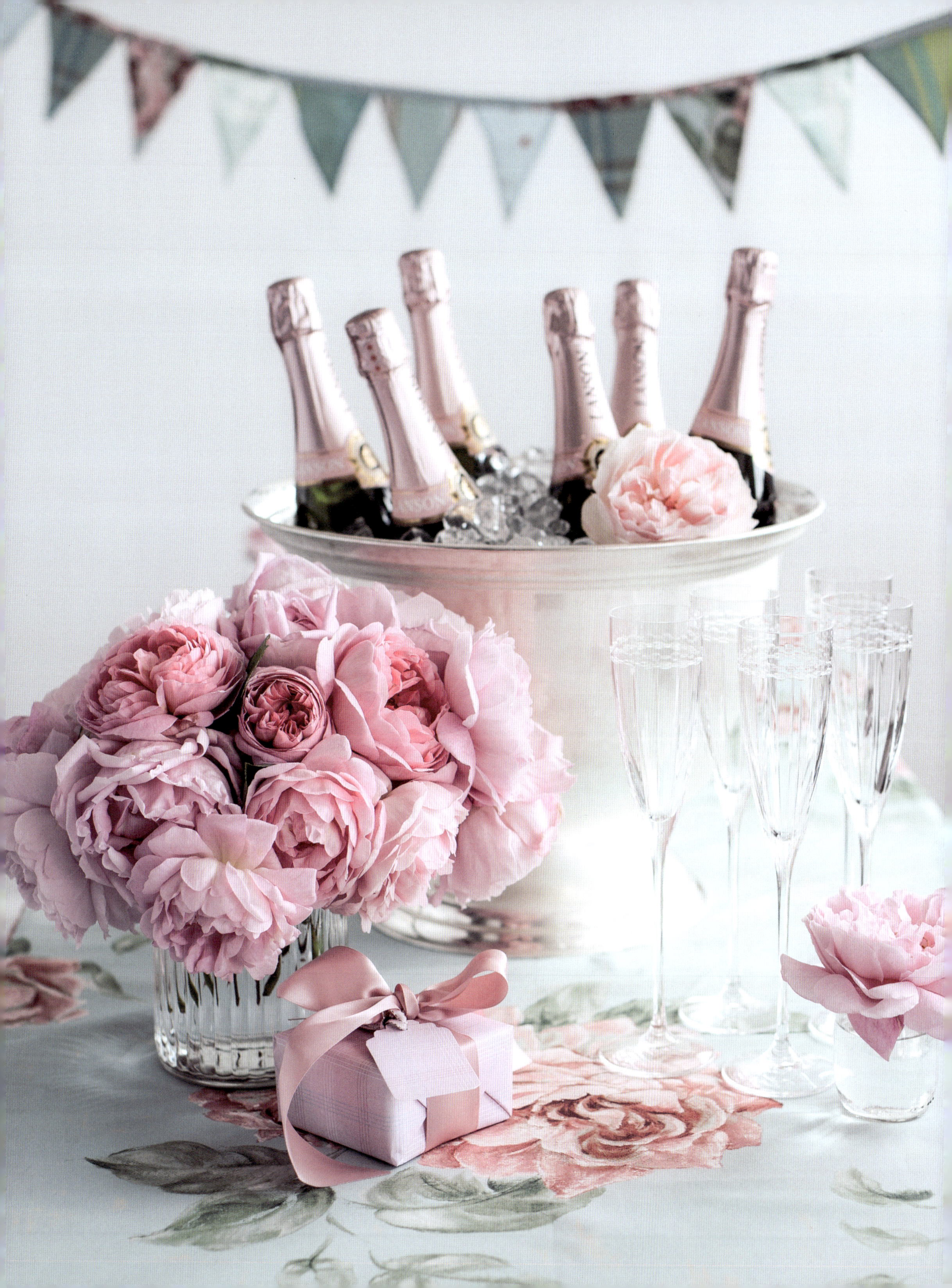

Blue and white make for a particularly restful and, on occasion, sophisticated combination, whether for the table, a guest bedroom or any place where you want to add an element of tranquillity. That effect is achieved with white Avalanche roses simply arranged in small blue-tinted glass bottles (top left) and again with the same roses, freesias and lilac shown off to perfection (below and right) against cool blue and white table linen.

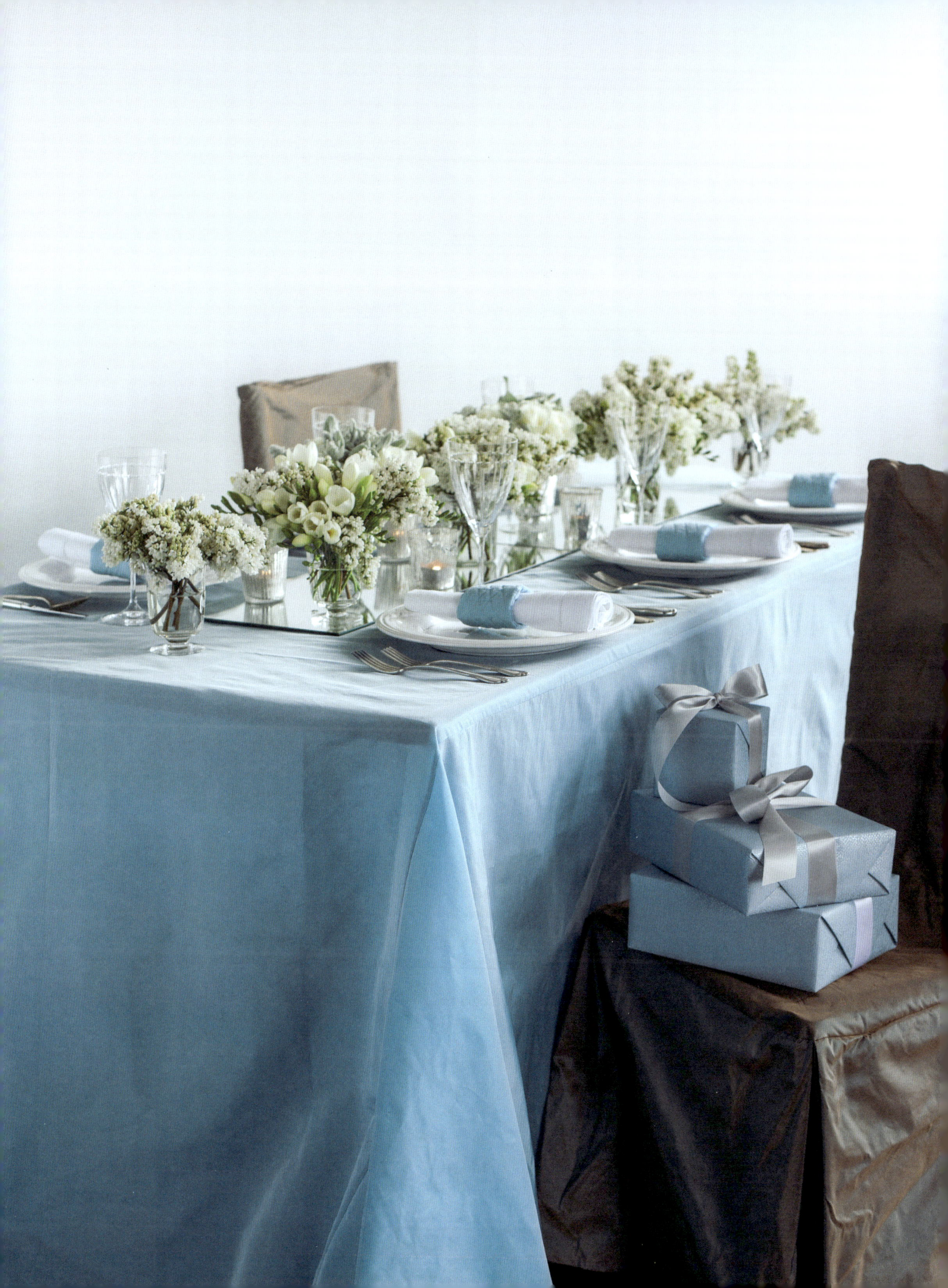

Delicate bone china provides a pretty yet dainty setting for a cluster of creamy white Vendella roses.

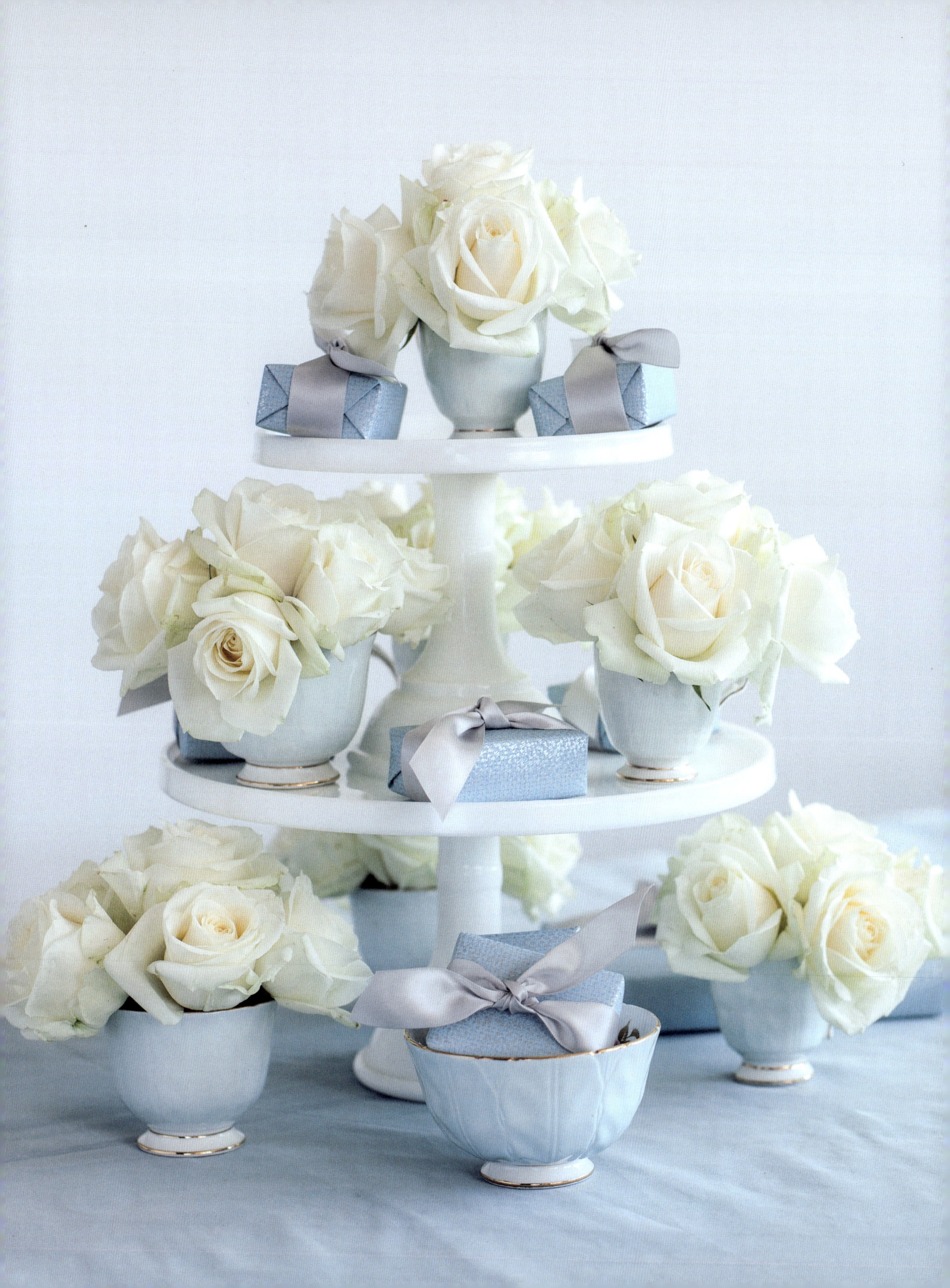

Just living is not enough. One must have sunshine, freedom and a little flower.

Hans Christian Andersen

It's almost impossible to improve on nature's work, which is why it's so important to make the flowers themselves the heroes as illustrated by these bunches of lilac set off in a collection of glass bottles. The bottles themselves don't have to be antique pieces nor do they all need to match; what does matter, however, is that they're sparkling clean inside and out.

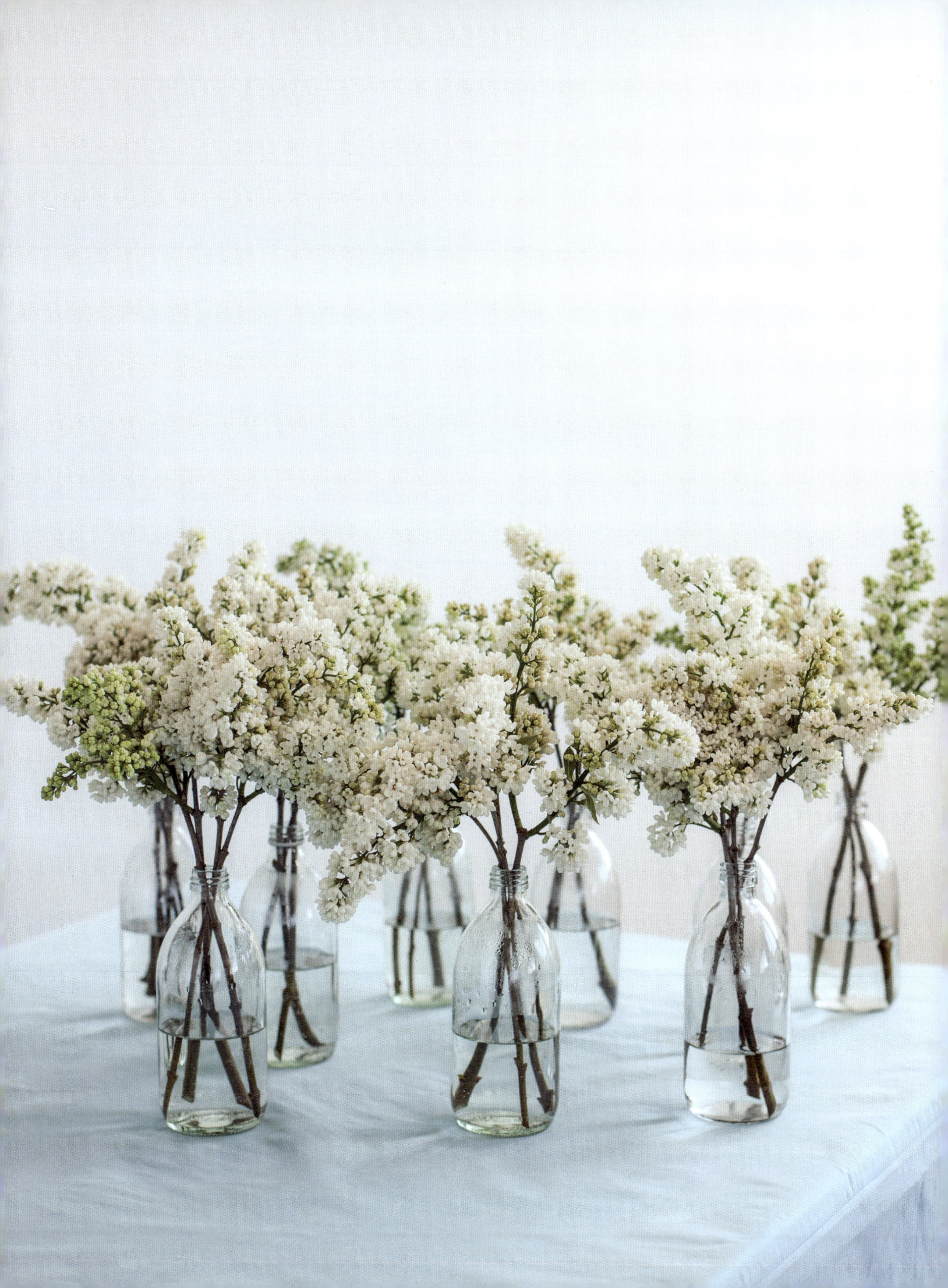

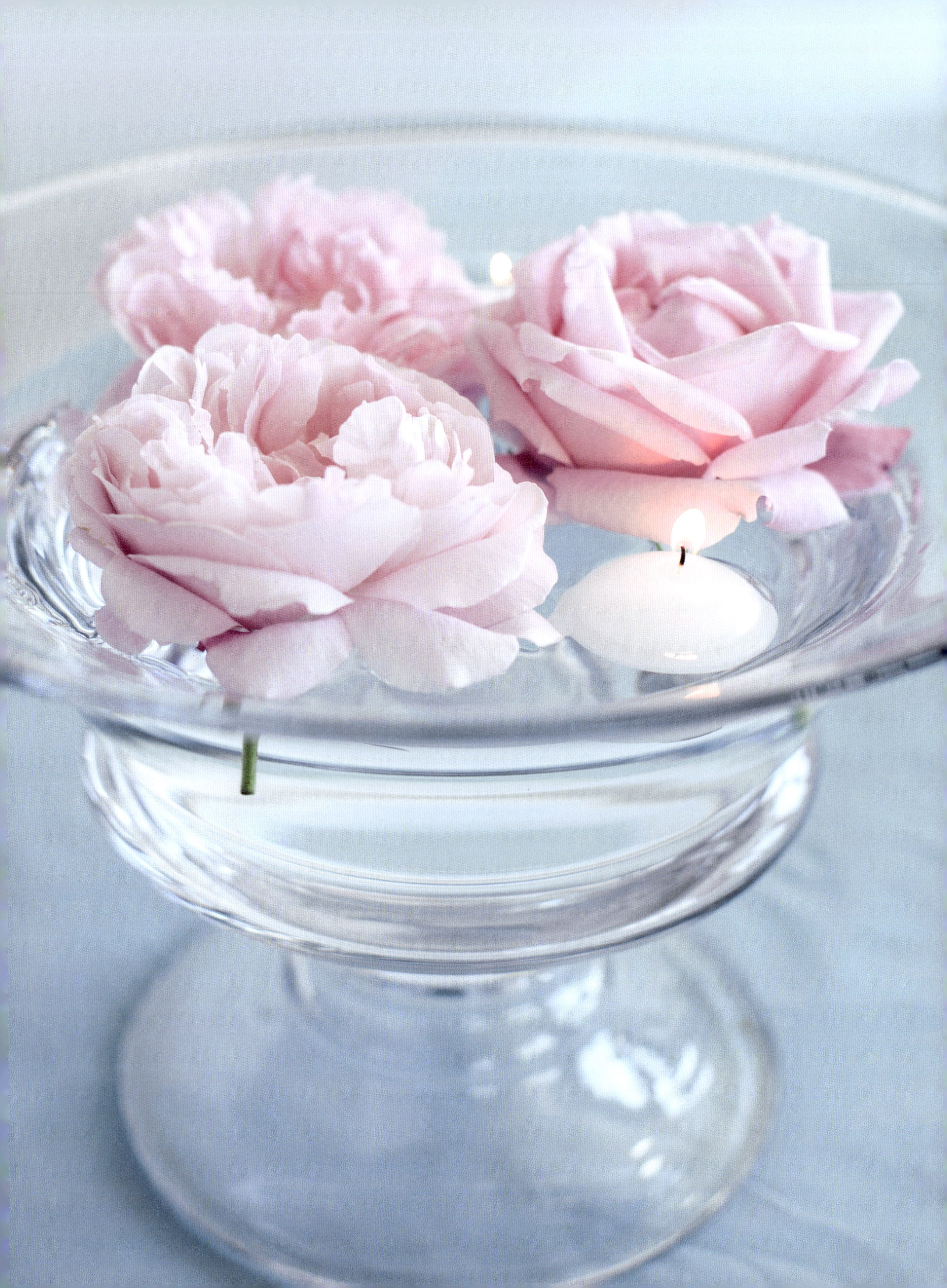

These next pages show off the pink perfection of garden roses and how they, too, have no need of elaborate vases or other vessels to show them off at their best. Pink is really the only colour when it comes to celebrating any event associated with love.

Spring

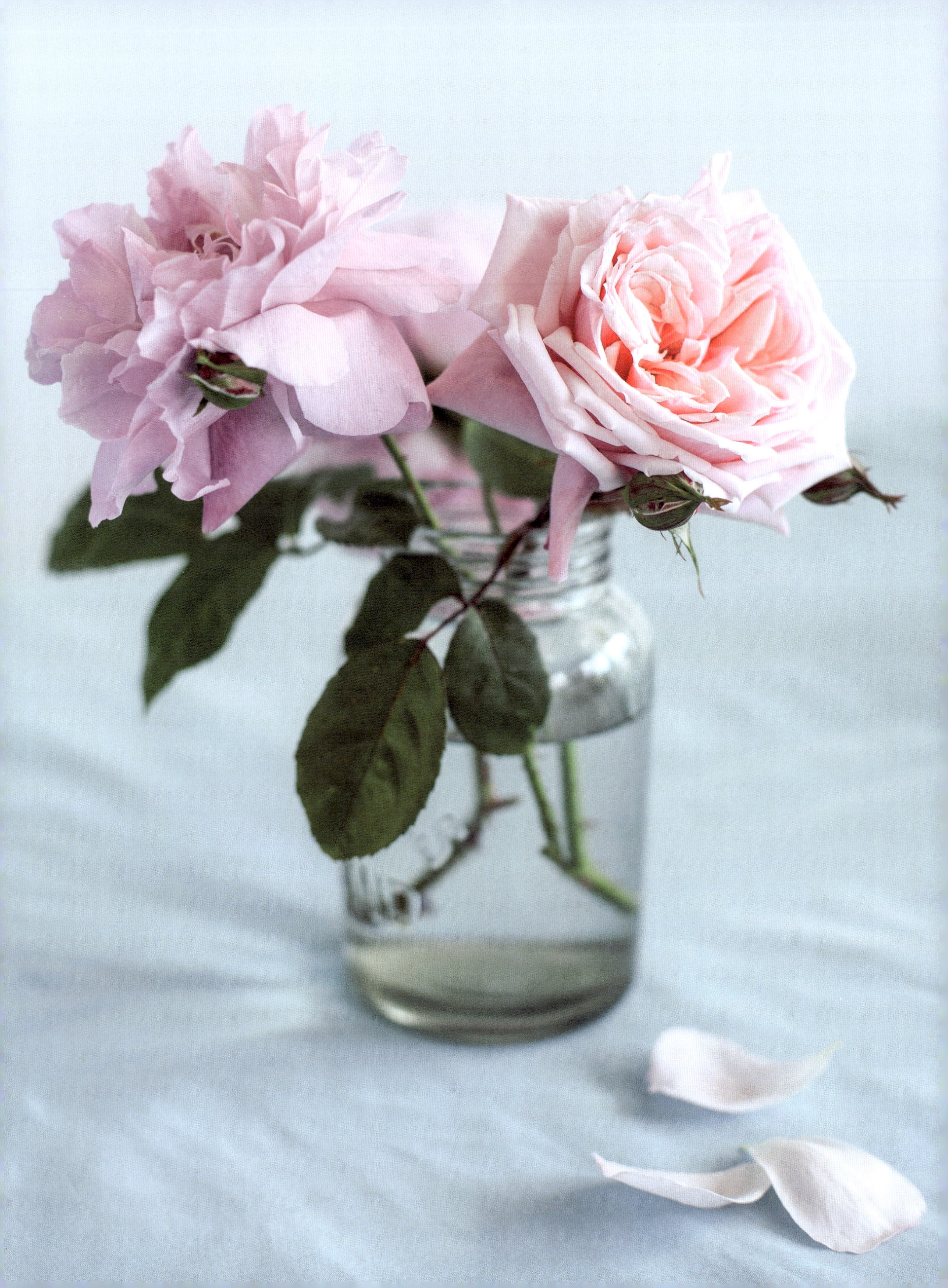

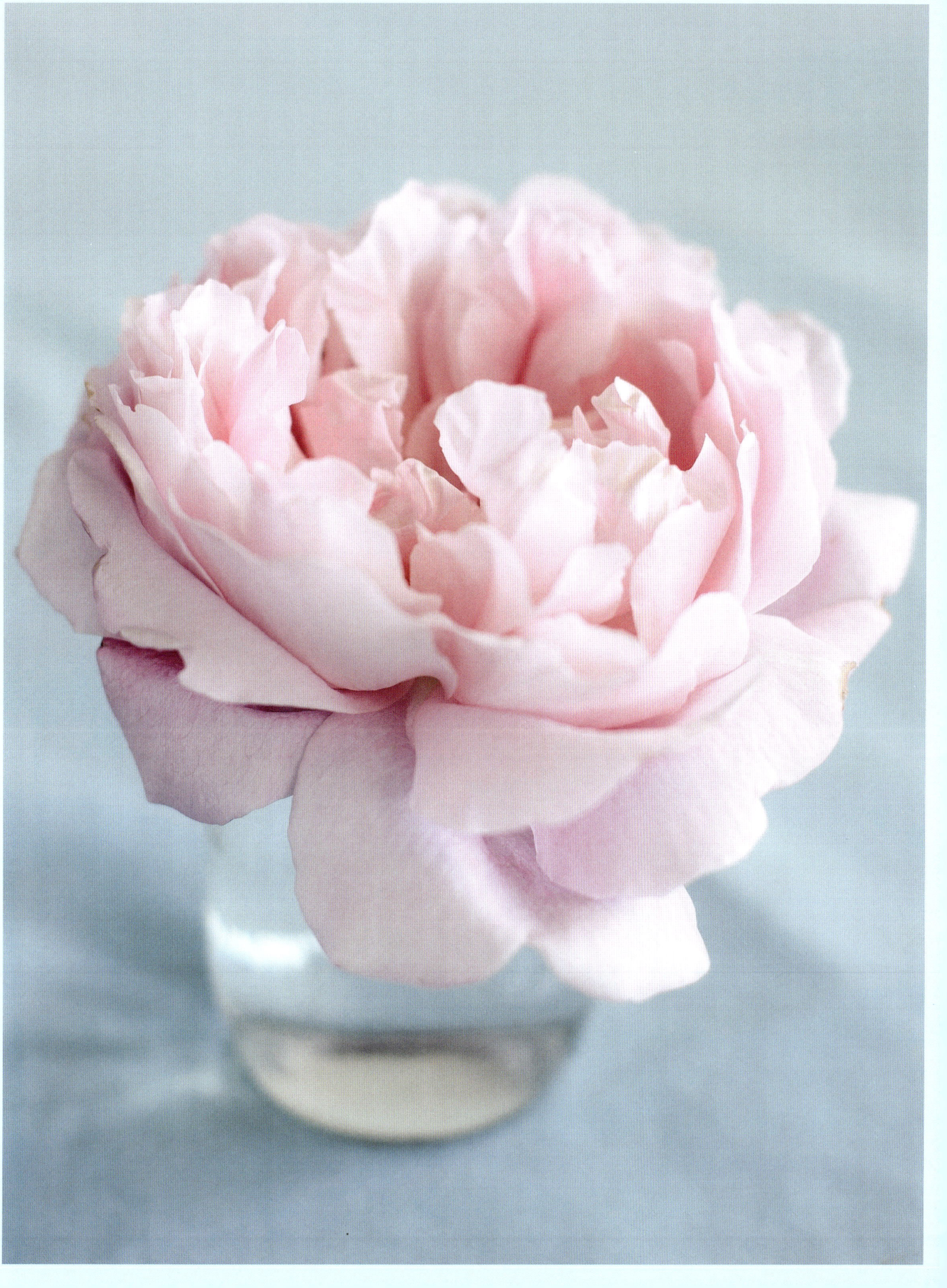

The arrival of peonies in late spring is truly an occasion to rejoice, not least because of the way those tightly furled flowers gradually relax to reveal a complex layering of petals that eventually opens out to form what can only be described as sheer floral opulence.

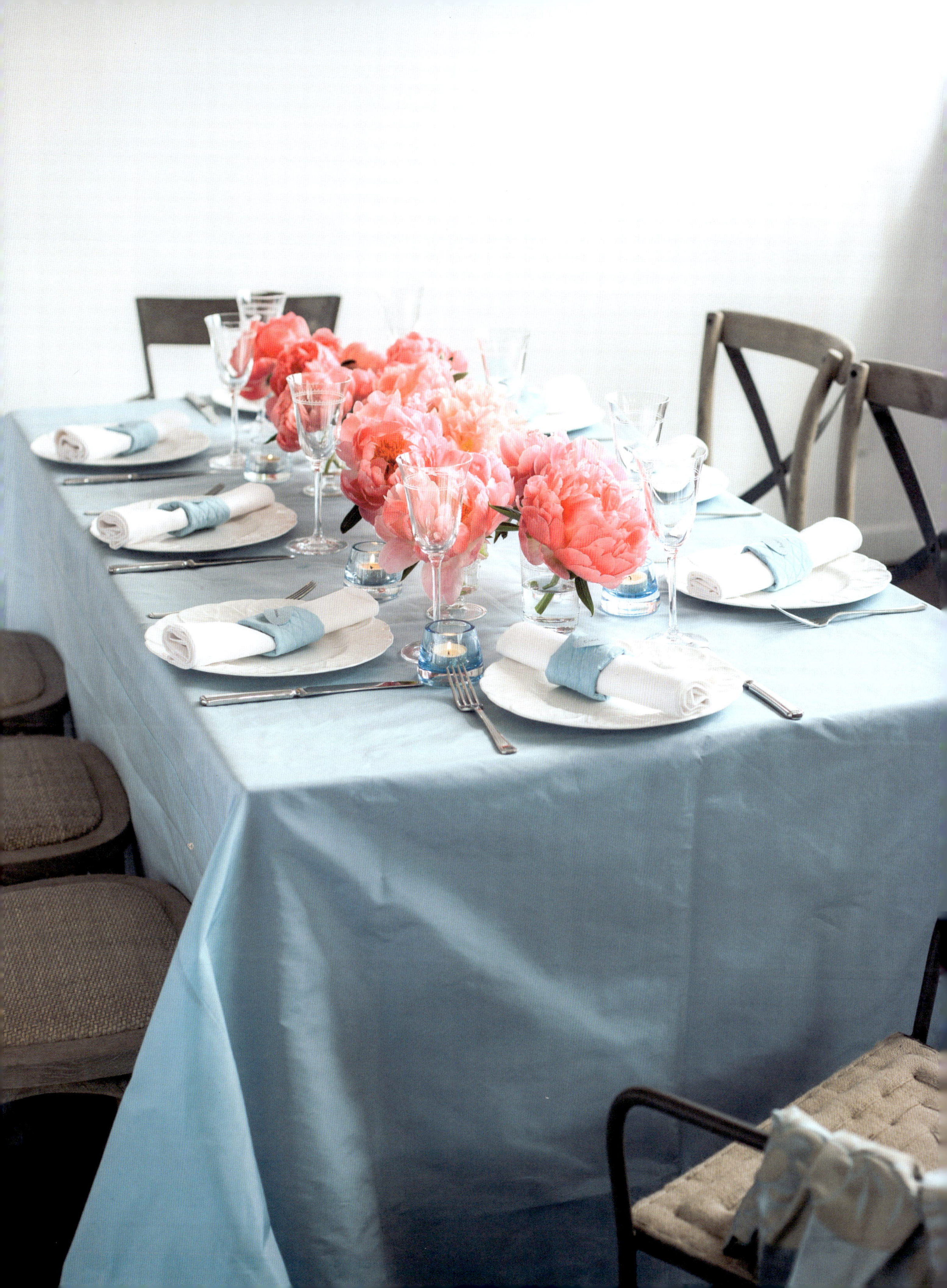

Every flower is a soul
blossoming in nature.

Gerard de Nerval

As spring progresses, more varieties of flowers become available which of course provides plenty of opportunities to mix and match without any one colour ever overwhelming the others. The simple but effective cones that enhance the table setting on the right contain a fragrant mix of sweet peas, roses and hyacinths.

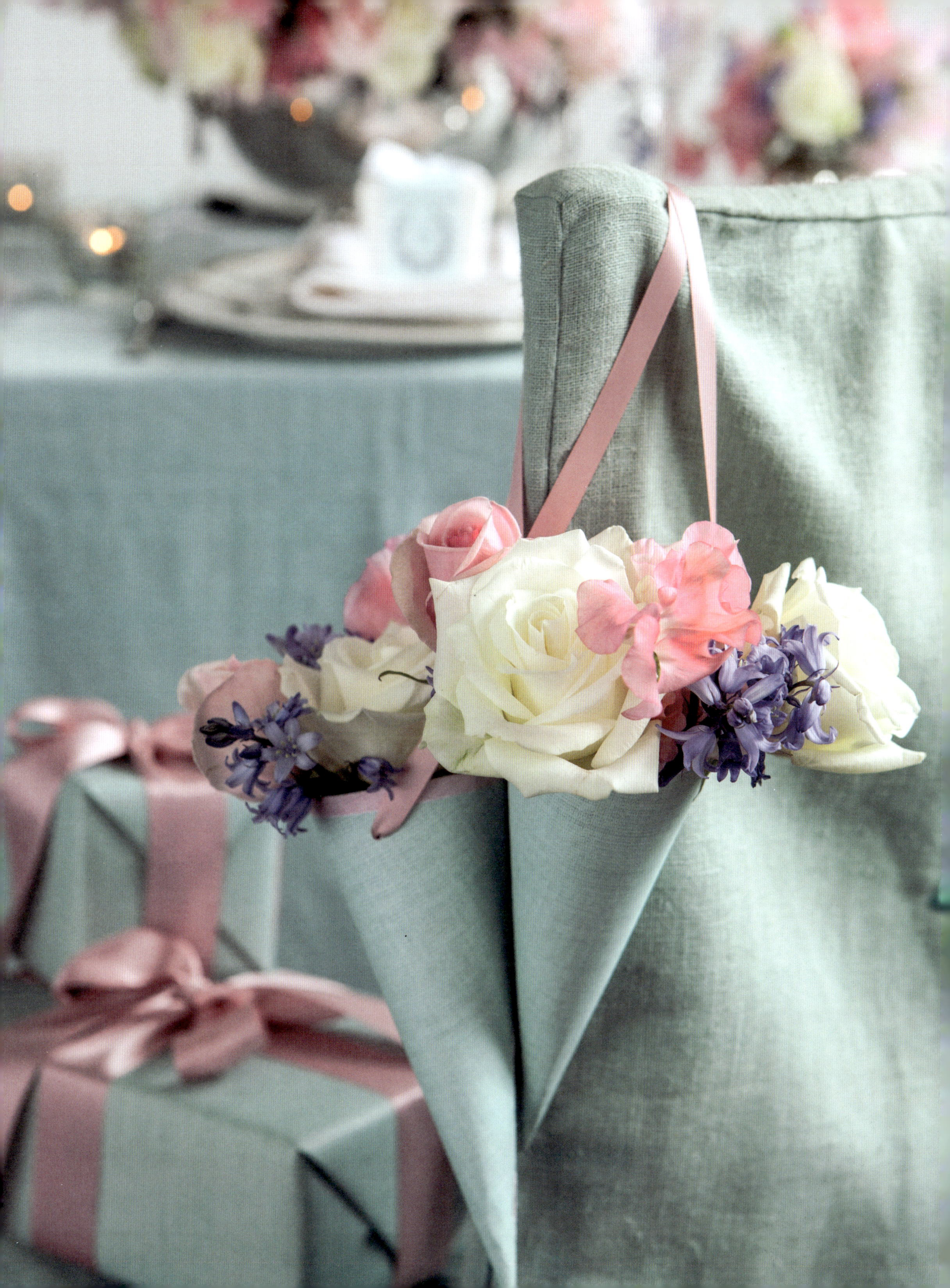

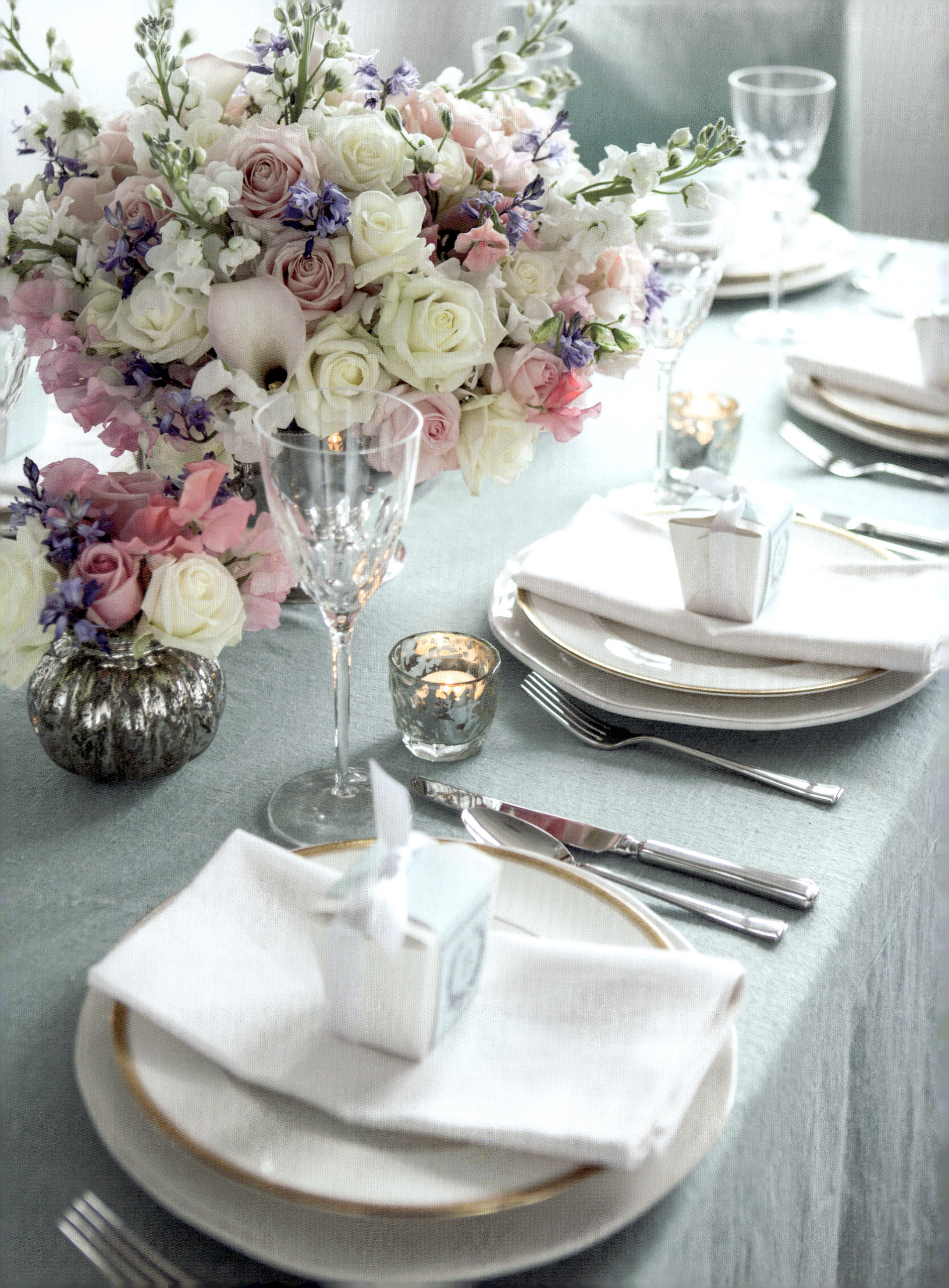

The colours of the floral cones on the previous page are complemented on the left (and subsequent pages) by a magnificent centrepiece comprising baby calla lilies, stock, a variety of cream and pink roses, sweet peas and hyacinth, while Lydia spray rosebuds soften a drinks tray.

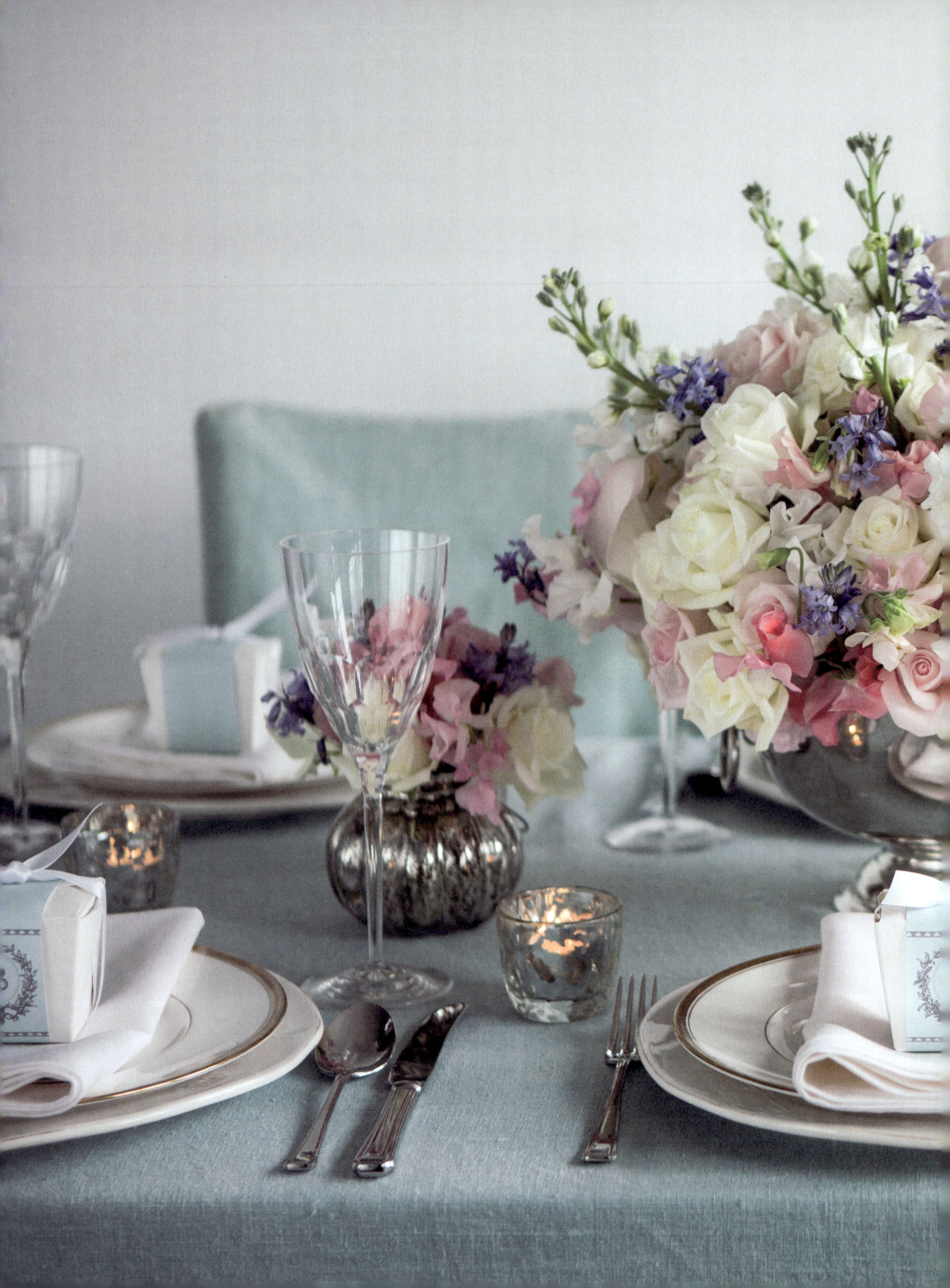

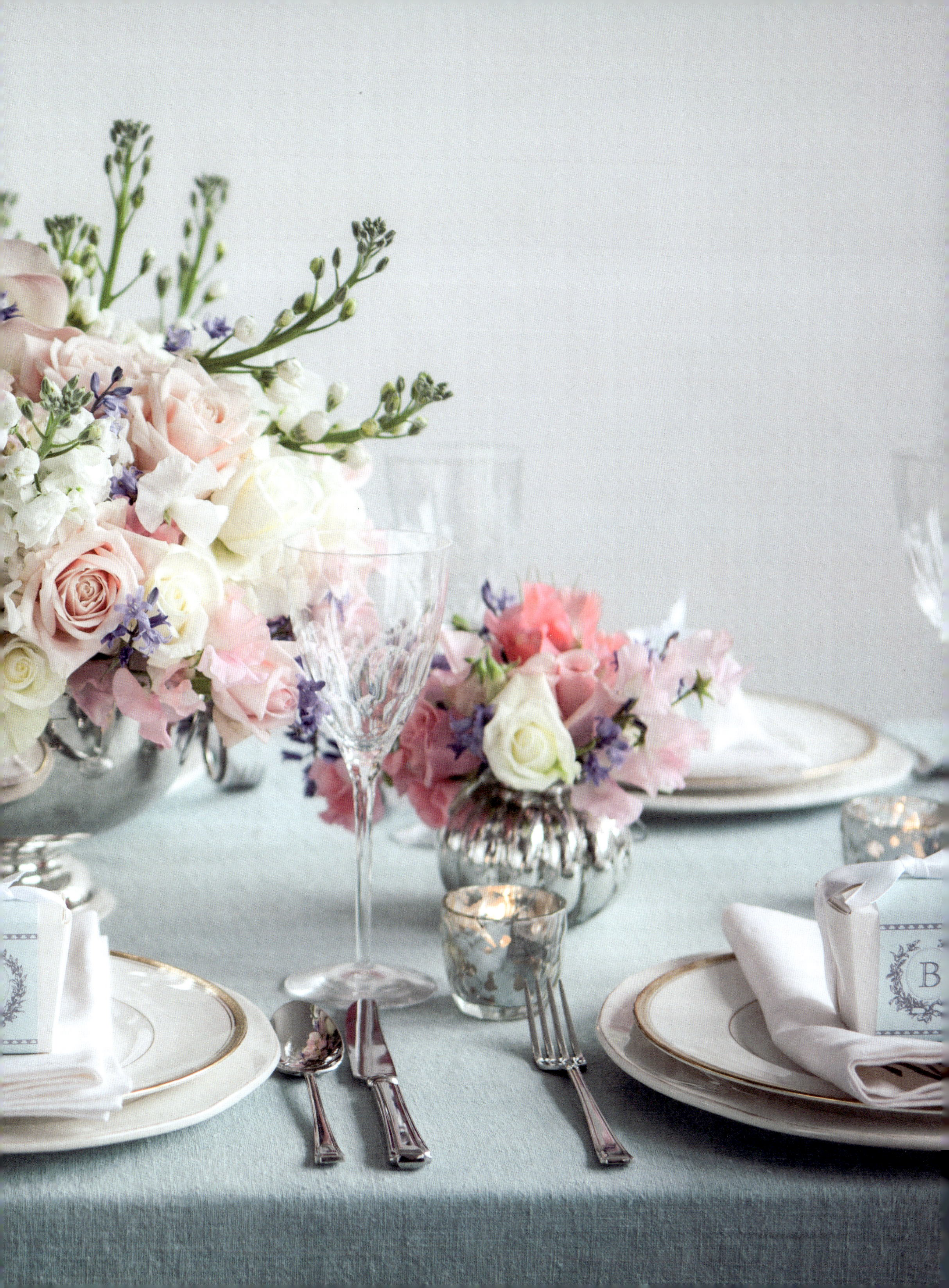

Spring

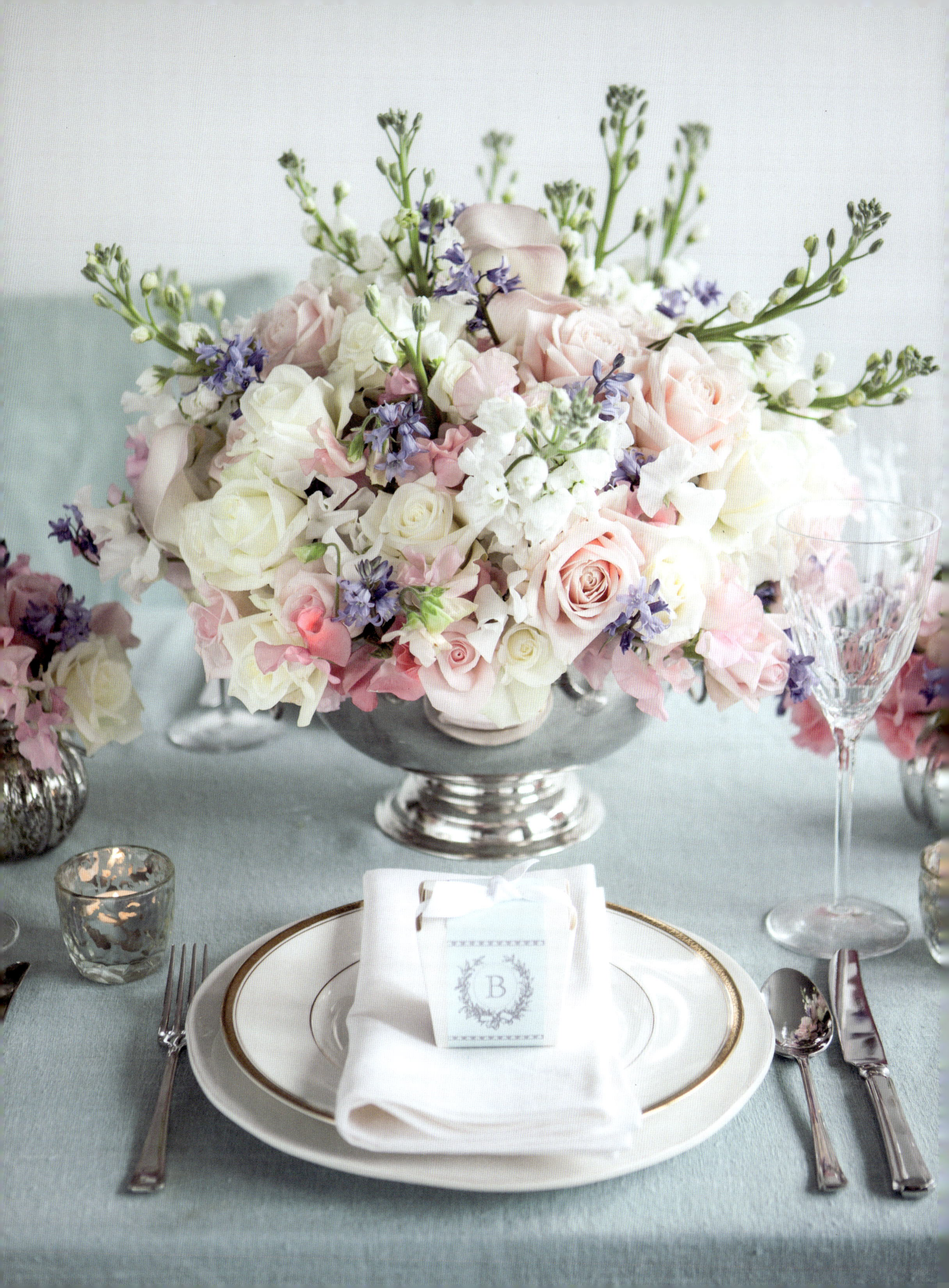
B

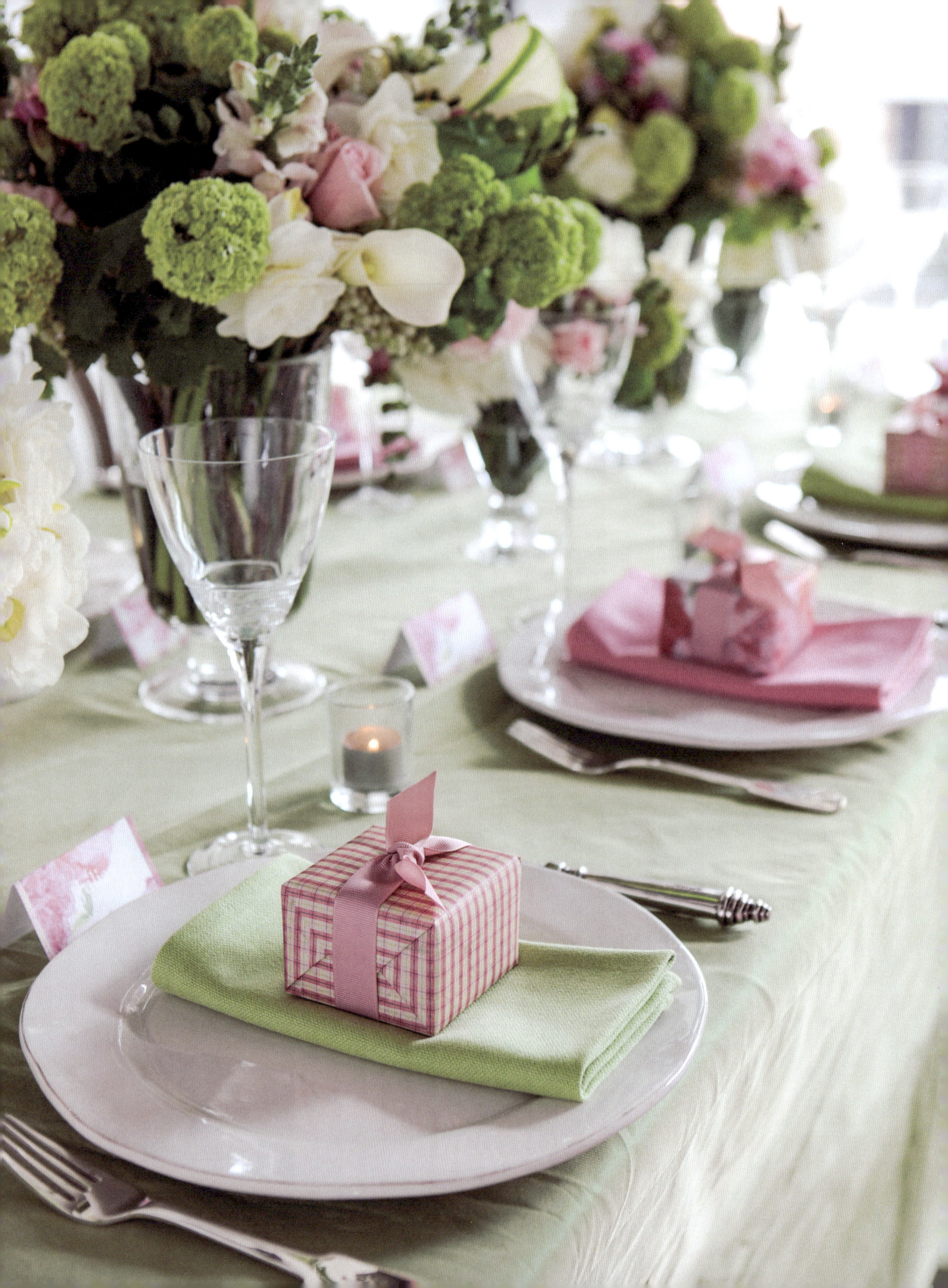

Large and small arrangements of calla lilies, roses, daffodils, snapdragons and snowball viburnum placed next to plates of dainty morsels, all set against calm green taffeta table linen, can be a delicious feature of any celebratory table setting, especially in springtime when the clear green of viburnum comes into its own. Each vessel has been selected so that the rich green of the stems is just as visually prominent as the blooms above them.

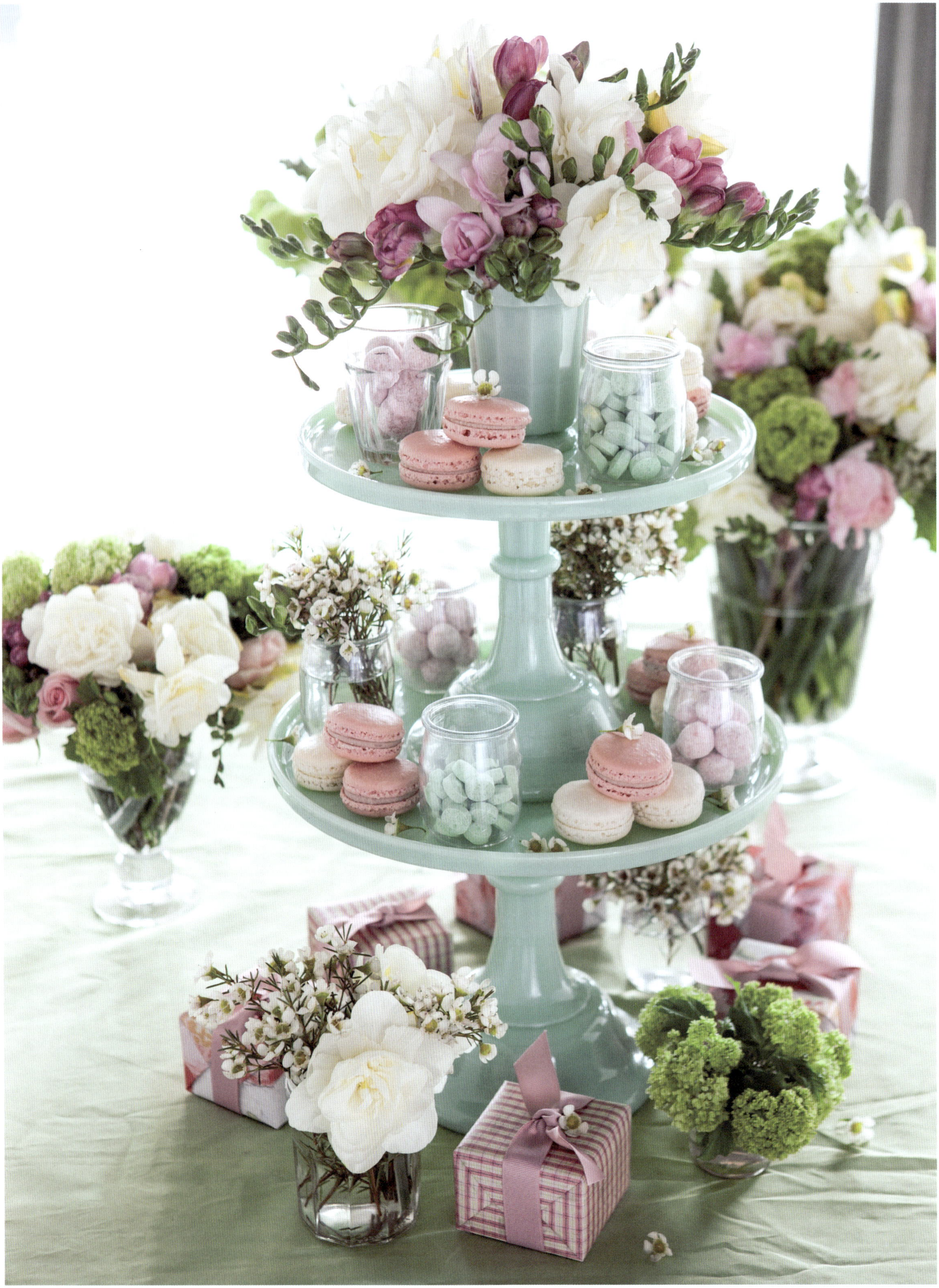

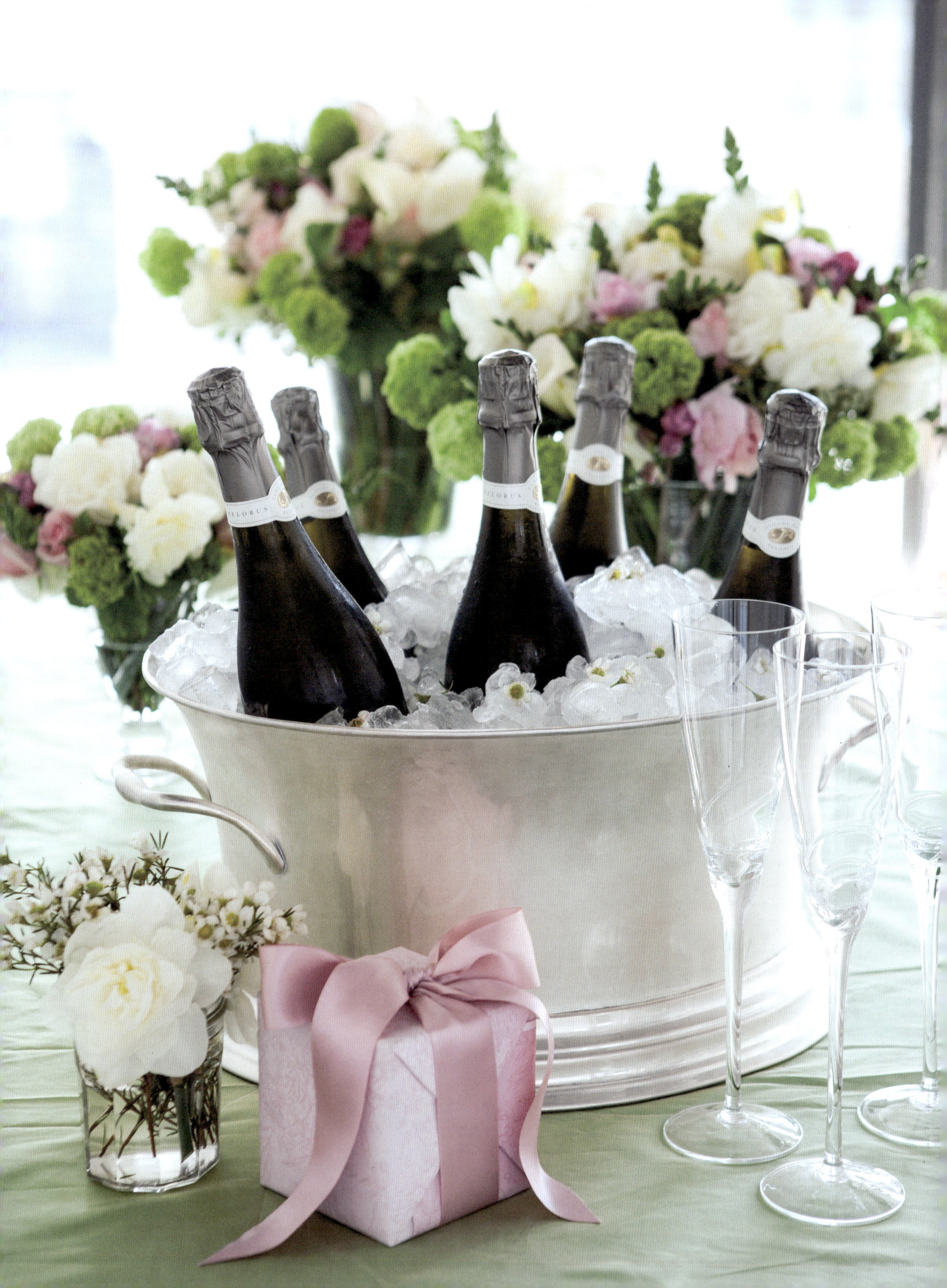

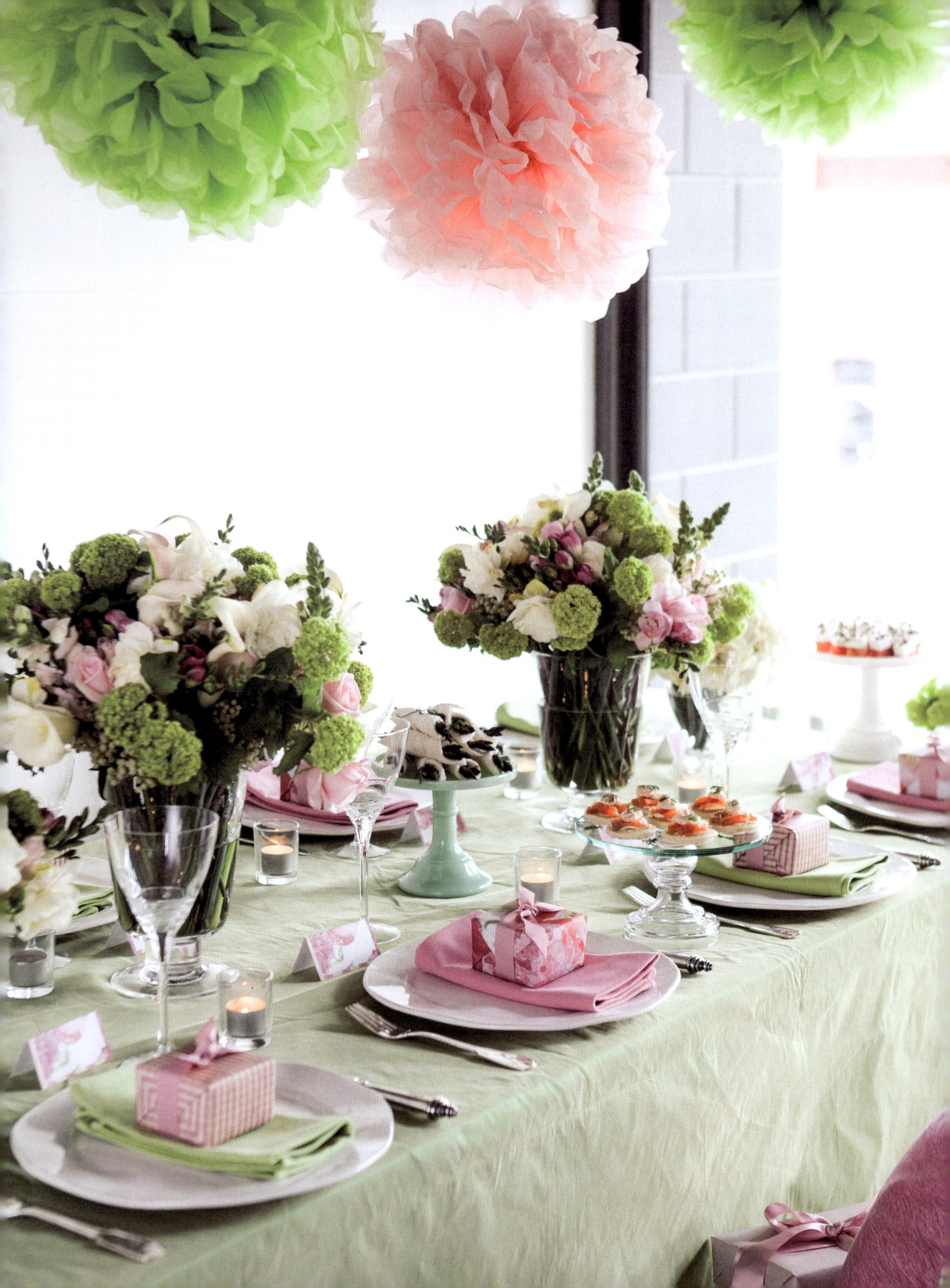

When you take a flower in your hand and really look at it, it's your world for the moment. I want to give that world to someone else. Most people in the city rush around so, they have no time to look at a flower. I want them to see it whether they want to or not.

Georgia O'Keeffe

Spring

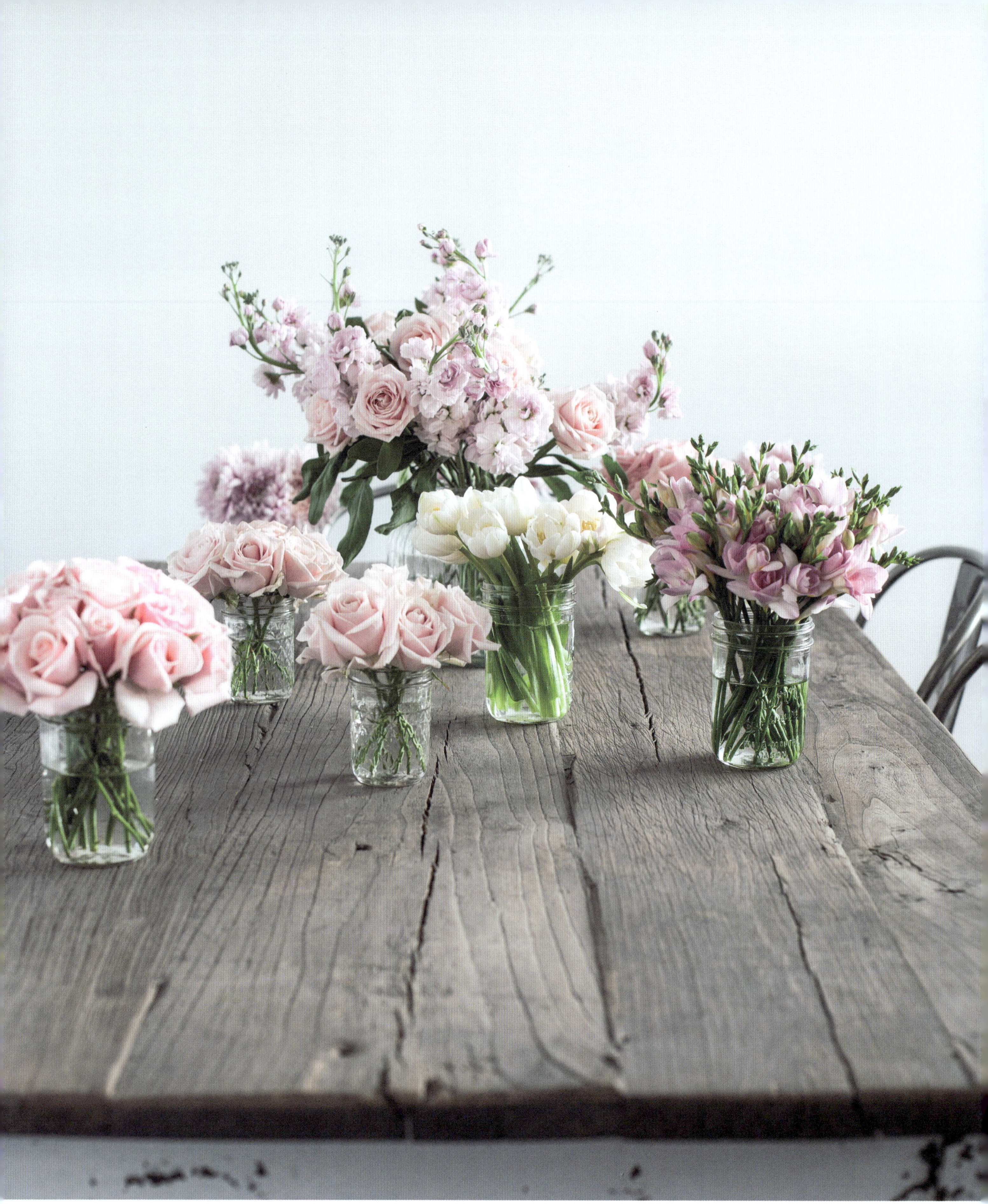

Once again, pink blooms and fresh green stems are enough to make a statement in themselves. The flowers seen here and overleaf include freesias, roses, tulips, stock and chrysanthemums.

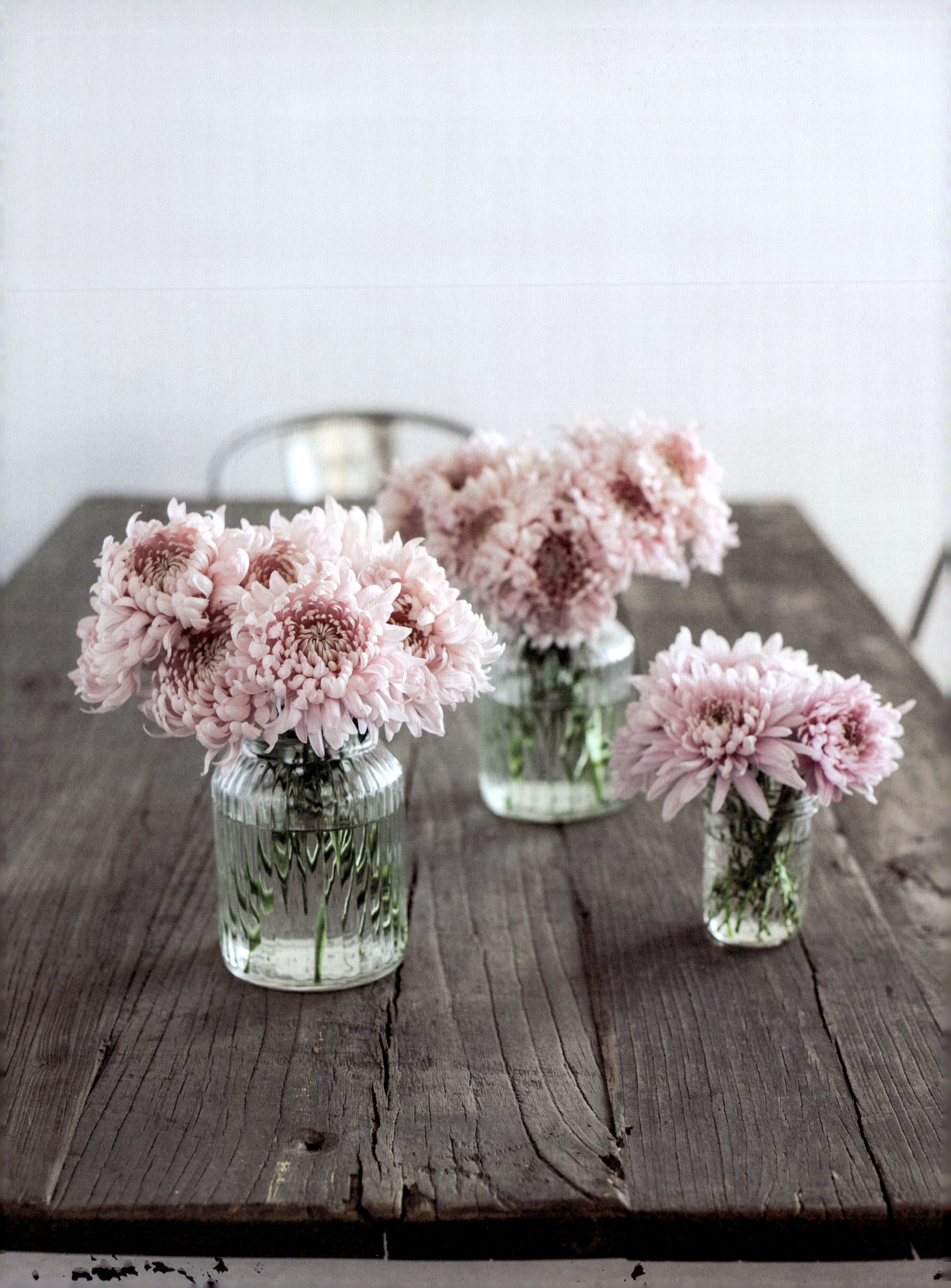

The flower is the poetry of reproduction. It is an example of the eternal seductiveness of life.

Jean Giraudoux

The slightly more elaborate arrangements seen here and in the following pages continue a celebratory theme but strive to remain as simple as possible. Exquisite details are the keynotes such as the wreath on the opposite page that is made up of roses, freesias and carnations with a little lamb's ear to add a touch of green foliage, all of which are designed to elicit a 'wow' response. Overleaf can be seen a perfect example of this in the form of a chilled wine container that has been decorated with flowers.

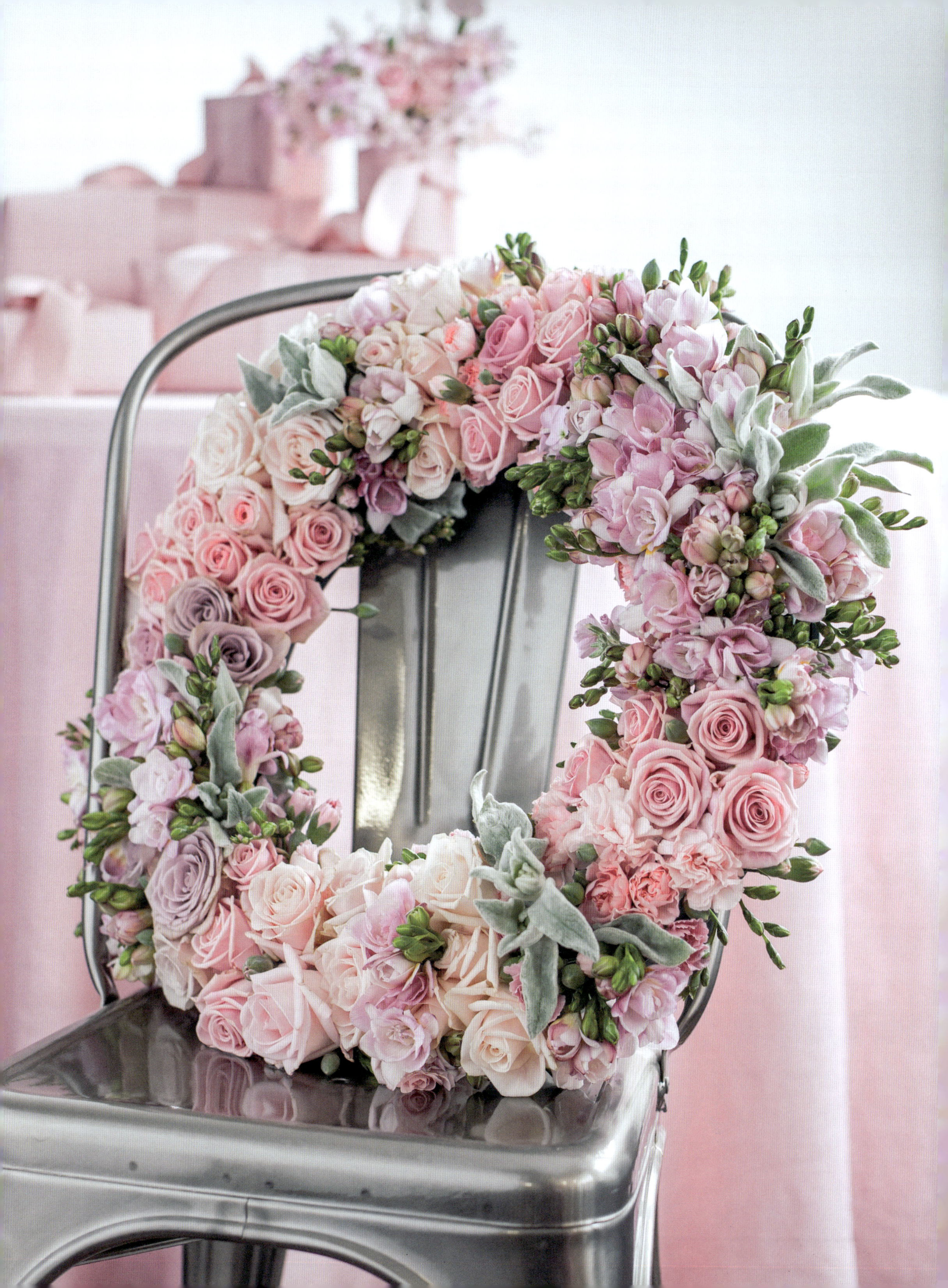

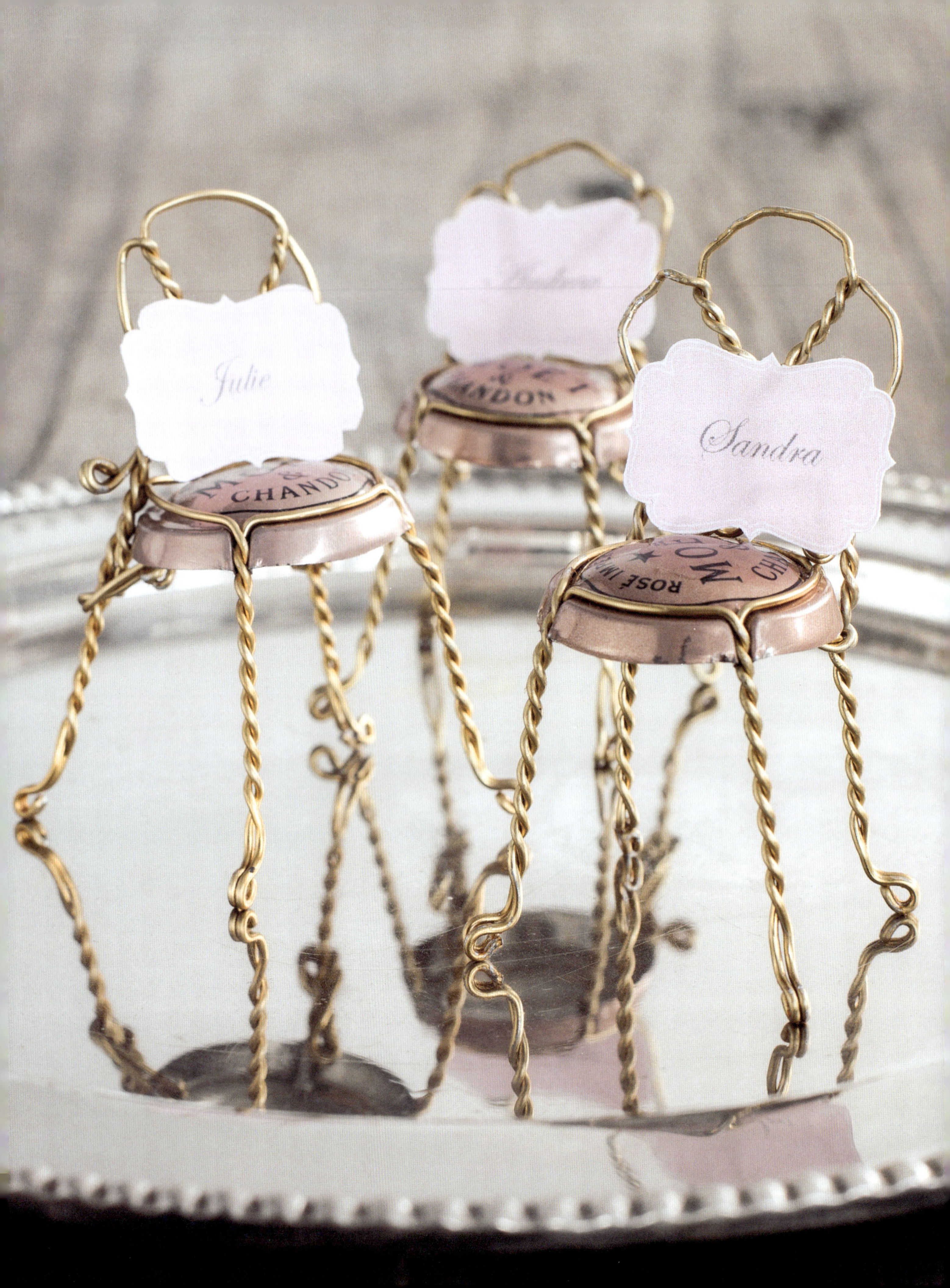
Julie
Sandra

Interestingly, the style of container chosen to hold the wine is actually less important than the palette of colours used to showcase the contents, in this case delicately blended and scented sweet peas, roses, tulips and anemones.

Overleaf are several options for special table settings featuring roses, stock, snapdragons and tulips on pages 76 and 77; and rosebuds and roses complemented by a carnation on pages 78 and 79.

Spring

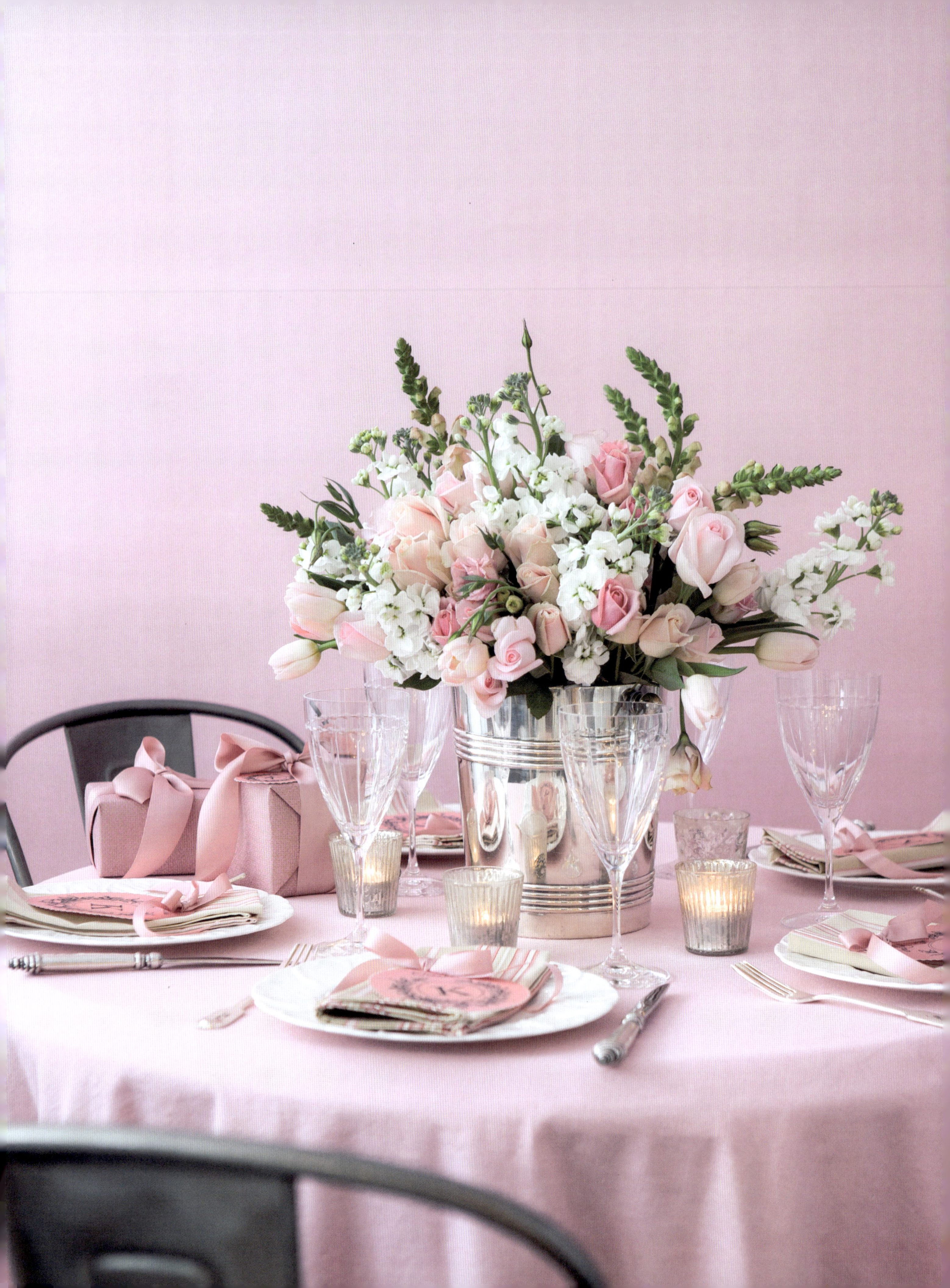

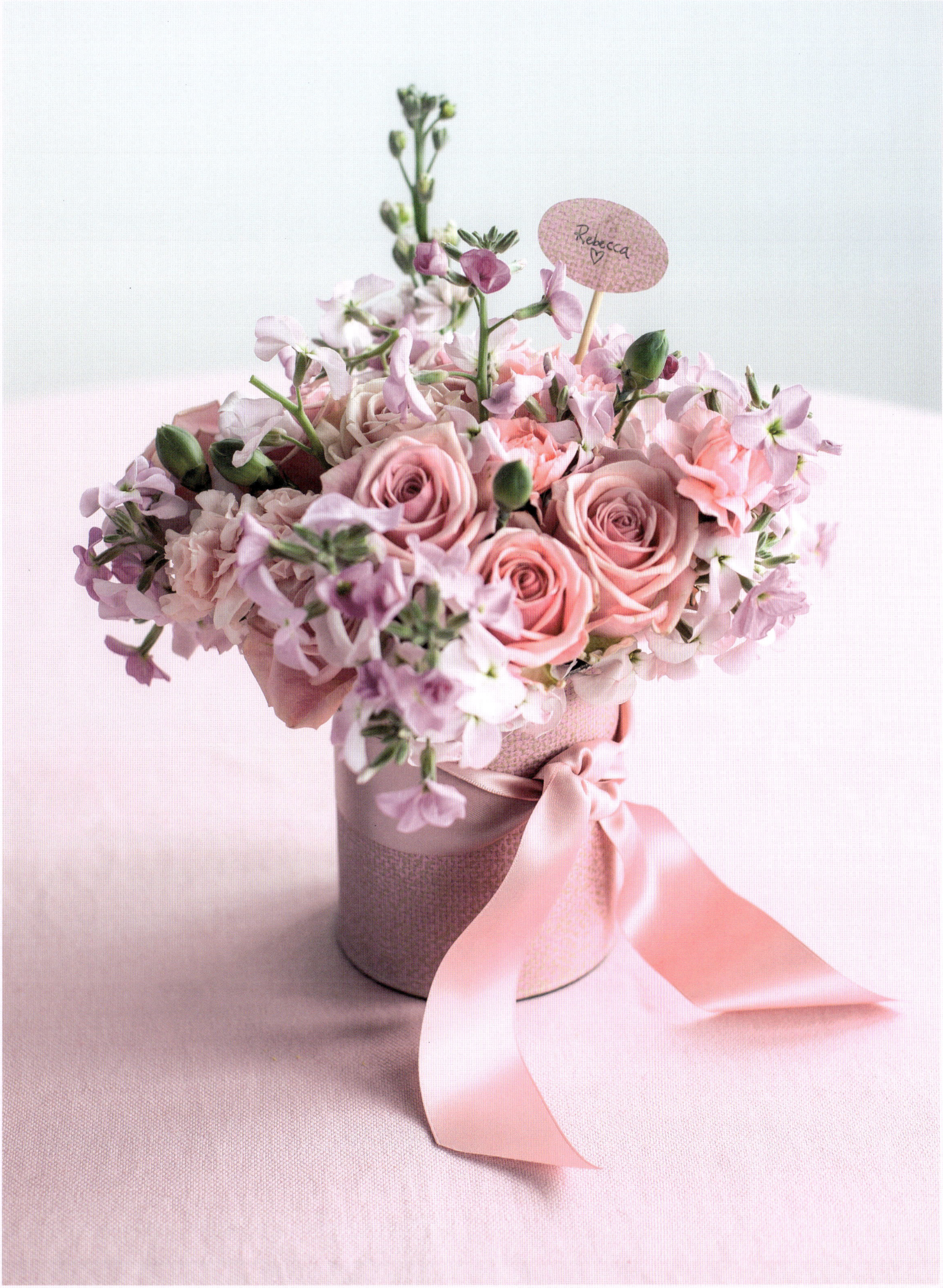
Rebecca

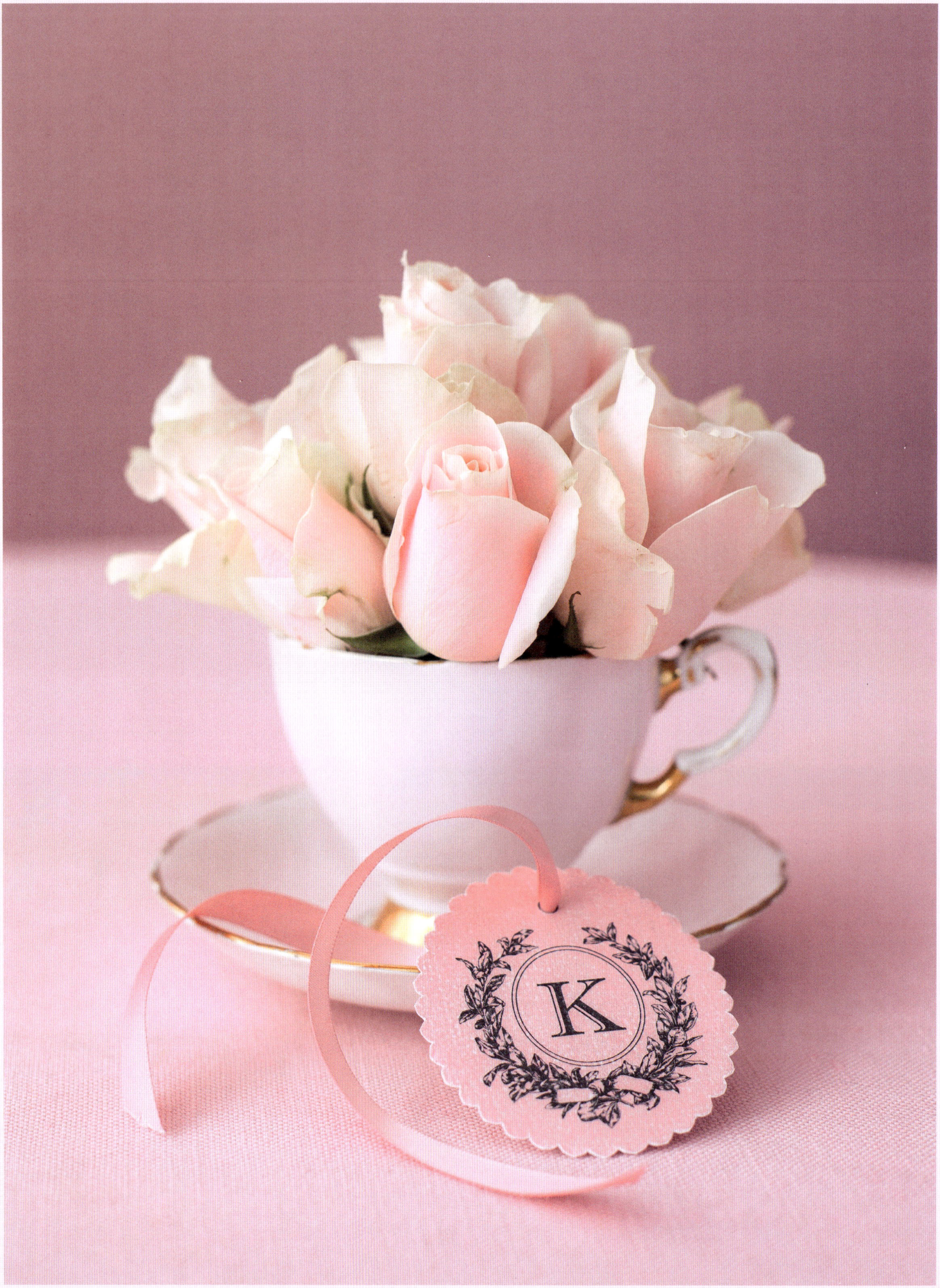
K

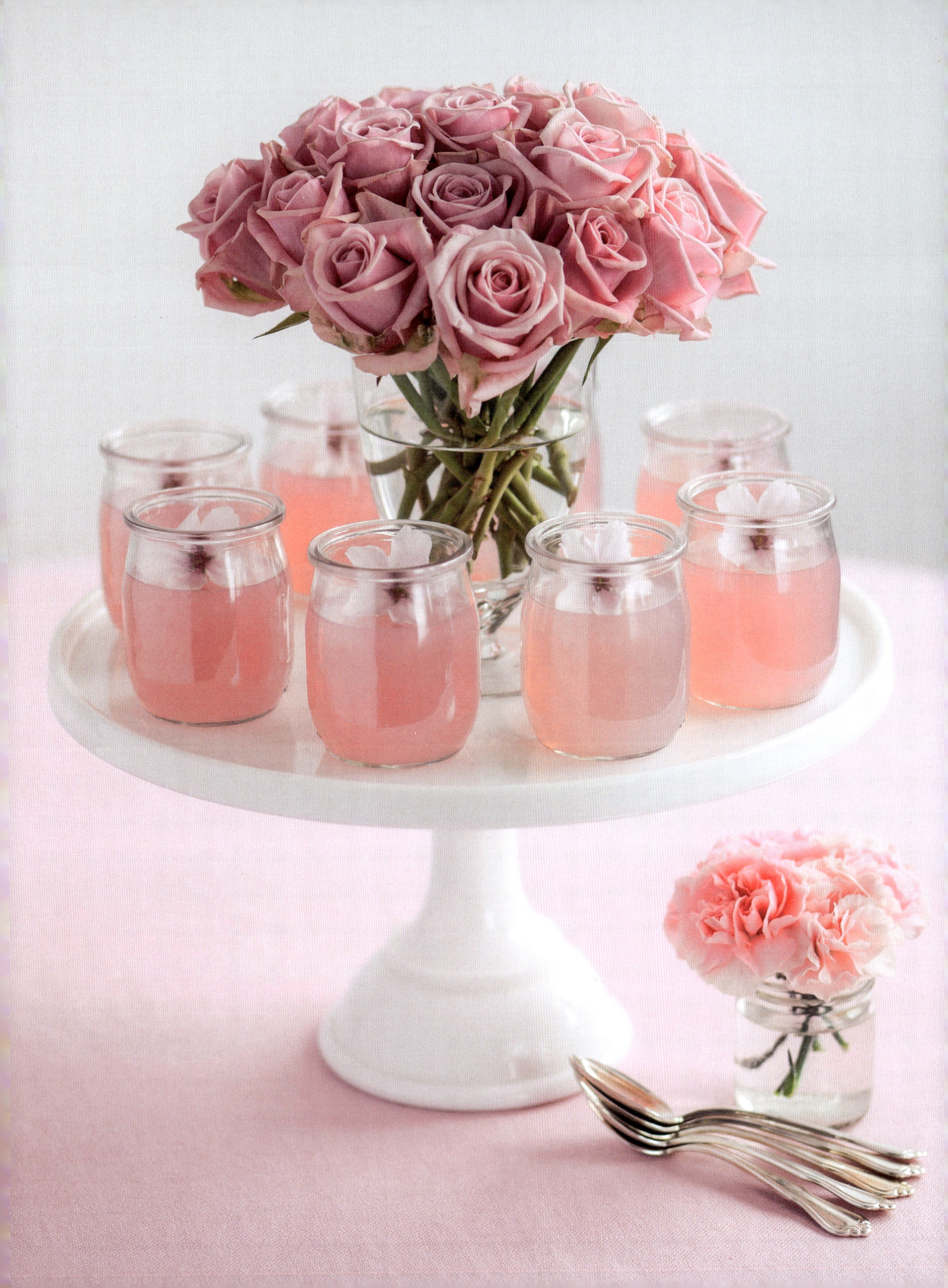

Scent can play an important part in an exquisite setting such as the sweet fragrance of these roses that will not be released until the glass cloche is lifted. Always use the appropriate essential oil rather than fragrance when making scented candles like those surrounding the roses and stock on the following page.

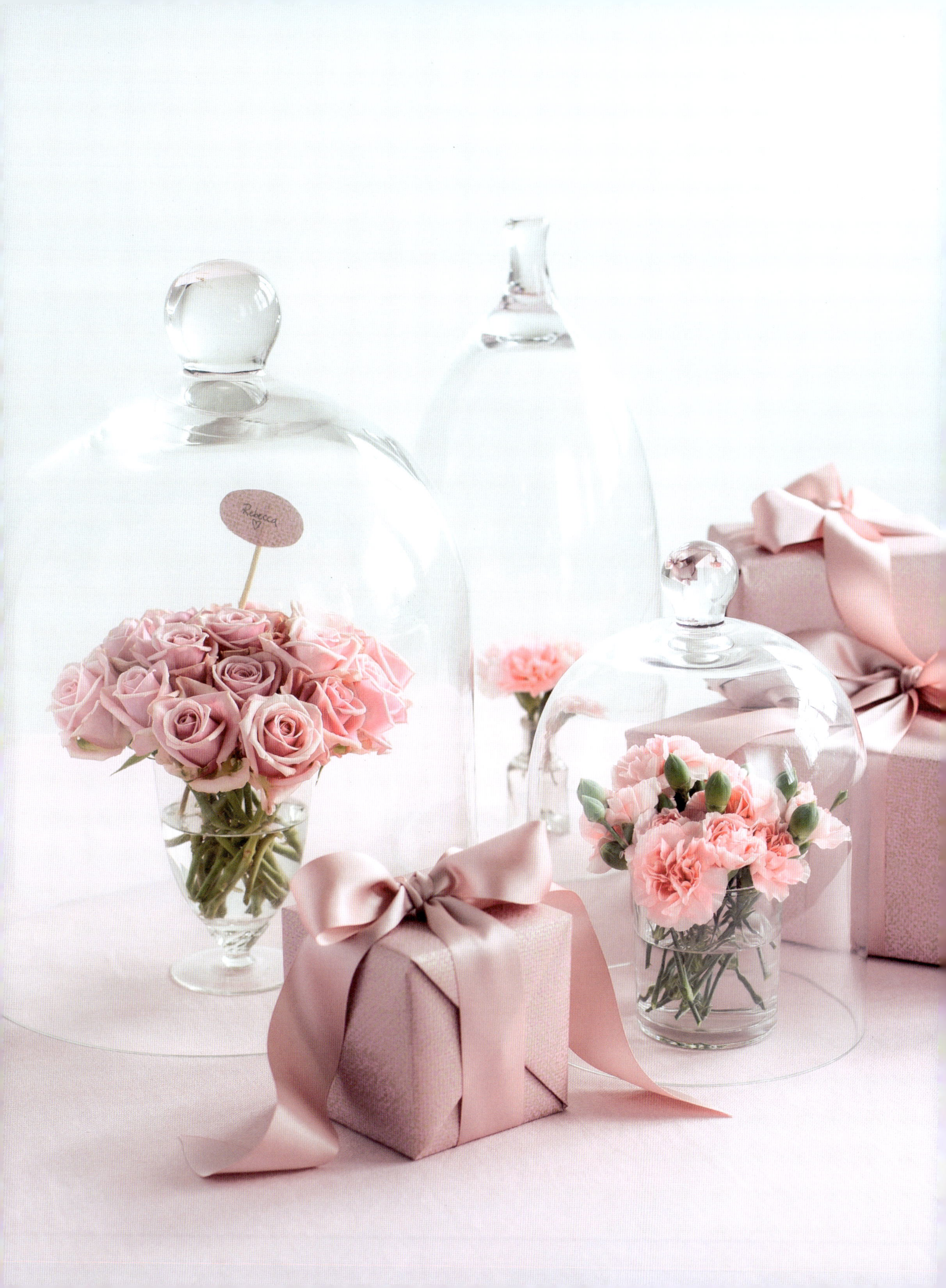
Rebecca

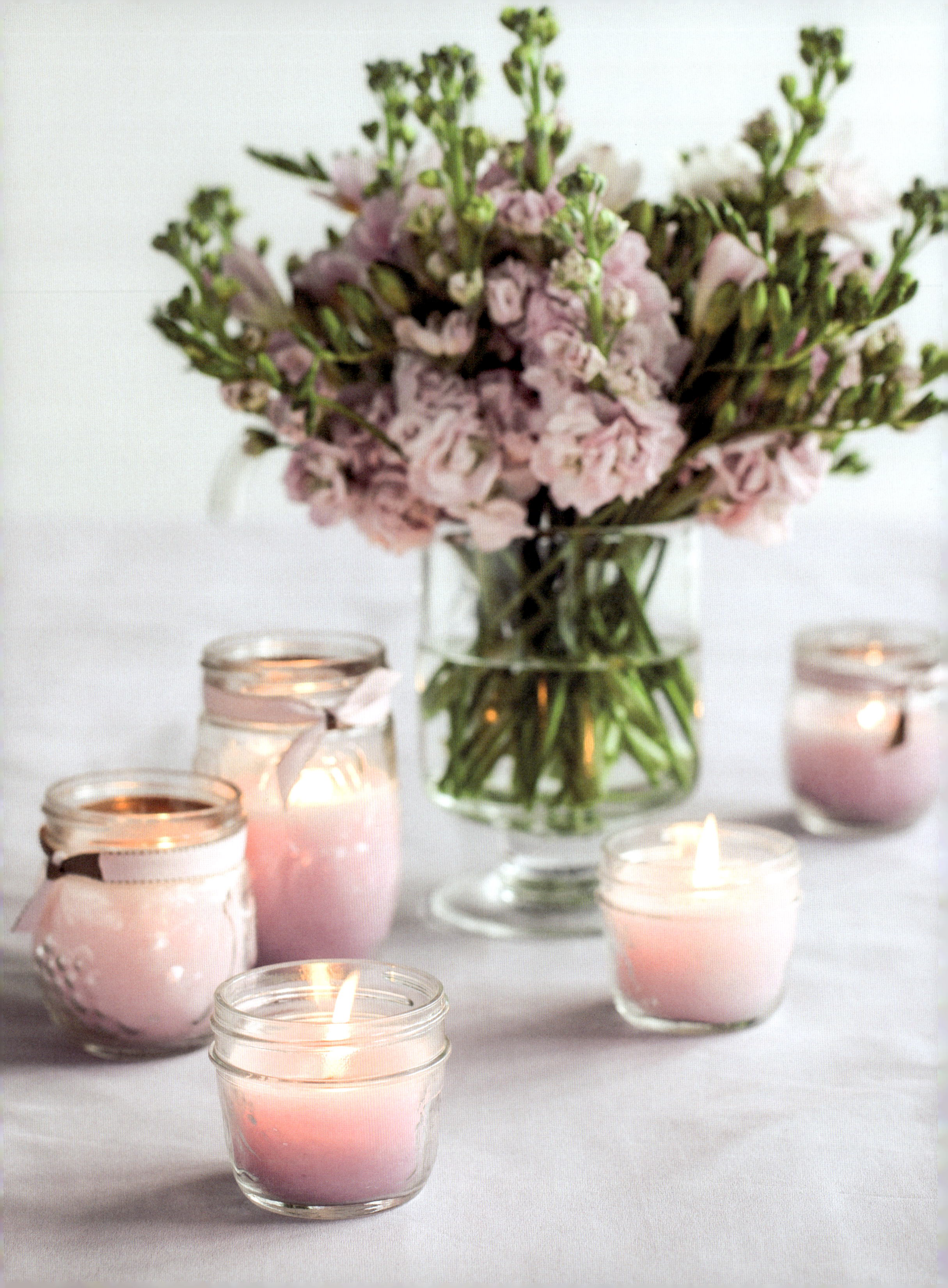

Loveliest of lovely things are they
On earth that soonest pass away.
The rose that lives its little hour
Is prized beyond the sculptured flower.

William Cullen Bryant

Spring 83

Elegant bone china enhances the apple blossom shown above and the complex texture of the carnations on the right.

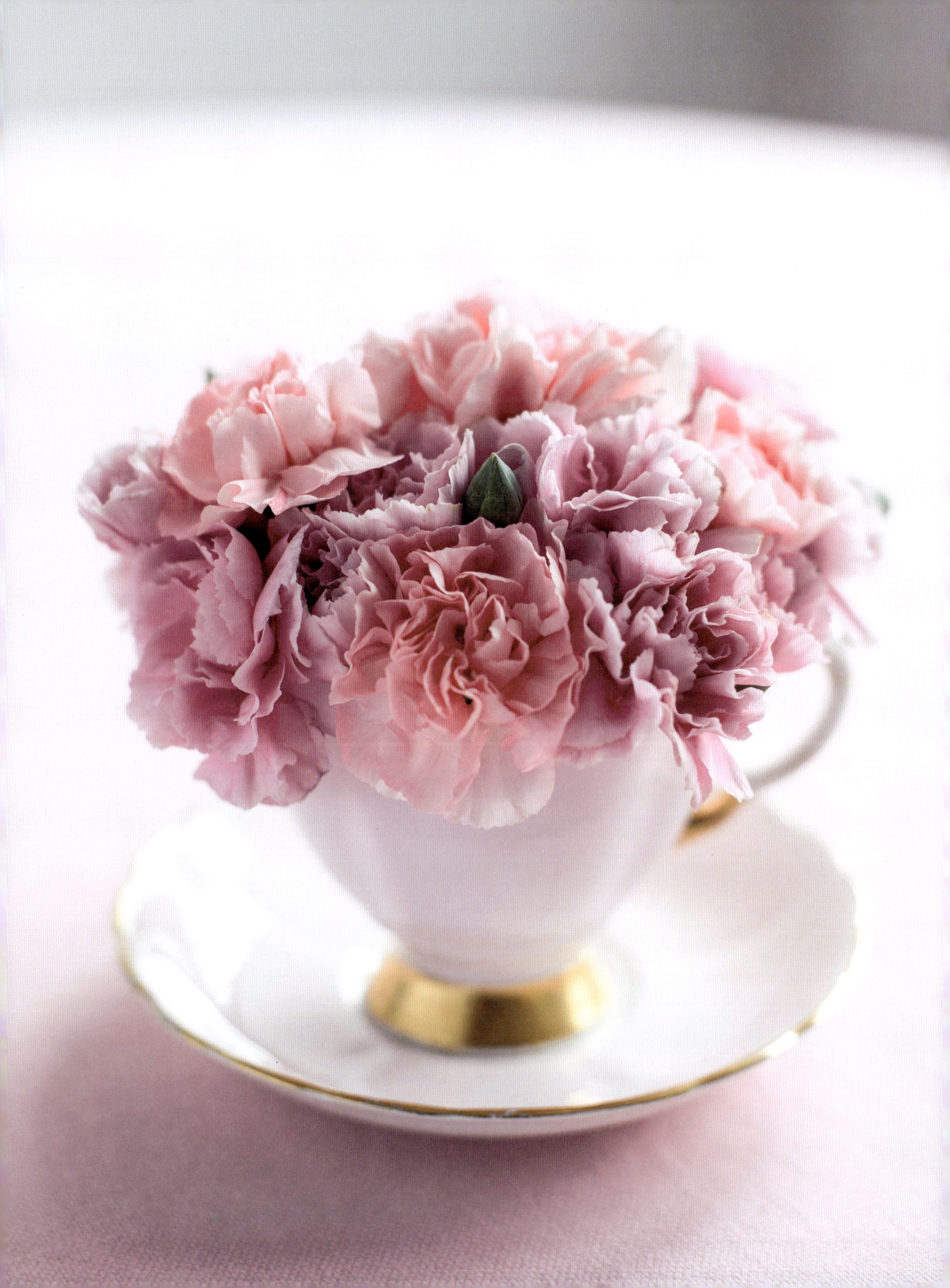

Apple blossom artfully arranged on these attractive cupcakes is set off to perfection on a plain white cake stand while the arrangements of tulips, roses and ranunculus on the left have been personalised to enhance a festive occasion.

Simple clear glass vases are all you need to showcase highly fragrant stock in complementary shades of pink as shown here.

Spring

Whether mixed together or used alone, camellias, delicately pastel hued roses, tulips and carnations are the ultimate feminine table accessory.

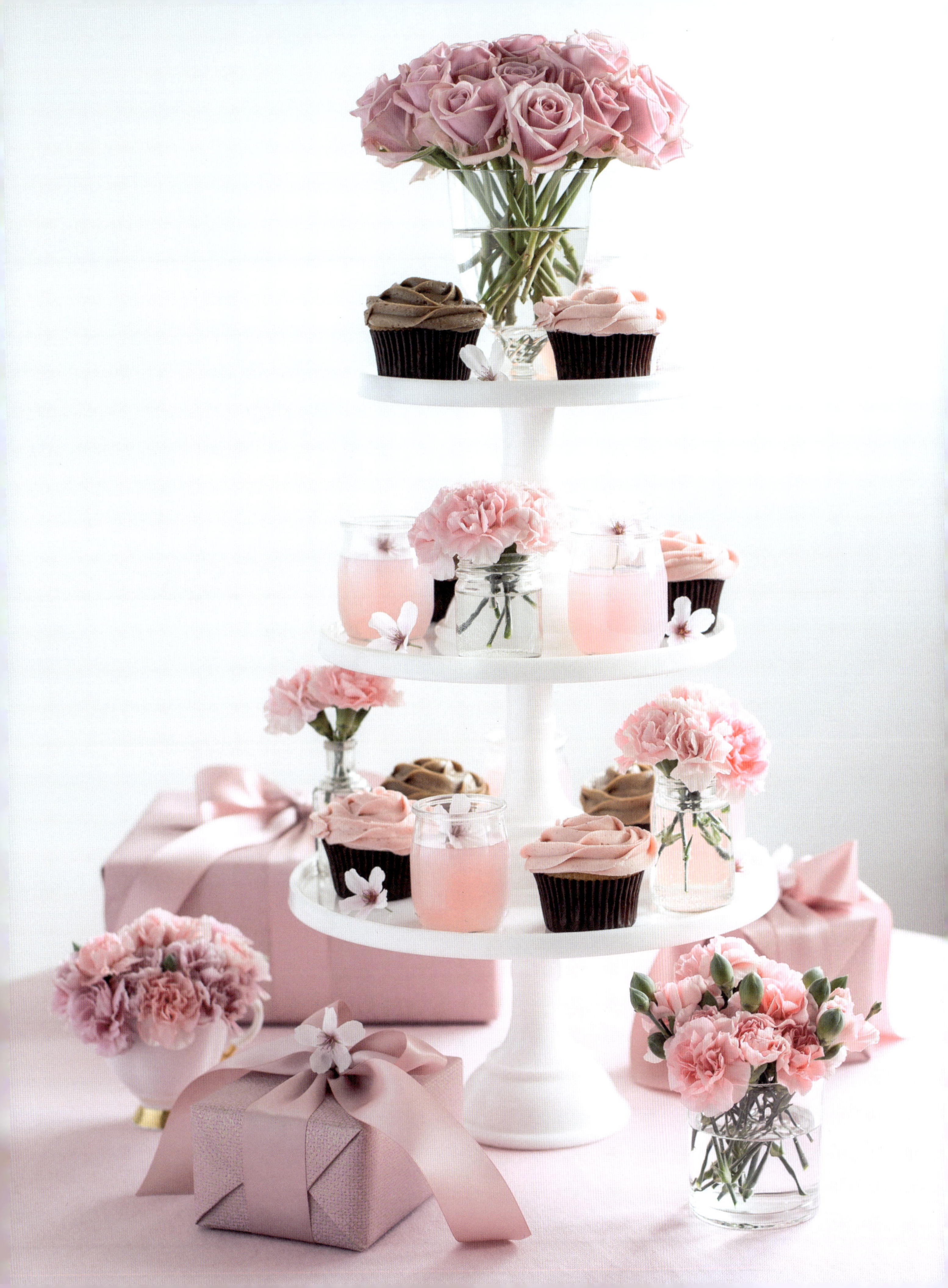

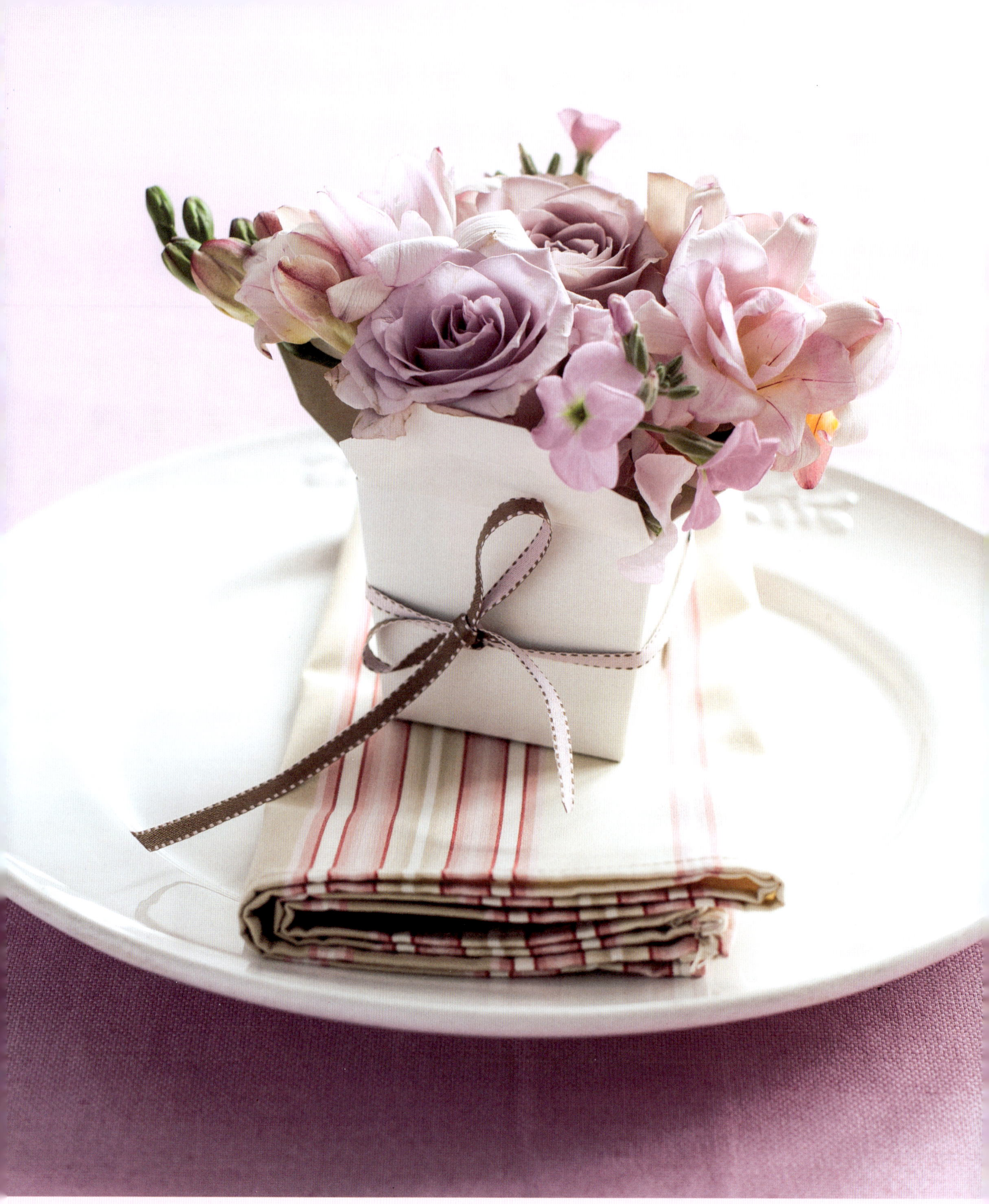

Use your imagination when choosing how best to set off your spring flowers. A stark white cardboard food container is the perfect foil for the colours and textures of this mixture of stock, roses, tulips and freesias shown on the left, while a plain glass jar holding pink rosebuds on a cake stand is enhanced by home-made jellies.

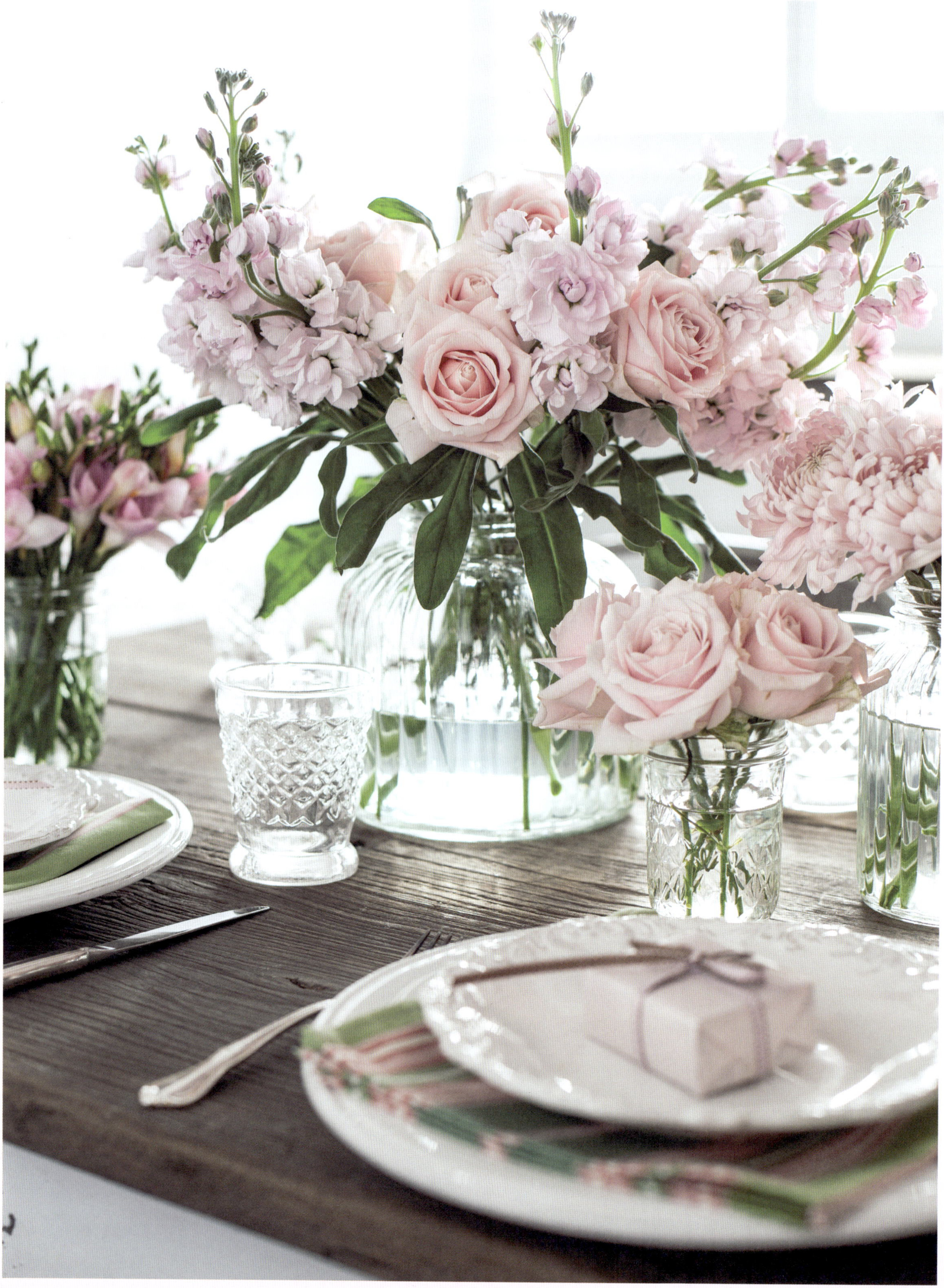

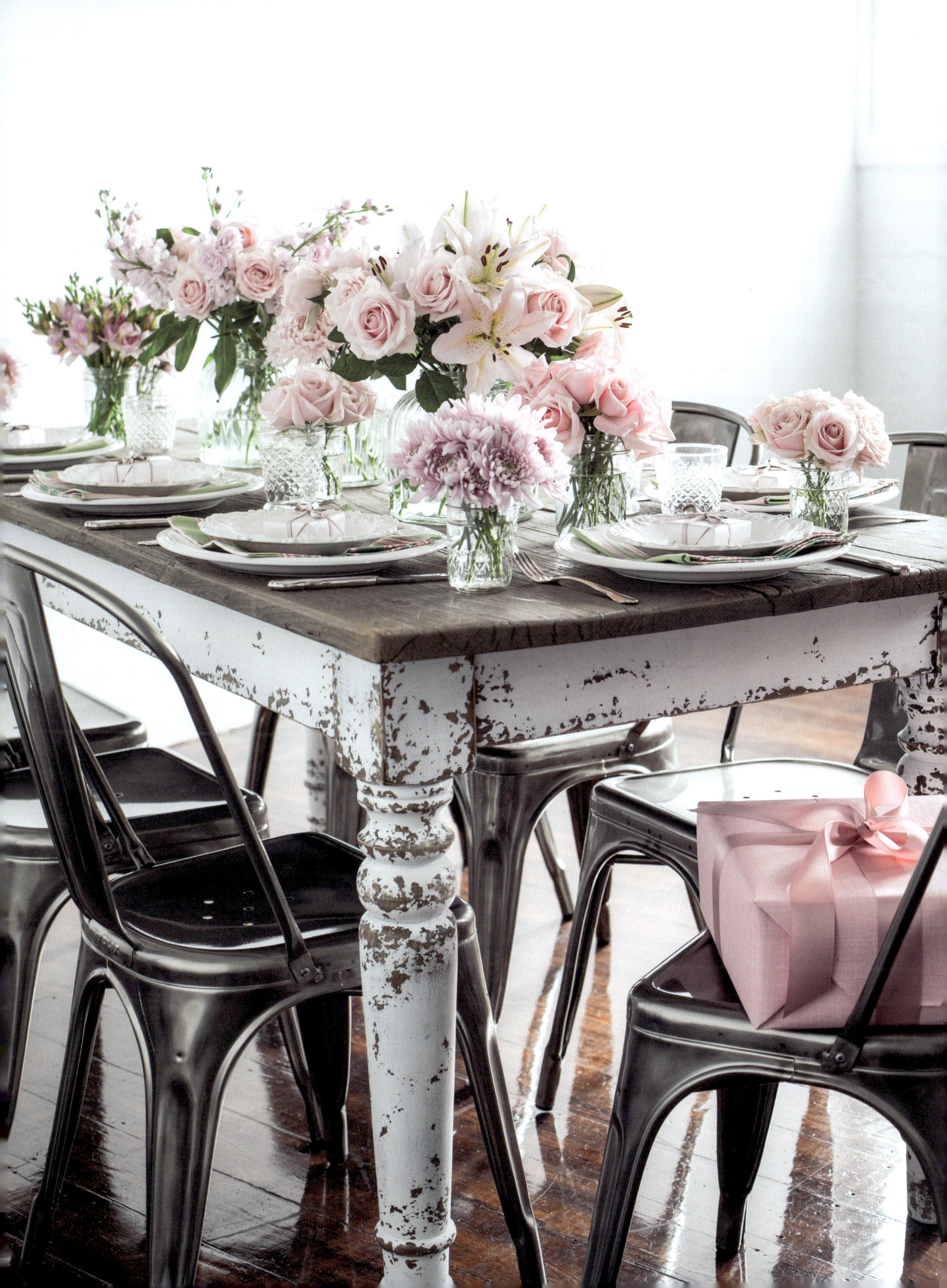

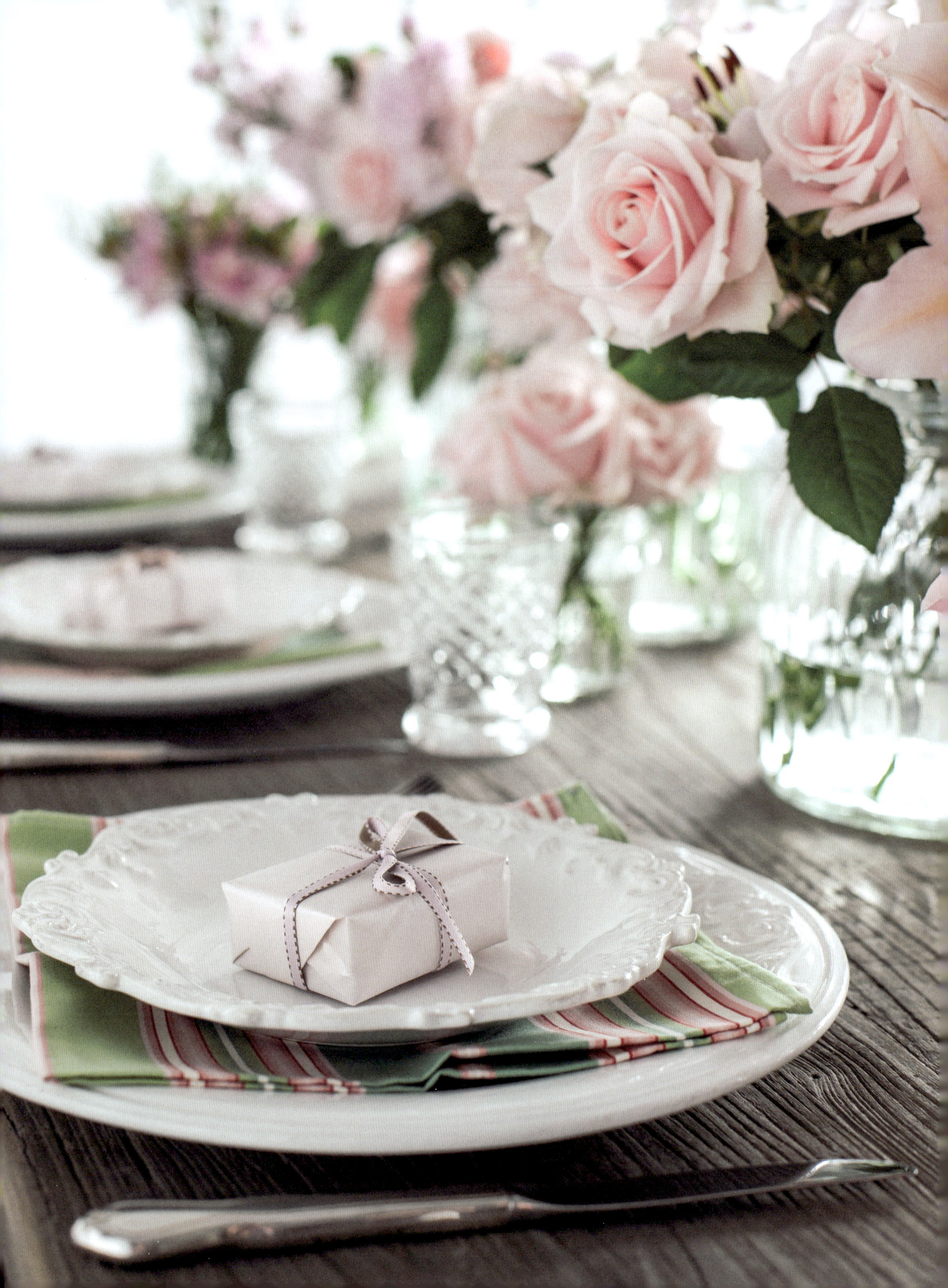

Both here and on the previous pages, an extravagant mix of scented pink blooms topped off by a simple sprig of blossom transforms a plain table into a place to celebrate and rejoice. Plain glass vases and drinking glasses are all that's required to display this glorious collection of Oriental lilies, roses, chrysanthemums, stock and freesias.

As the season moves through its paces and the weather slowly turns warmer, it's time to start playing with stronger colours such as these deeply hued roses set off by the fresh green of viburnum and pale green carnations.

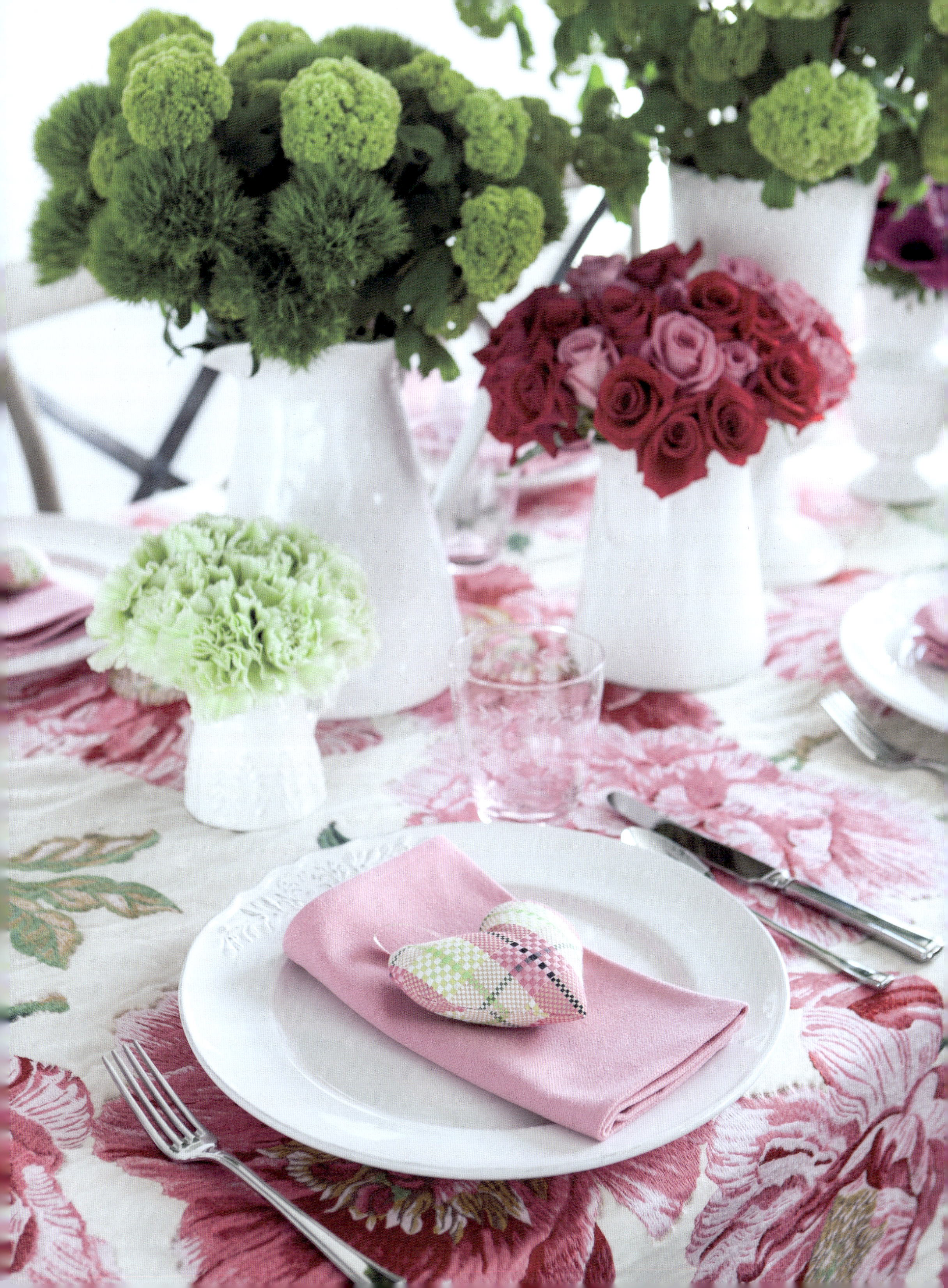

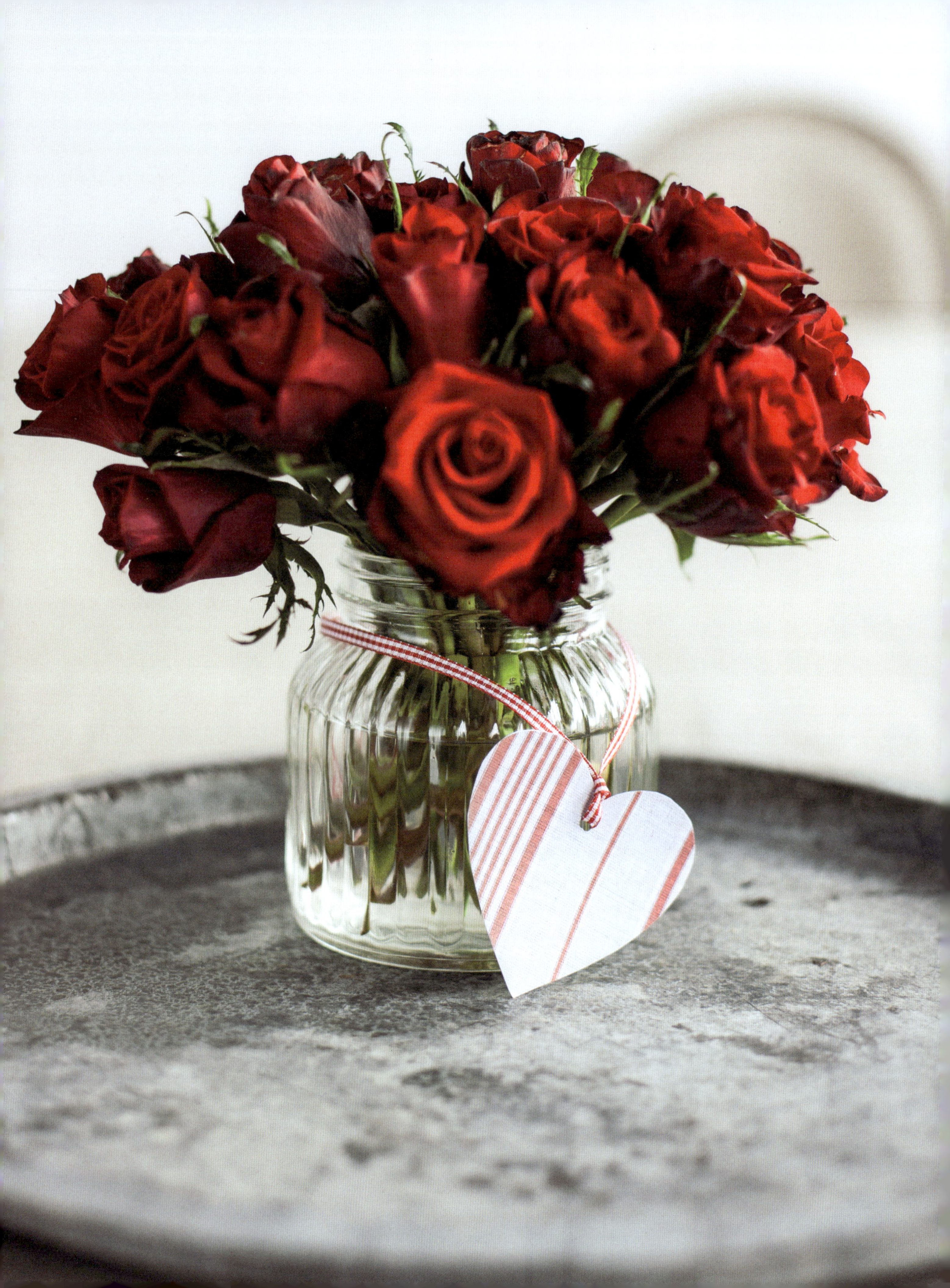

Choose a simple but striking container to show off the rich colours of the roses on the left and the tulips above. Nothing else in the way of foliage is required.

Lift everyone's spirits with this riot of colour featuring peonies, roses and cosmos.

The following pages illustrate how nothing in the way of an elaborate vase should distract the eye from exquisite peonies shown at their best in plain glass bottles or jars; hyacinths and tulips in white china; peonies and sweet peas also in plain glass.

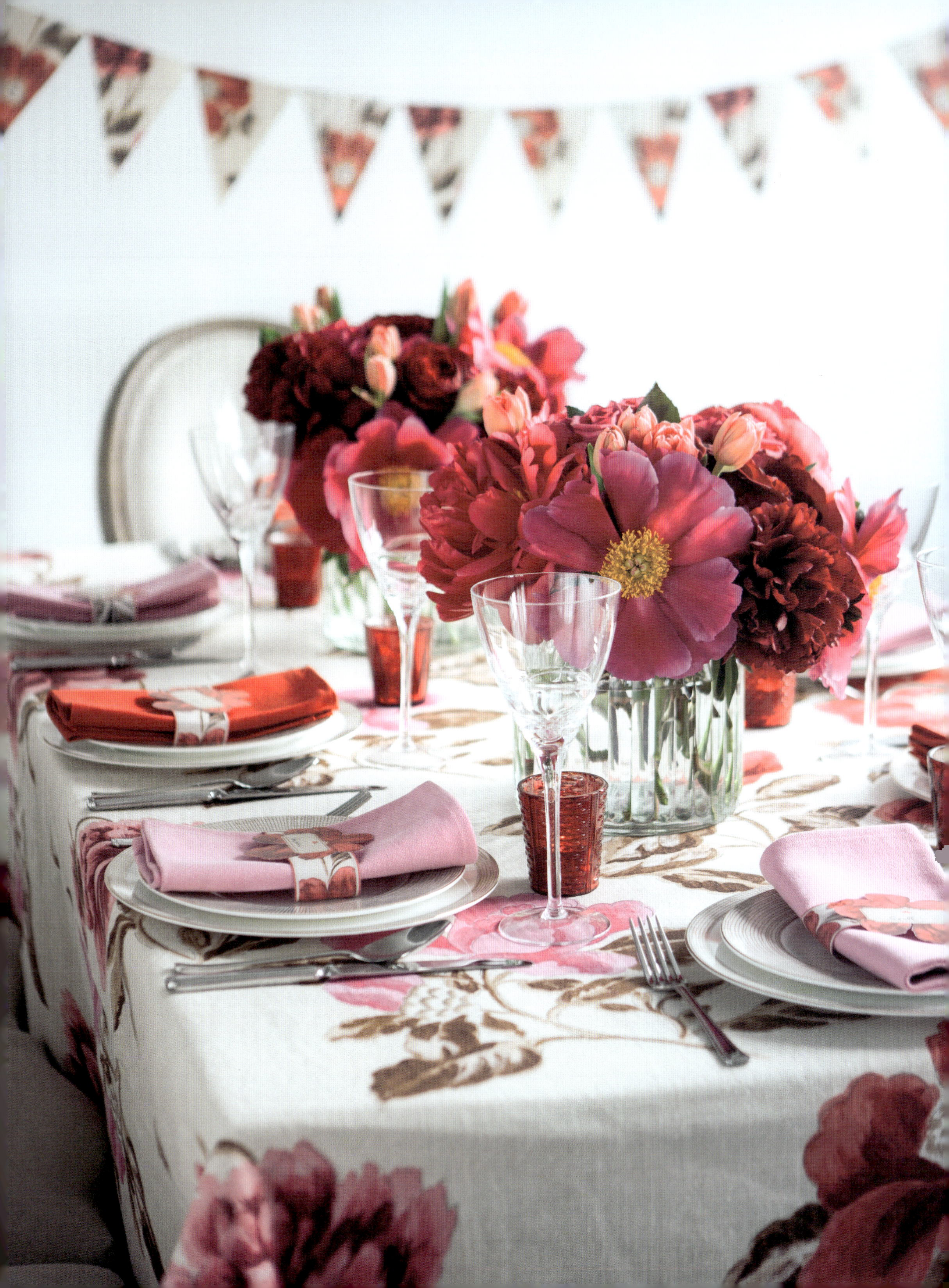

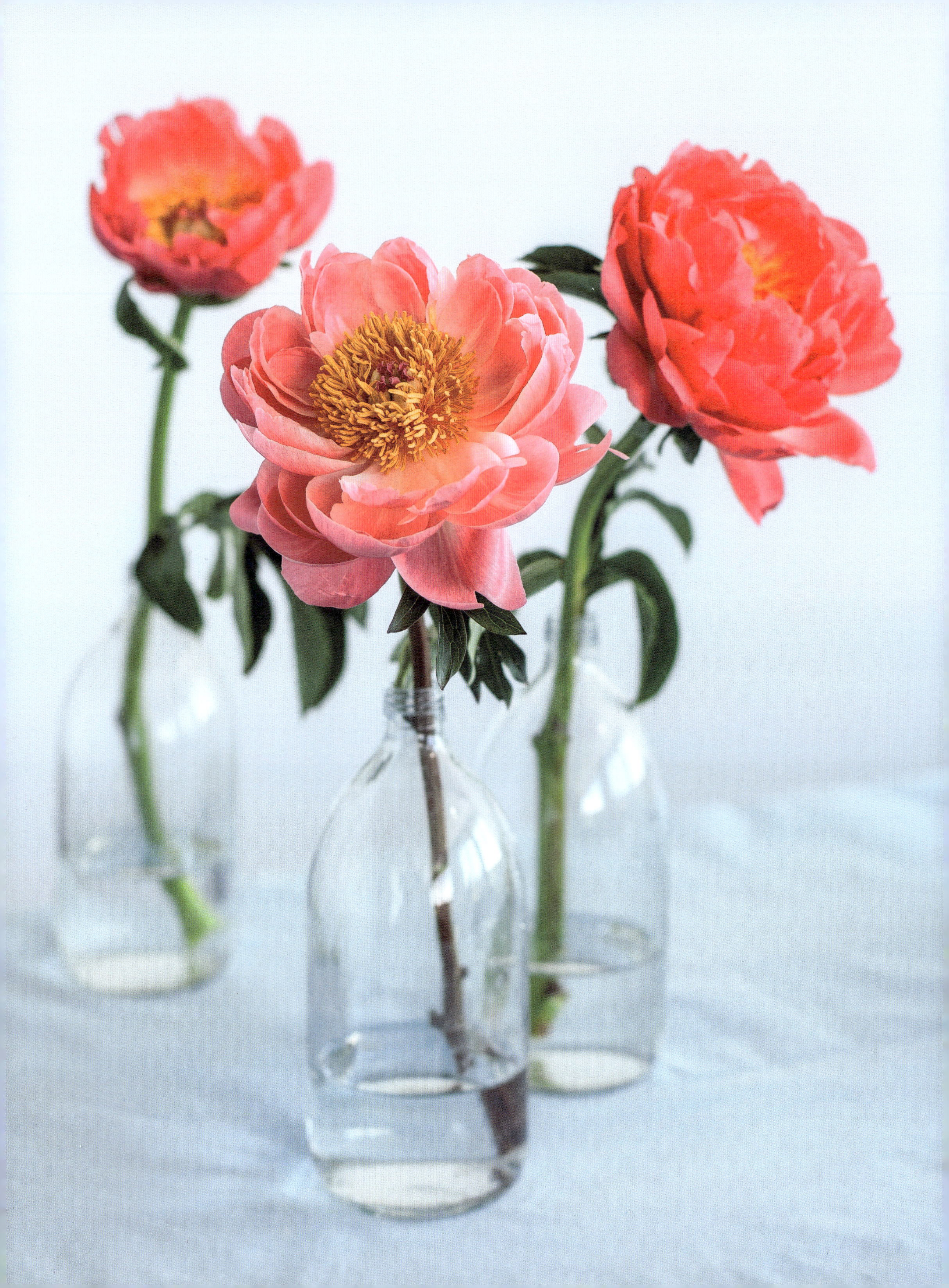

Spring 103

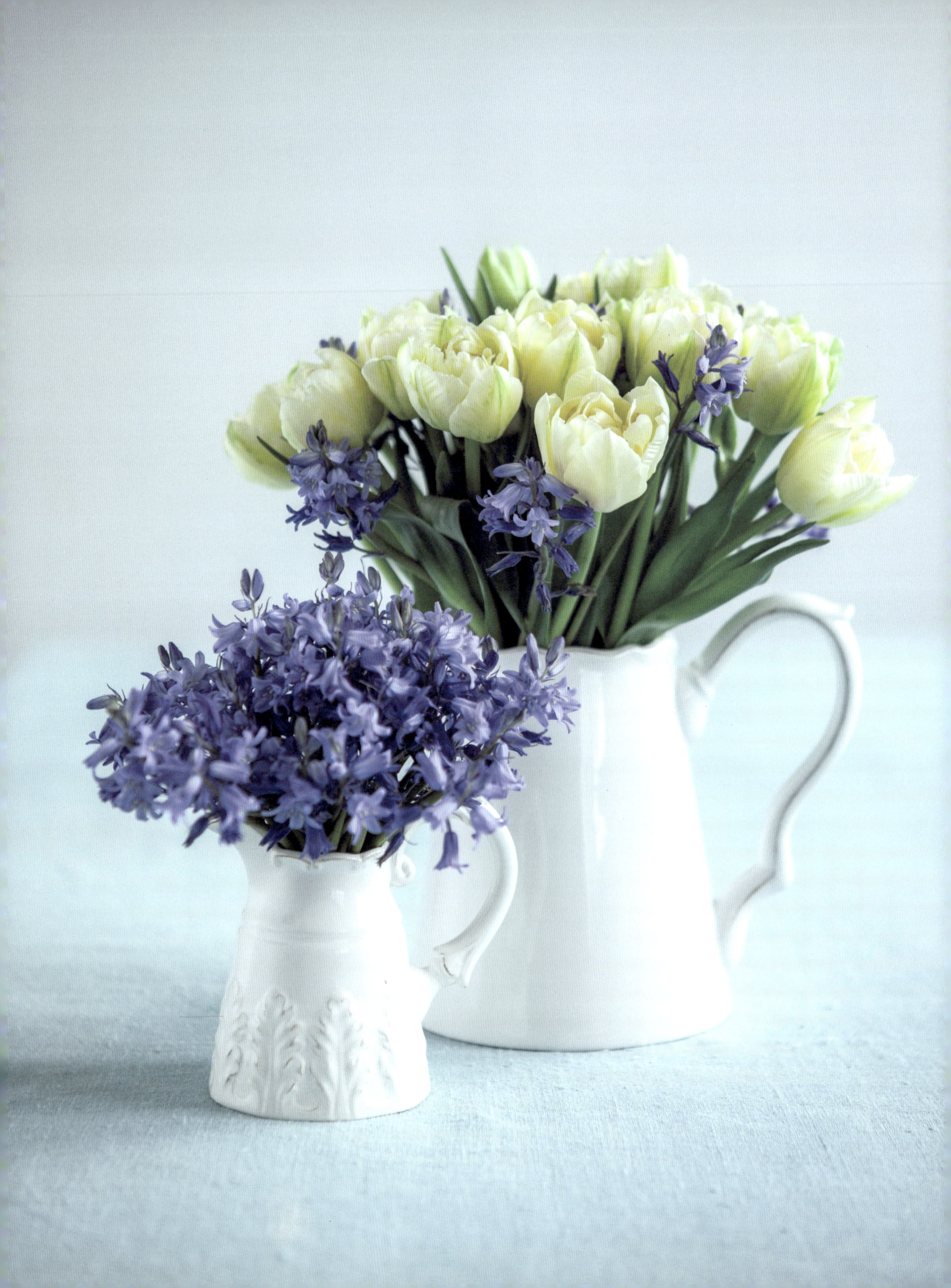

Spring 105

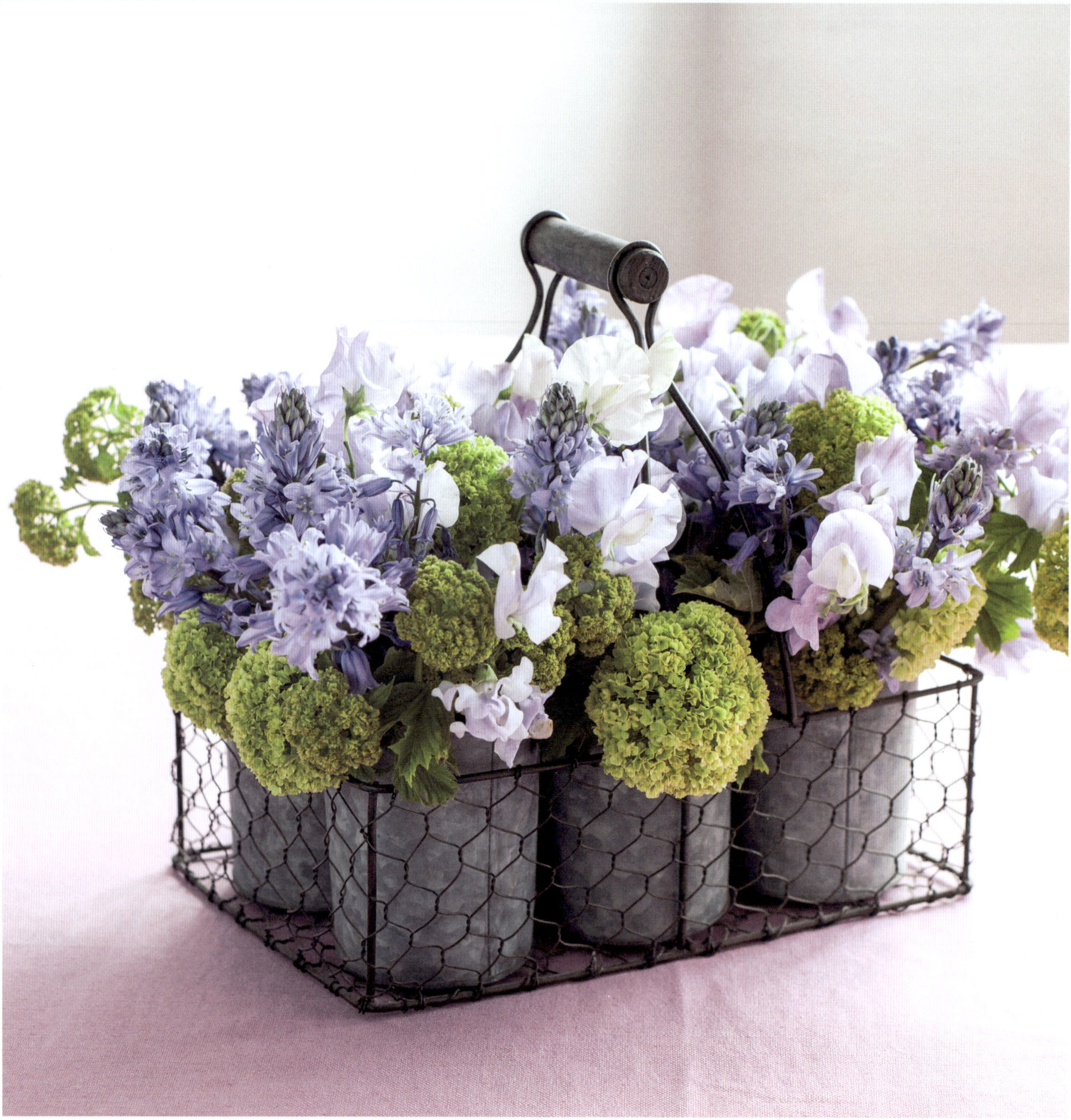

Simple arrangements featuring combinations of snowball viburnum, hyacinths, sweet peas, campanula and Bluebird roses can be placed anywhere in the house for effect, while small packages of beribboned snowball viburnum make exquisite little gifts for your guests to treasure.

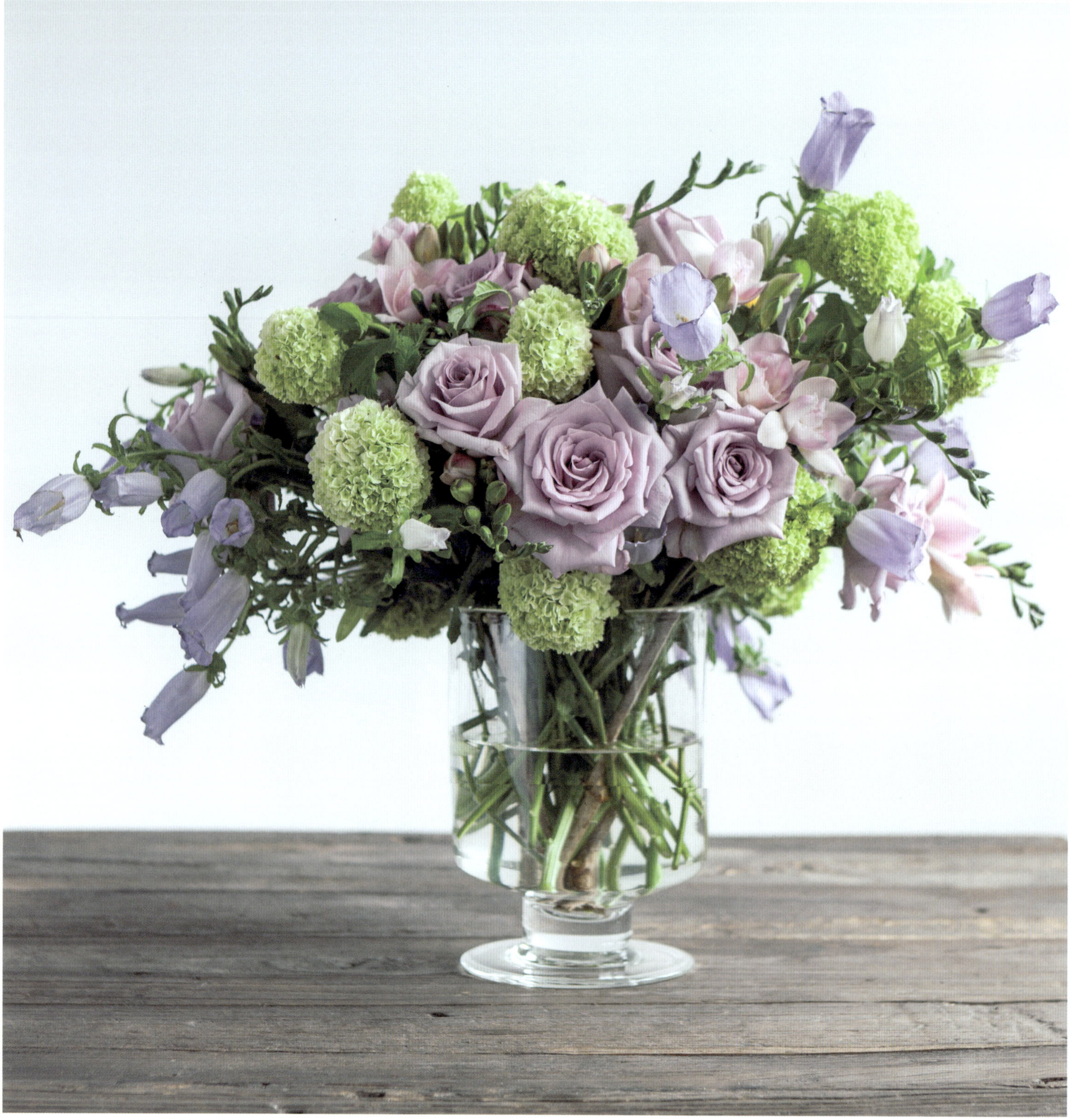

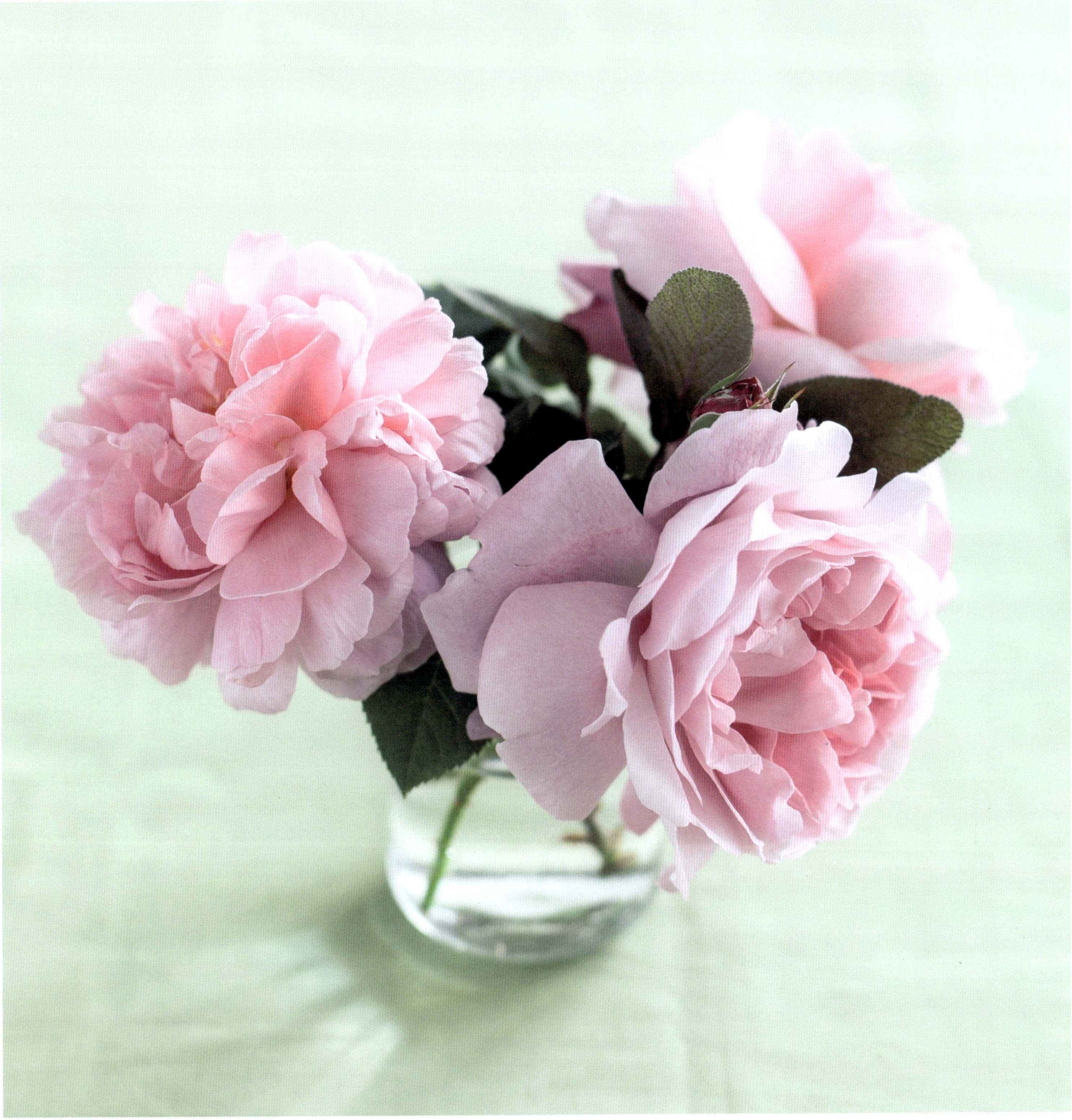

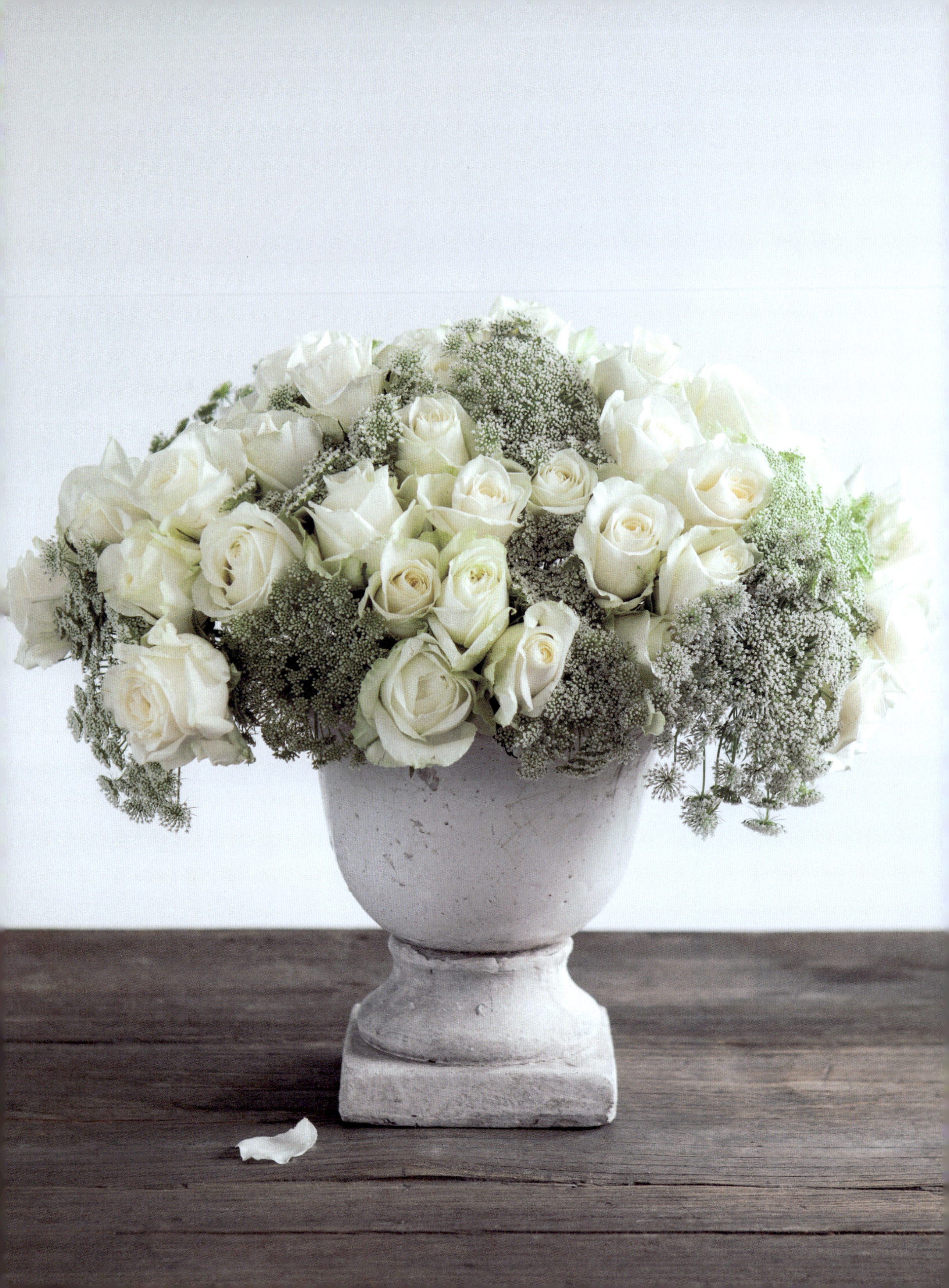

Spring 111

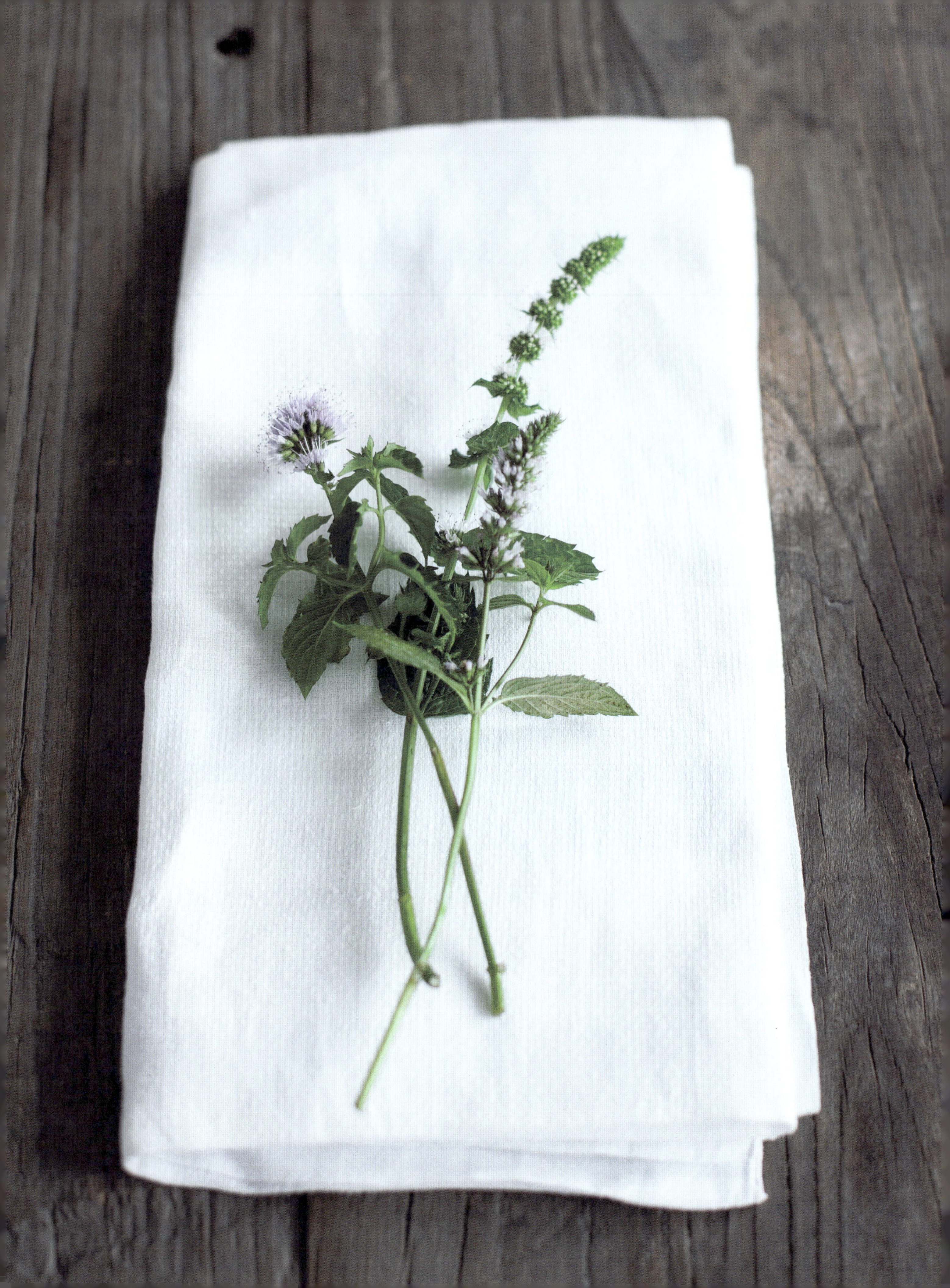

SUMMER

Bread feeds the body,
indeed, but flowers feed also
the soul.

The Koran

After the romance of spring, when it is as if so much of the earth is reborn, the warmer months of summer bring with them a more relaxed approach to life. Those first bursts of colour have now matured into an intense and sometimes fiery palette as demonstrated by flowers such as zinnias and dahlias.

This intensity of colour can be seen in many roses, too; it's not long before those delicate spring hues are replaced by summer's rich deep offerings. And as the summer solstice approaches it's as if all these blooms sense a deadline by which they must achieve their boldest and brightest tints.

The garden is a great place to be at this time of year, not least because whatever you have encouraged to grow will be at its best about now. And because flowers are usually plentiful and well priced at this time of the year, purchase them fresh from your local seller, then you can easily give any arrangement your own touch by including some home-grown foliage to add colour and texture.

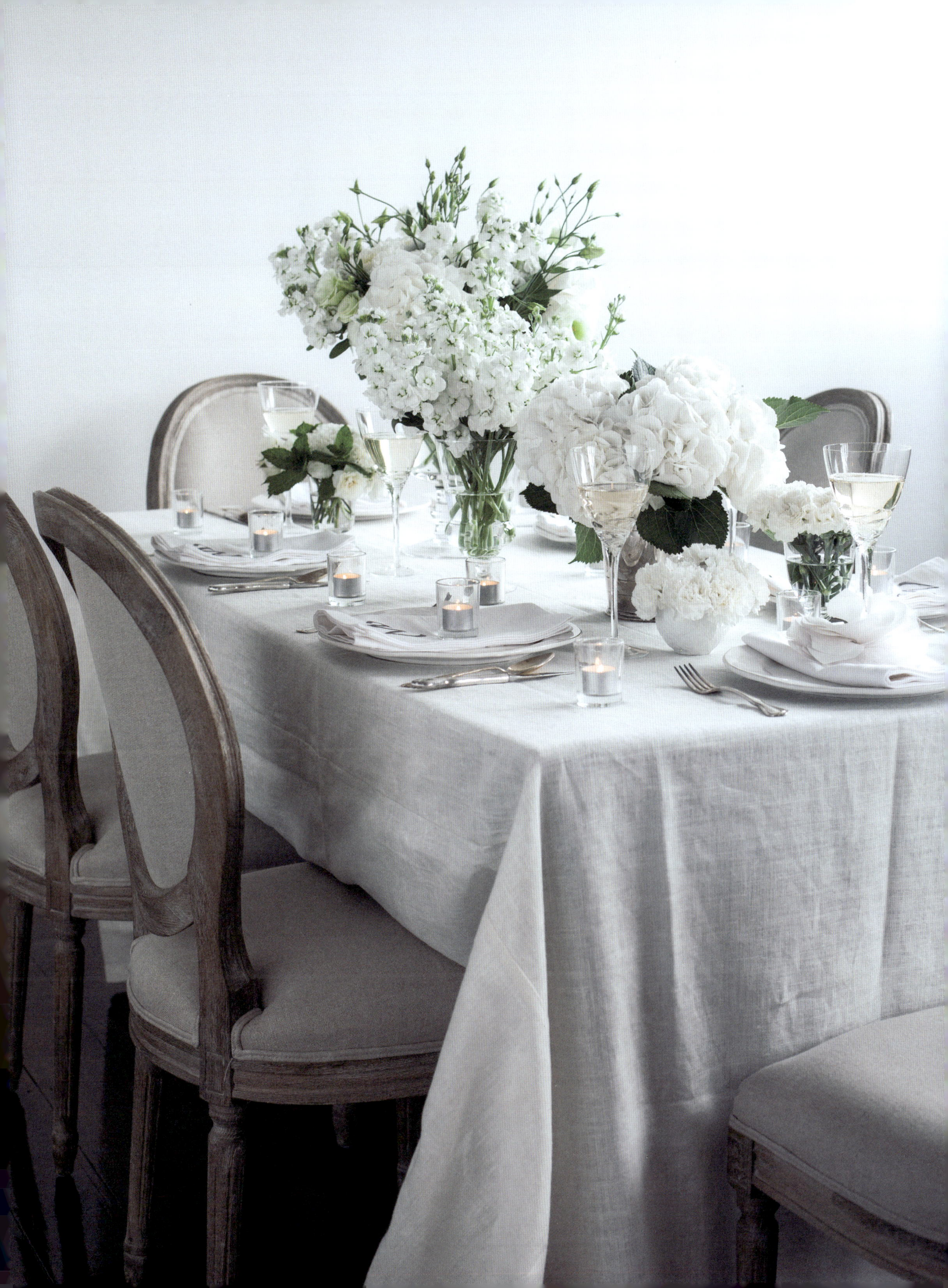

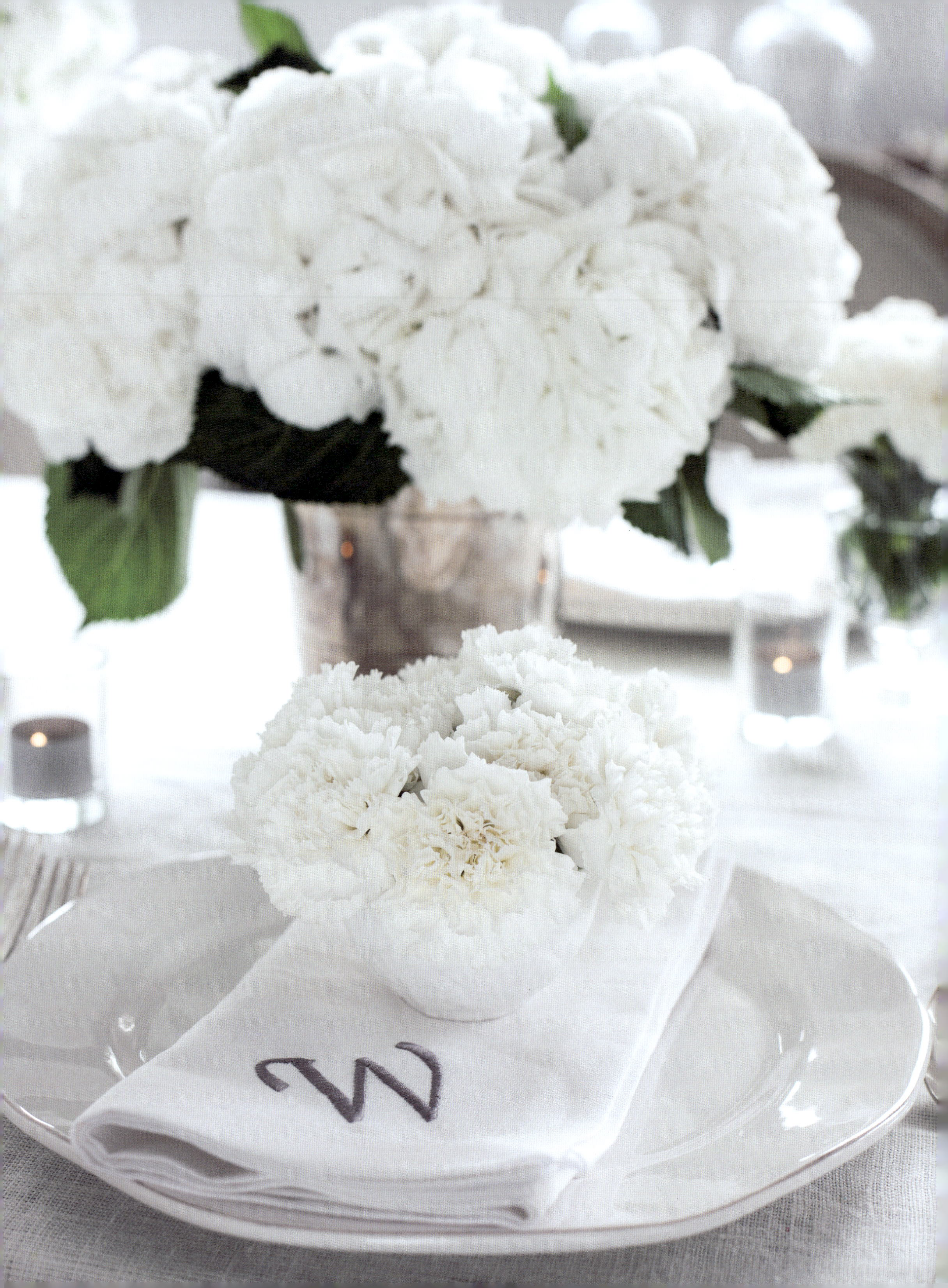

Although many flowers are at their brightest at this time of year, summer's warmer temperatures also invite contrast, especially after you've spent time outdoors and feel the need for a cooler ambience.

Invoke a wonderful feeling of serenity with these cool and tranquil settings using white lisianthus, stock, standard carnations and hydrangeas grouped in plain glass or crystal and enhanced by the use of white table linen.

Candlelight and fresh flowers add a special touch of intimacy to any occasion; however, always keep the colour theme as subtle as possible. Tea light candles are a perfect addition to any special dinner table setting.

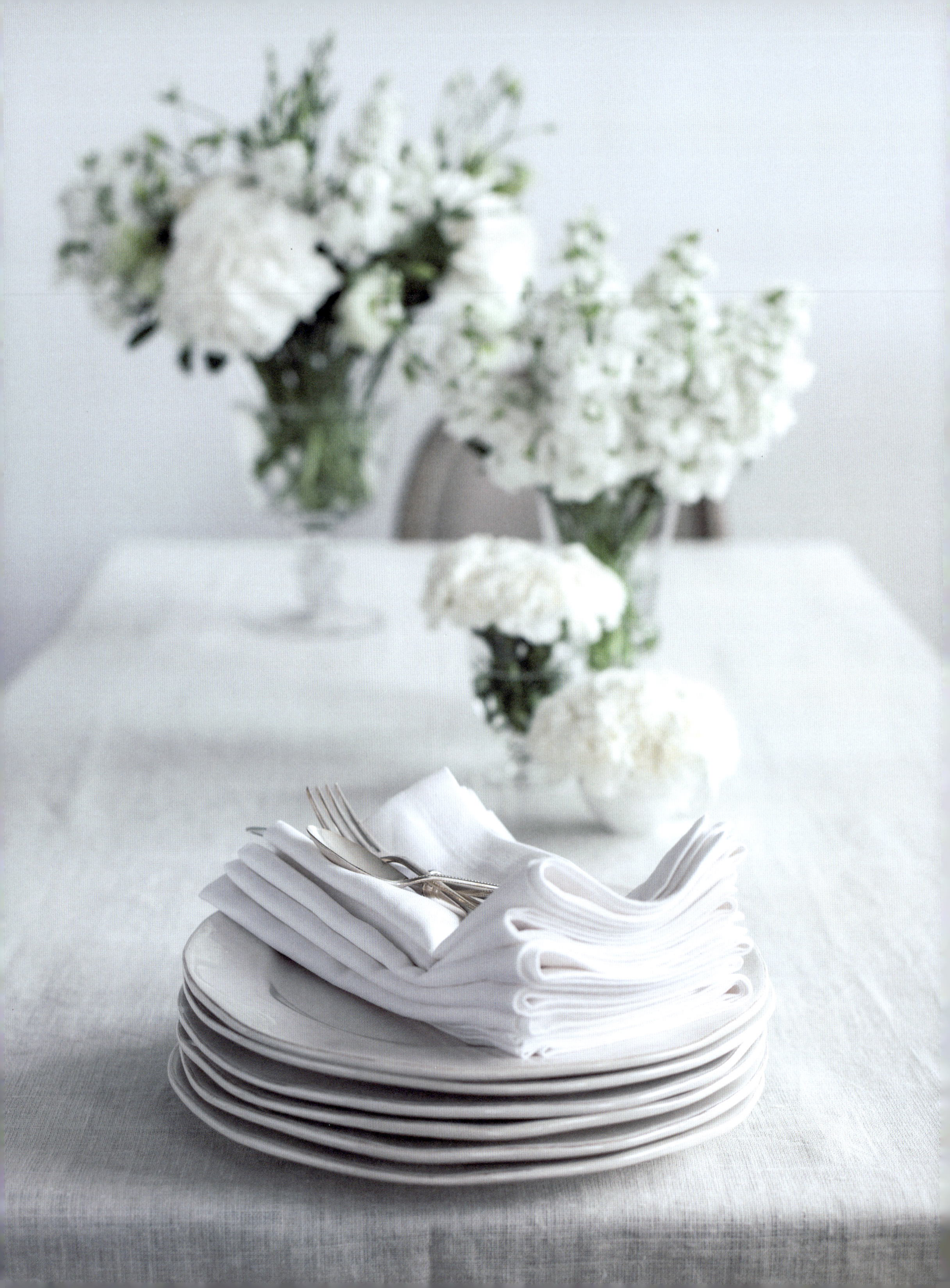

Sweetly scented white carnation flower heads enhance this serene white-on-white table setting.

You'll be surprised how much of what you already have in your cupboards can be used to set off a few gorgeous blooms such as delicate china and a silver ice bucket seen here above and right.

Summer 121

When wanting a simple less formal look, go for a handful of pansies or raid your herb patch. Flowering chives, mint and oregano make a charming and fragrant statement.

I know a bank where the wild thyme blows,
Where oxlips and the nodding violet grows,
Quite over-canopied with luscious woodbine,
With sweet musk-roses and with eglantine.

William Shakespeare

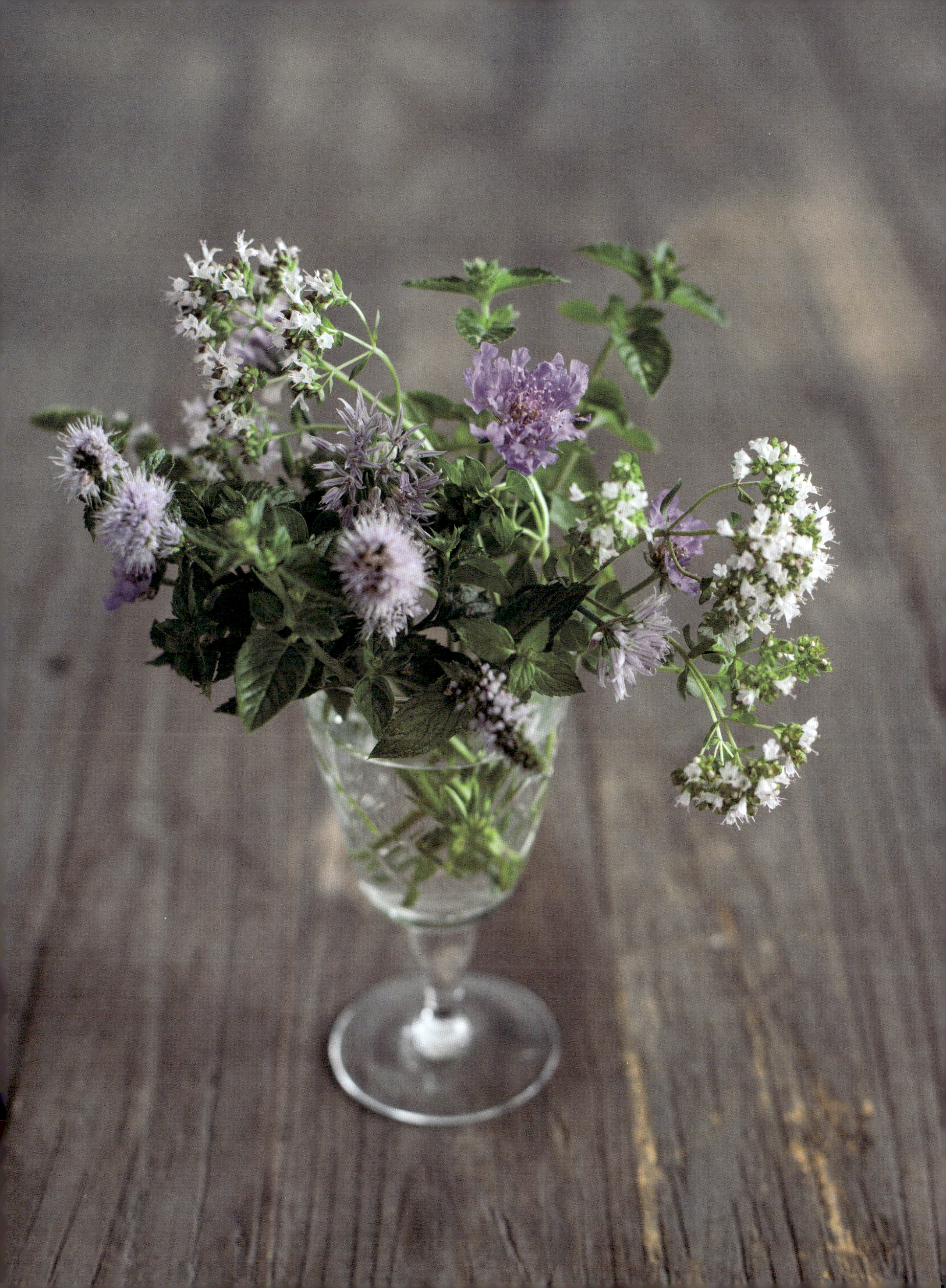

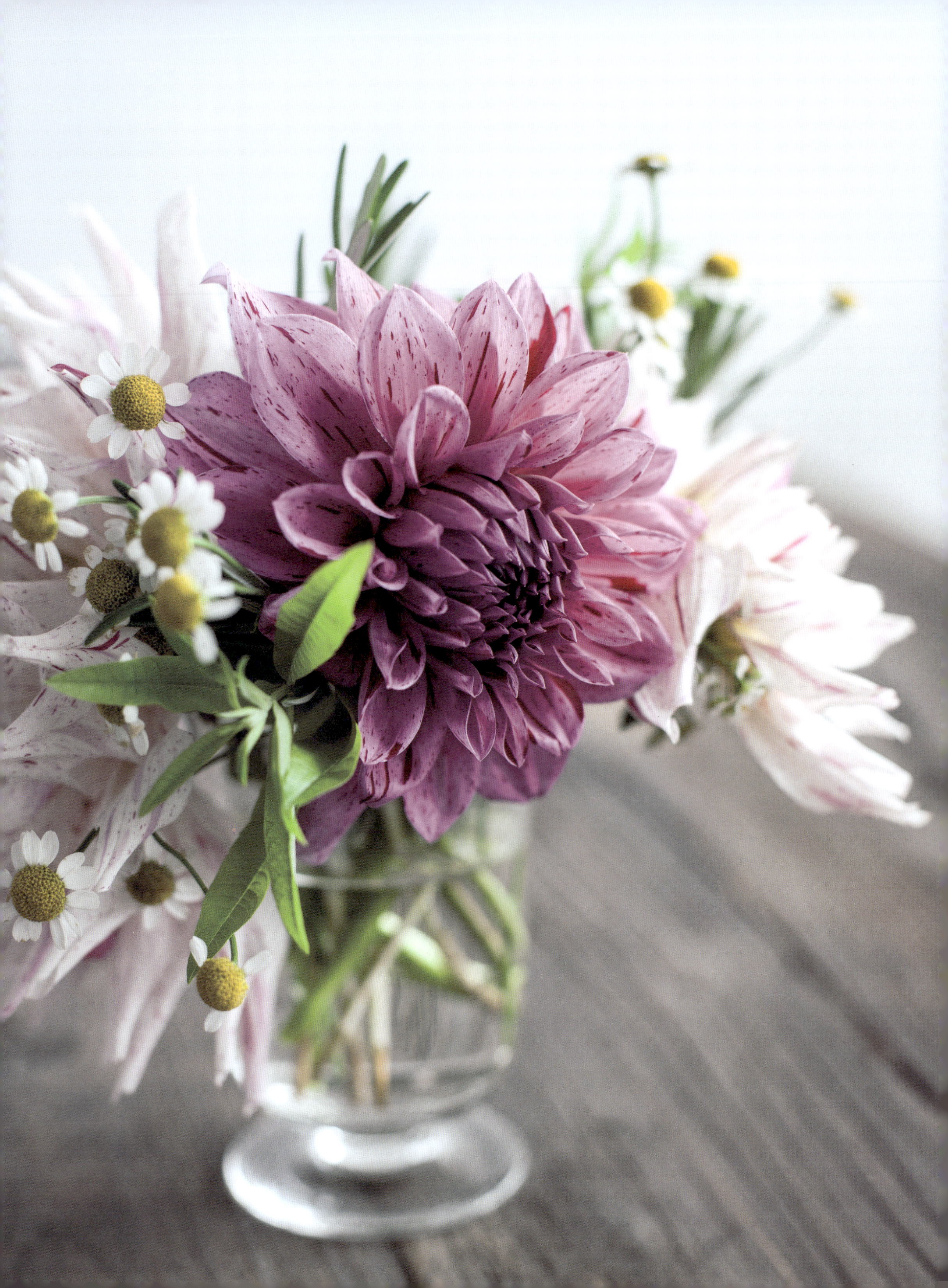

Dahlias come in an amazing array of colours that here blend perfectly with a little lemon verbena and some stalks of feverfew.

Flowers have spoken to me more than I can tell in written words. They are the hieroglyphics of angels, loved by all men for the beauty of their character, though few can decipher even fragments of their meaning.

Lydia M. Child

The pure simplicity of single white chrysanthemums is hard to surpass.

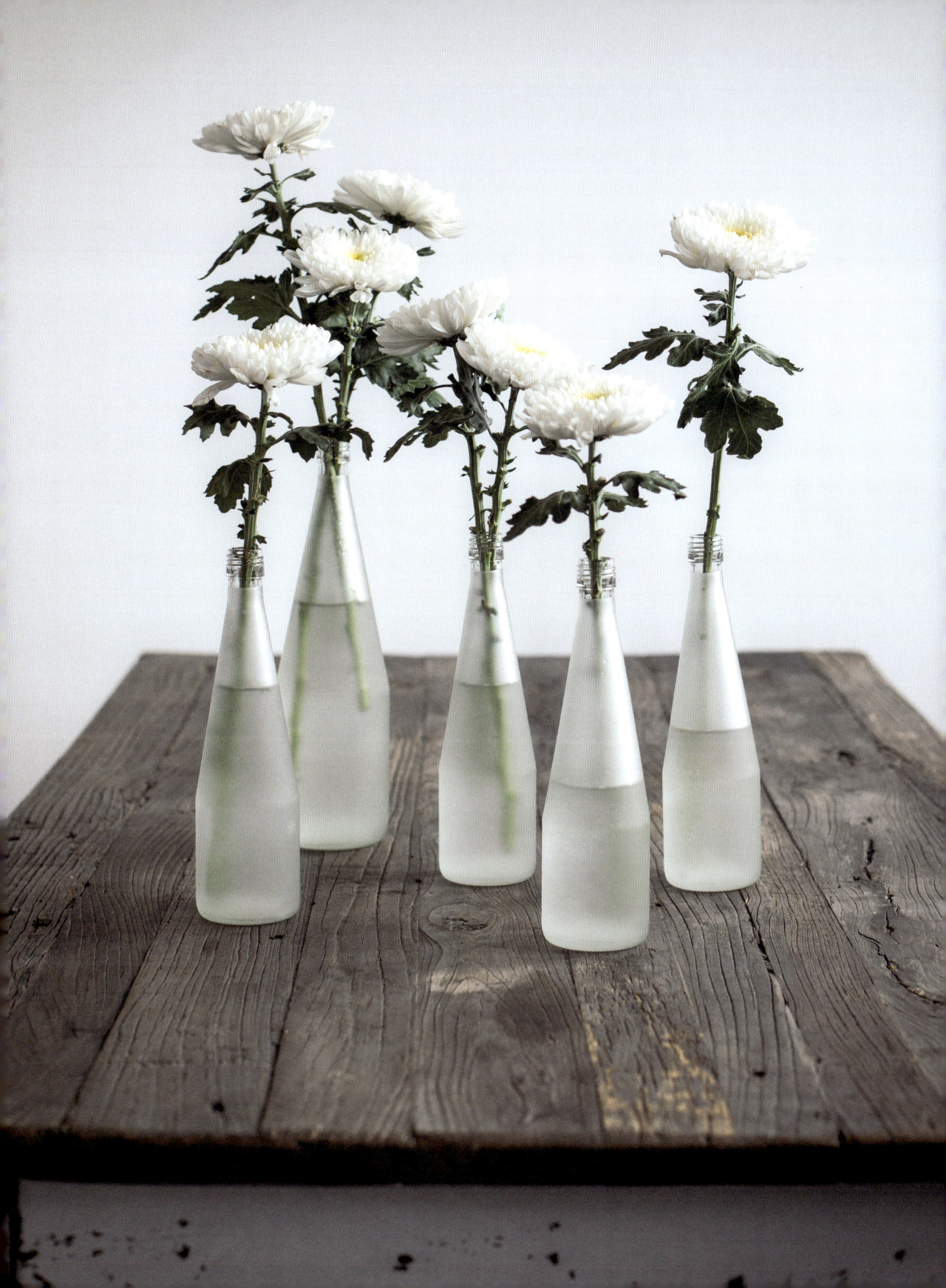

Loveliest of lovely things are they on earth that soonest pass away. The rose that lives its little hour is prized beyond the sculptured flower.

William B. Bryant

Over the next few pages a profusion of pink petals from garden roses mixed with commercially grown peonies – all arranged in the simplest of vessels on a damask cloth – create a very romantic and feminine ambience.

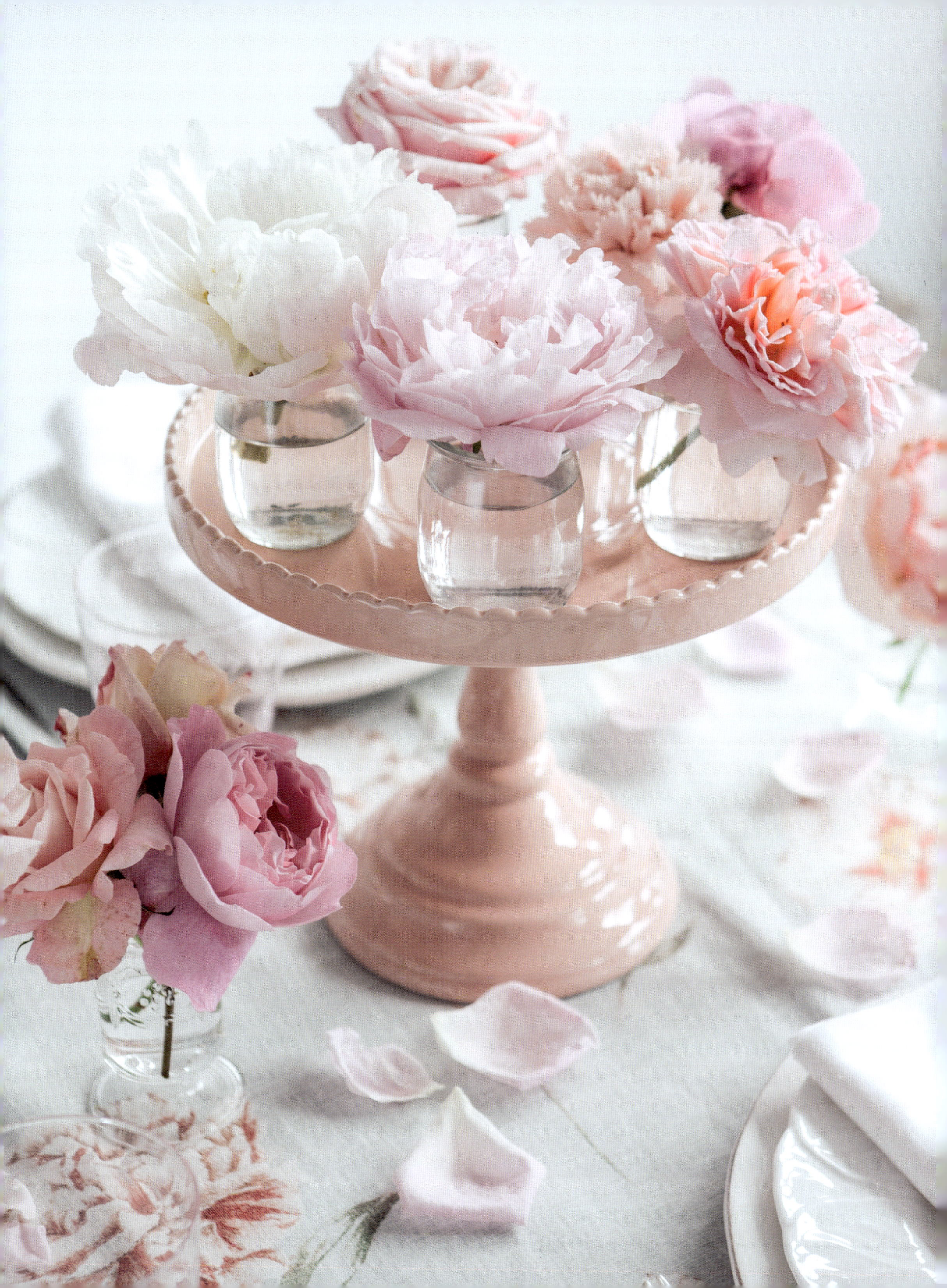

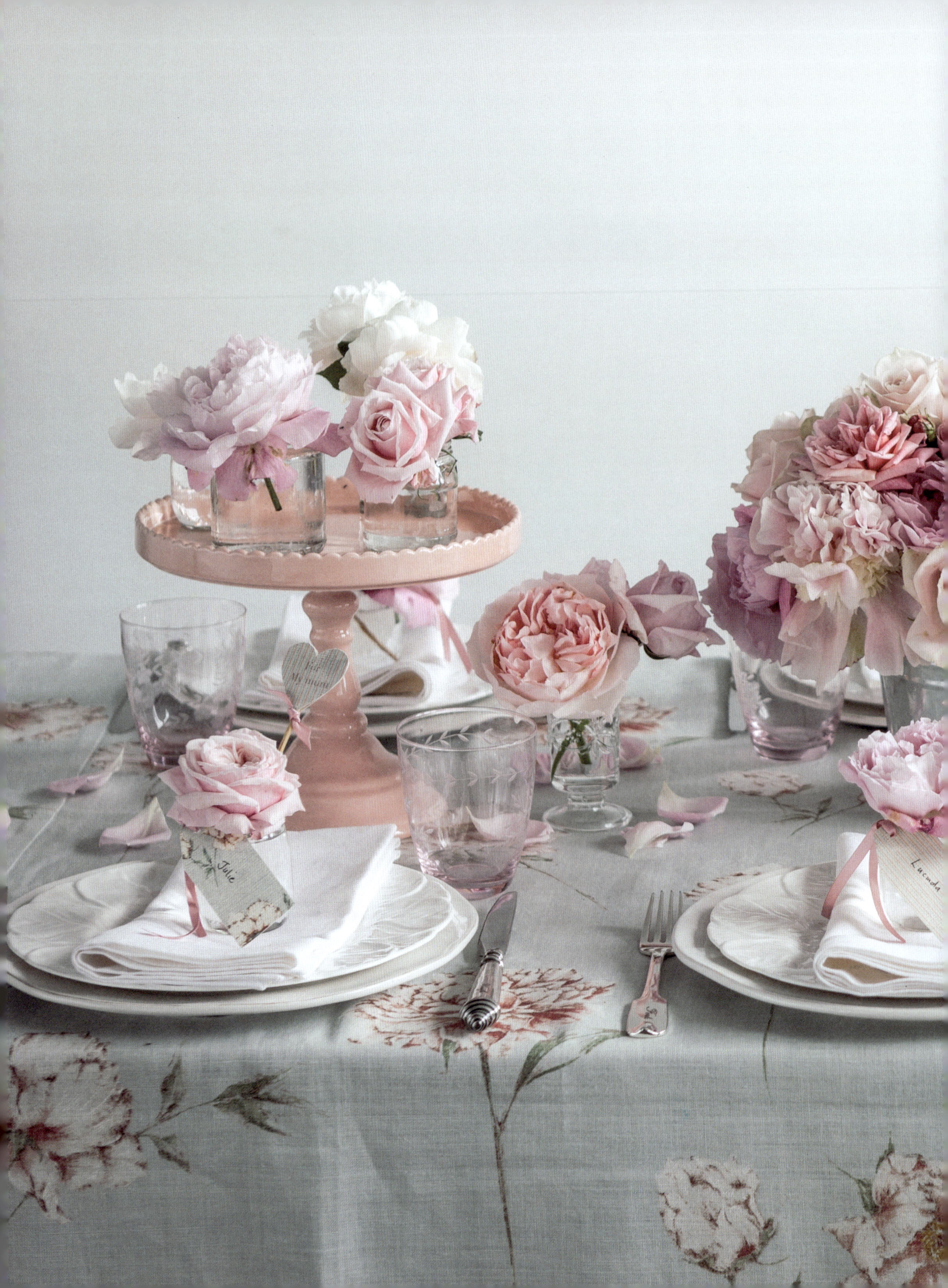
Julie

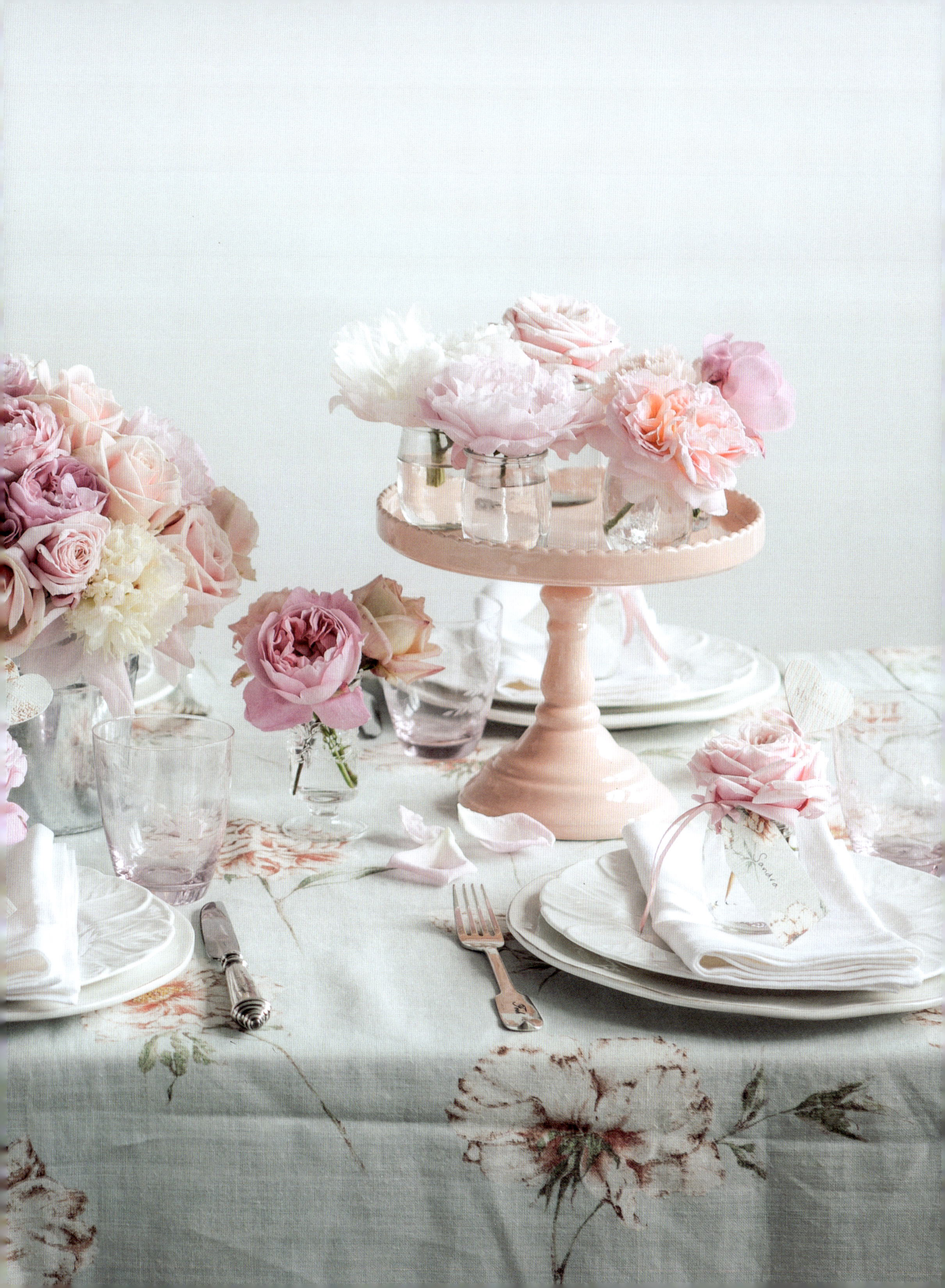

I'd rather have roses on my table
than diamonds on my neck.

Emma Goldman

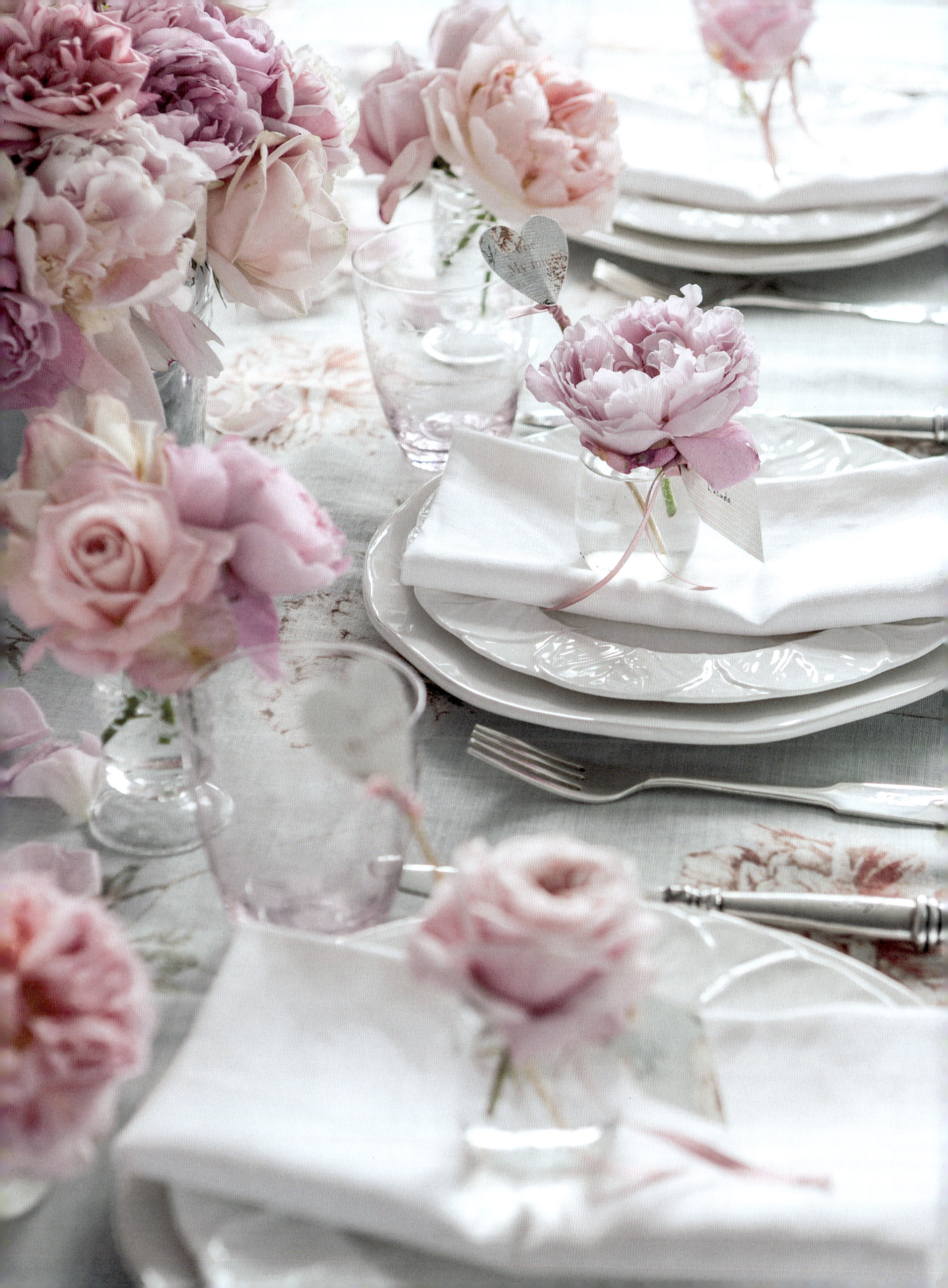

Gentle shades of pink are carried through to the other table decorations, some of which make ideal gifts for guests. And although the floral ice bucket looks to be a highly ambitious project, the main component apart from the flowers is time.

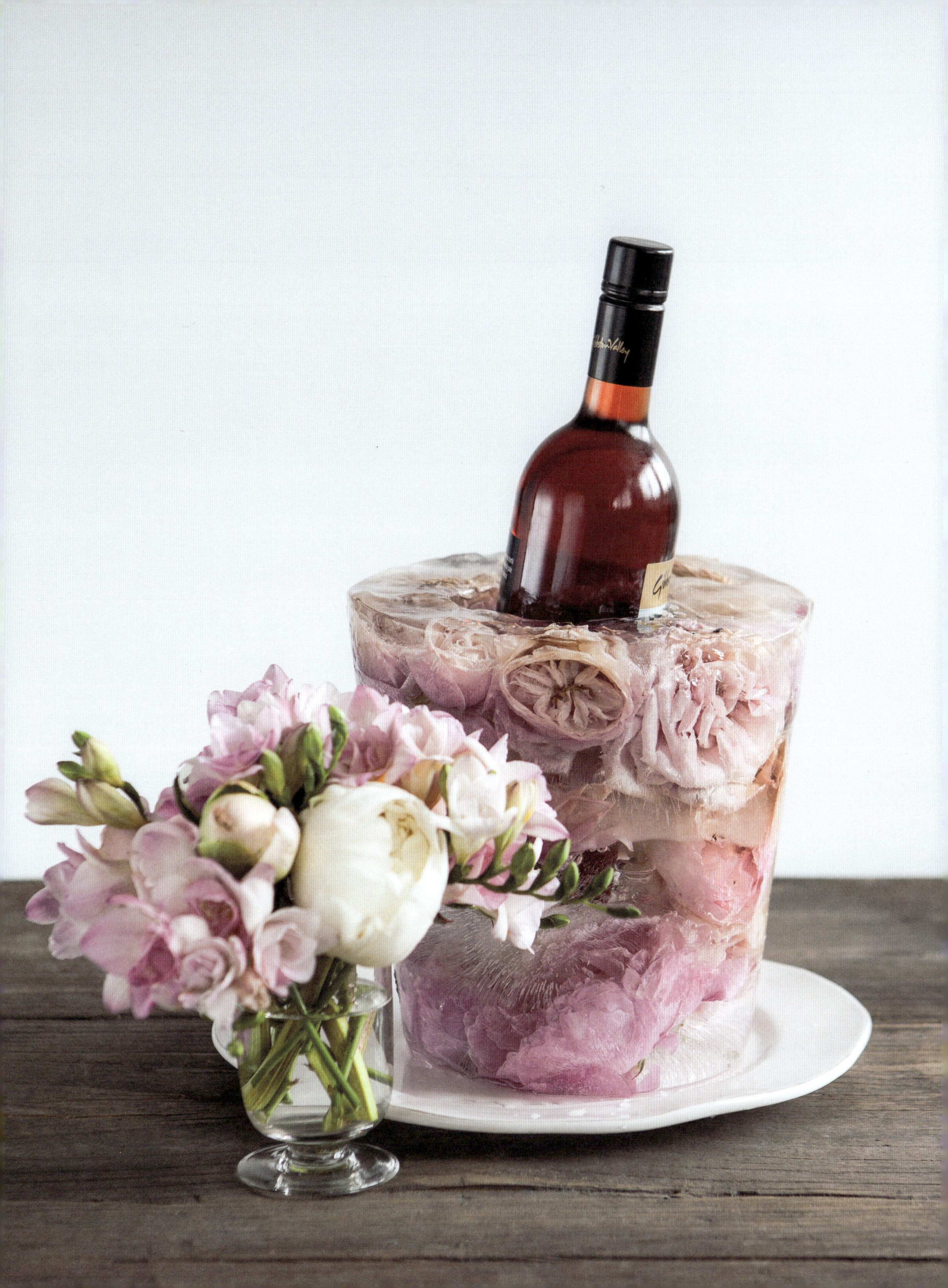

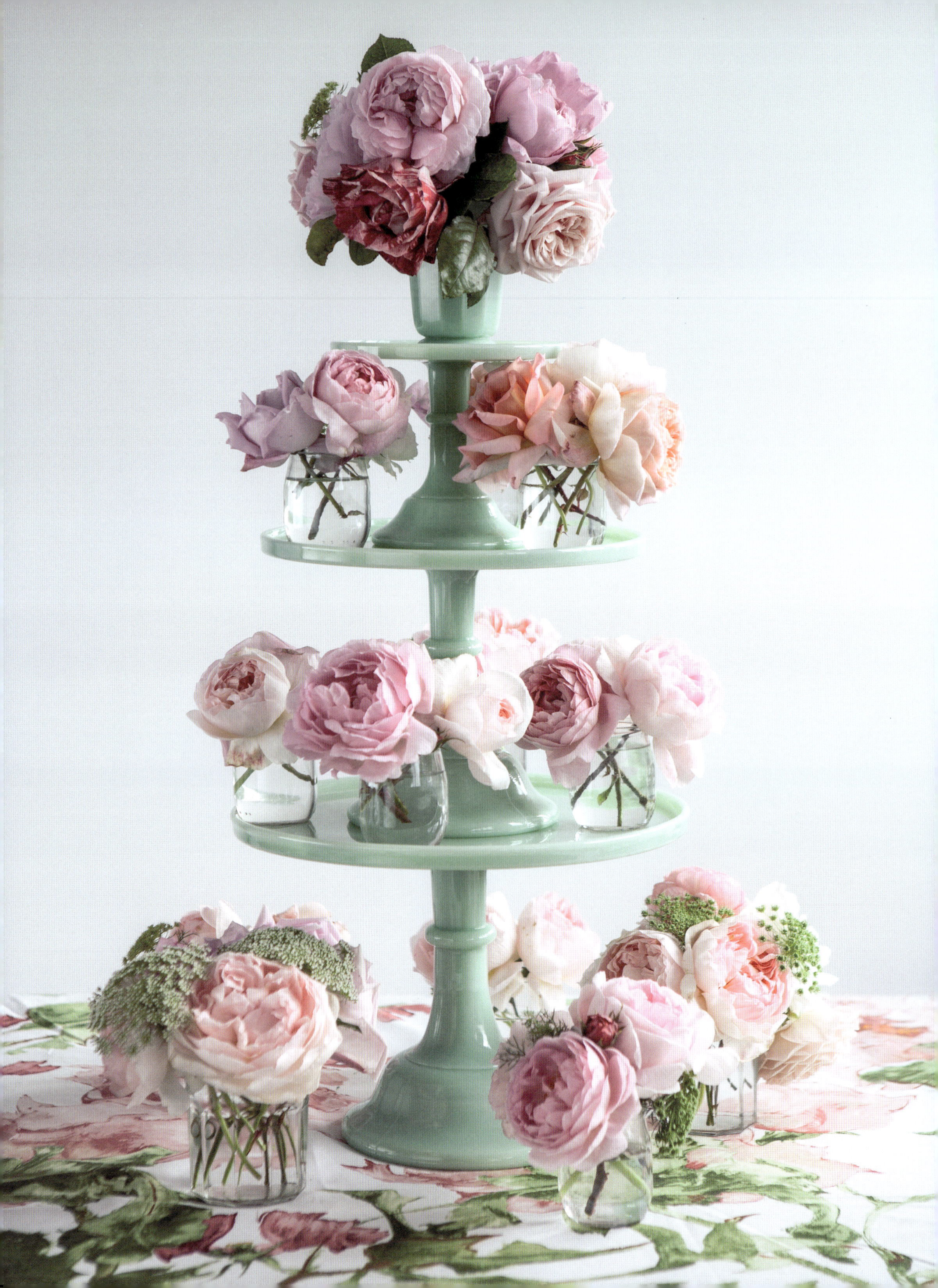

Pastel-coloured cake stands are the ultimate table accessory when you want to show off an abundance of floral perfection. This arrangement of garden roses with a peep of Queen Anne lace (left) works so well because of the simplicity of the plain glass jars in which the flowers are bunched.

To be overcome by the fragrance of flowers is a delectable form of defeat.

John Beverley Nichols

A scented rose wreath will lift even an ordinary occasion to a very special level, but if roses are not available, use any other flowers that appeal. The secret is to keep the colour palette simple and the textures uncomplicated.

Overleaf is another example of how to ensure that the flower rather than the container is the star of the show; in this case simple glass bottles allow the full drama of these peonies to be seen.

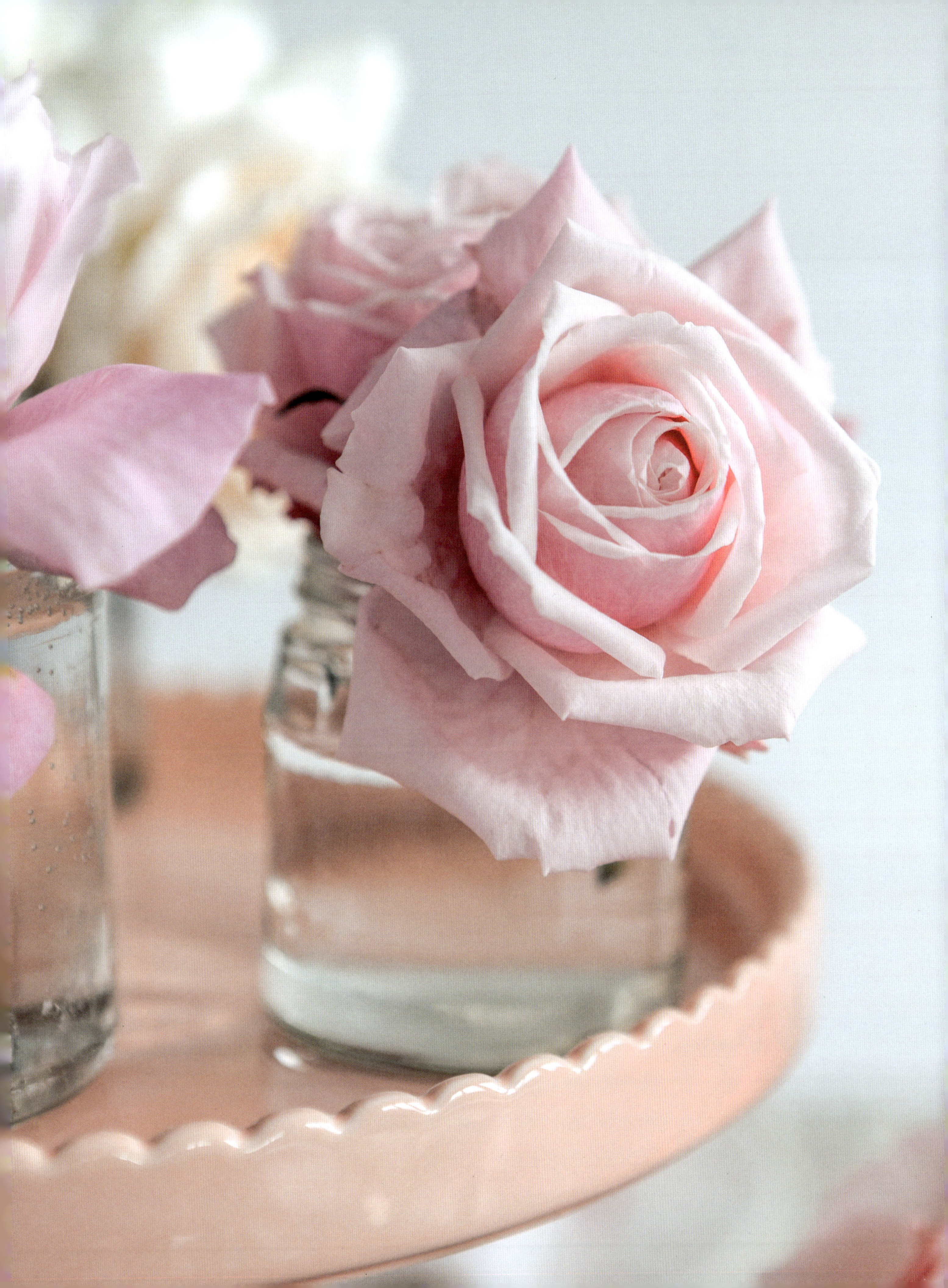

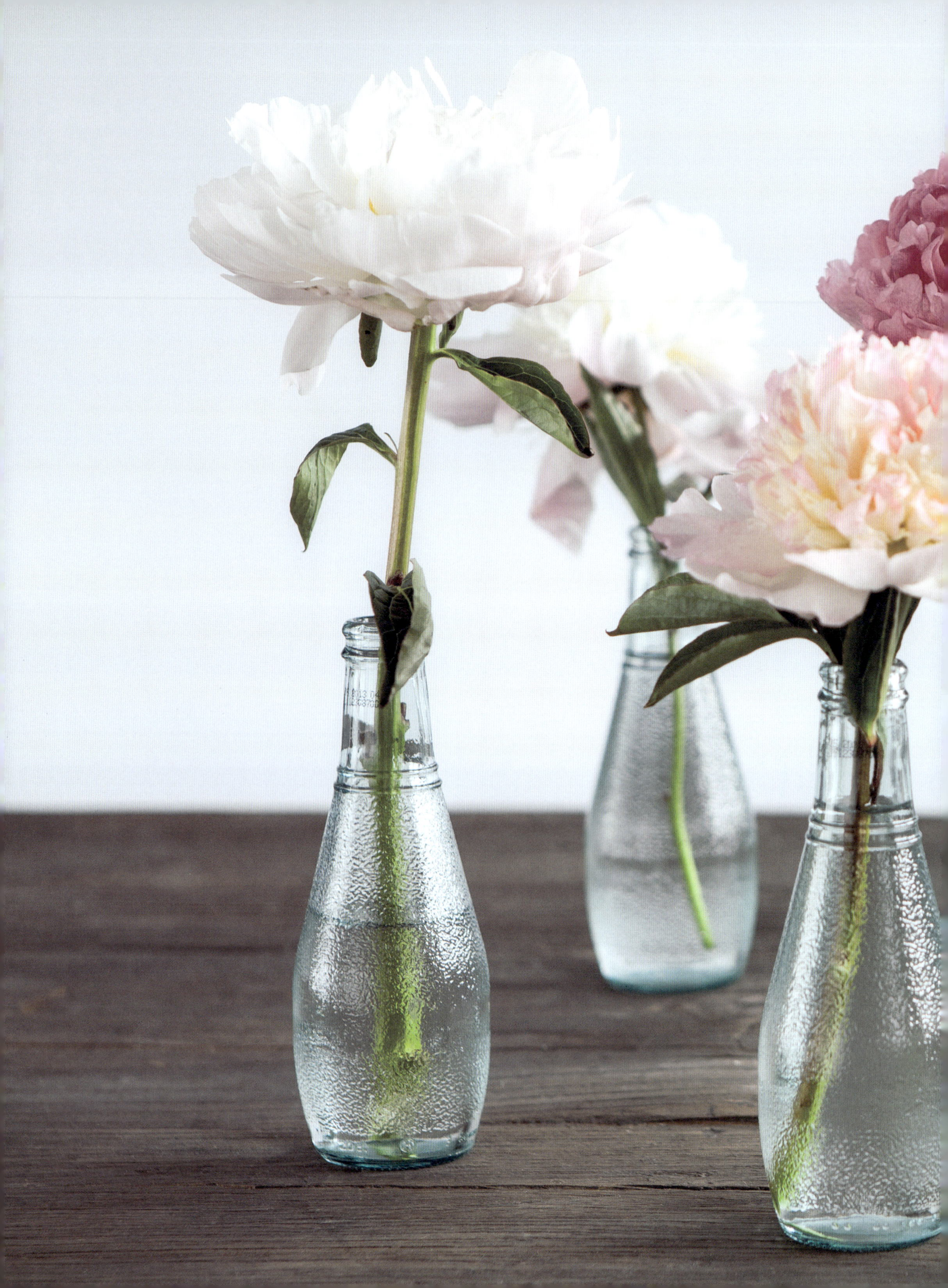

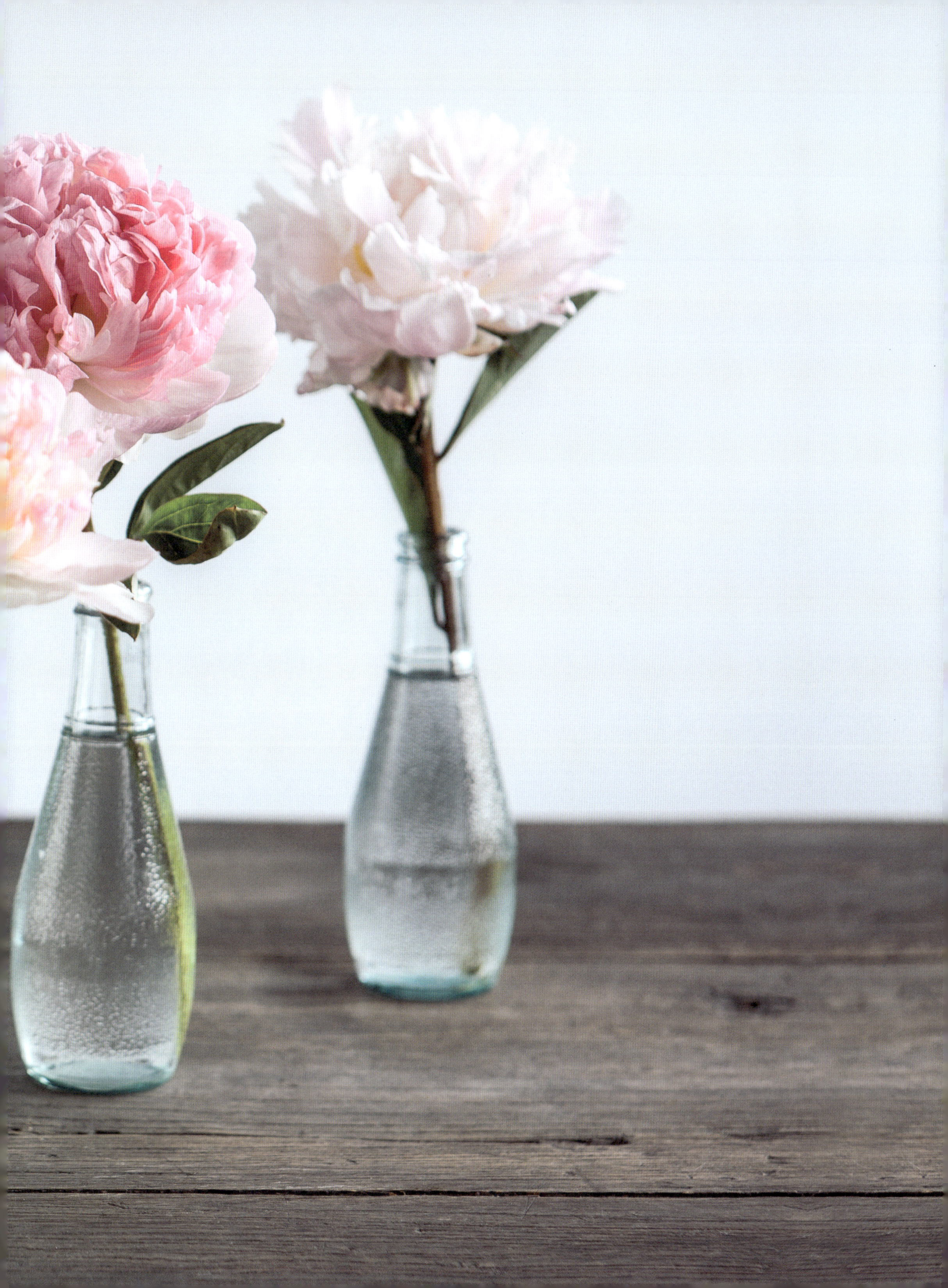

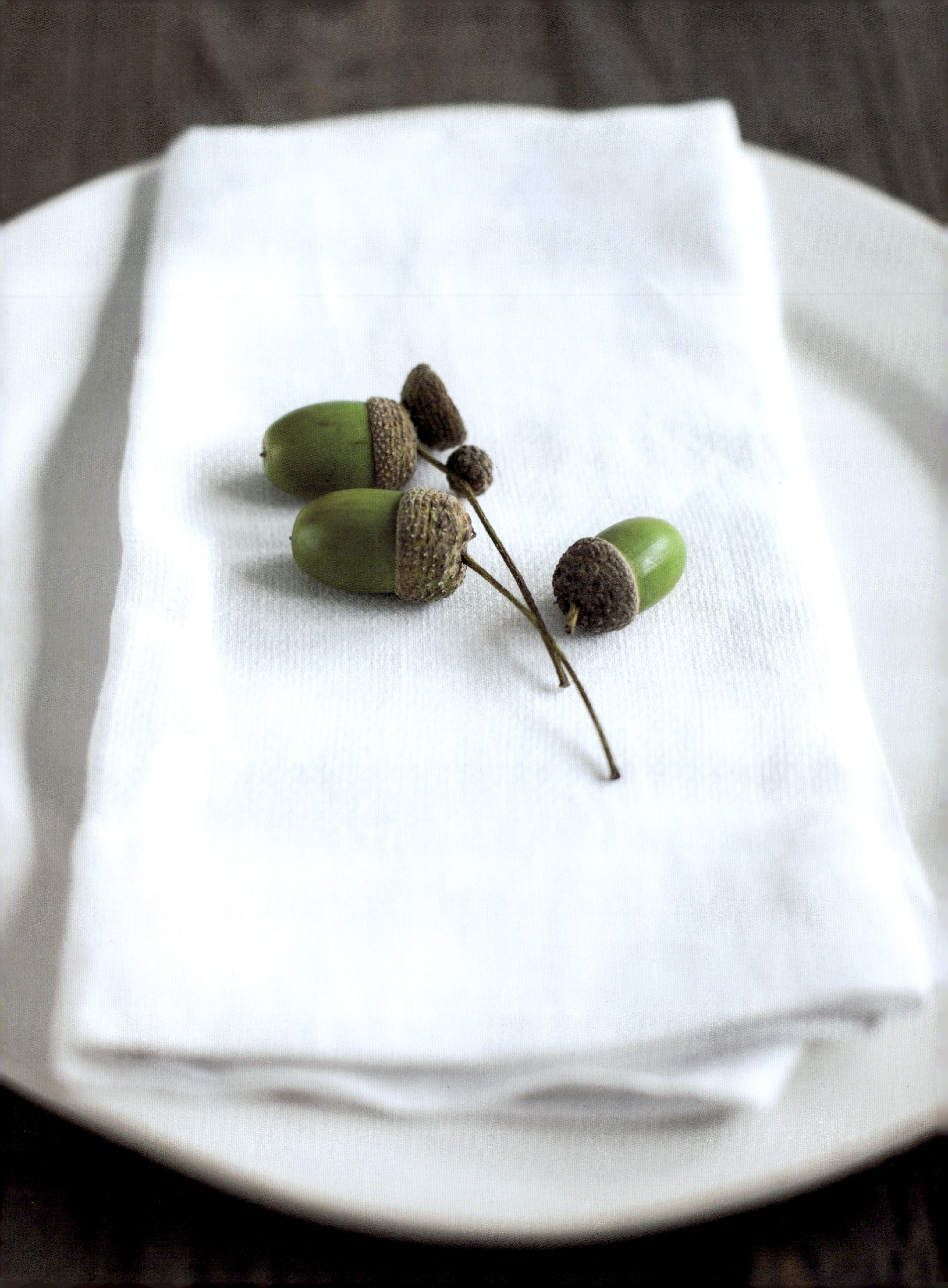

AUTUMN

I perhaps owe
having become a
painter to flowers.

Claude Monet

Nature's gifts during this bountiful season are many indeed. Probably at no other time of year are we so much aware of the colourful consequences of what we've planted in the soil. Take pumpkins, for example: during autumn it's as if they are growing before our very eyes; and many of the flowers available now seem to take their cue from those colours – burnt orange in particular.

Burnt orange, vibrant yellows and rich reds all complement each other in a manner unique to nature – they are colours that we can work with, too, as they are perfect for making a strong statement. However, keep those vessels and related containers as simple as possible so you don't detract from any of that earthy sensual boldness.

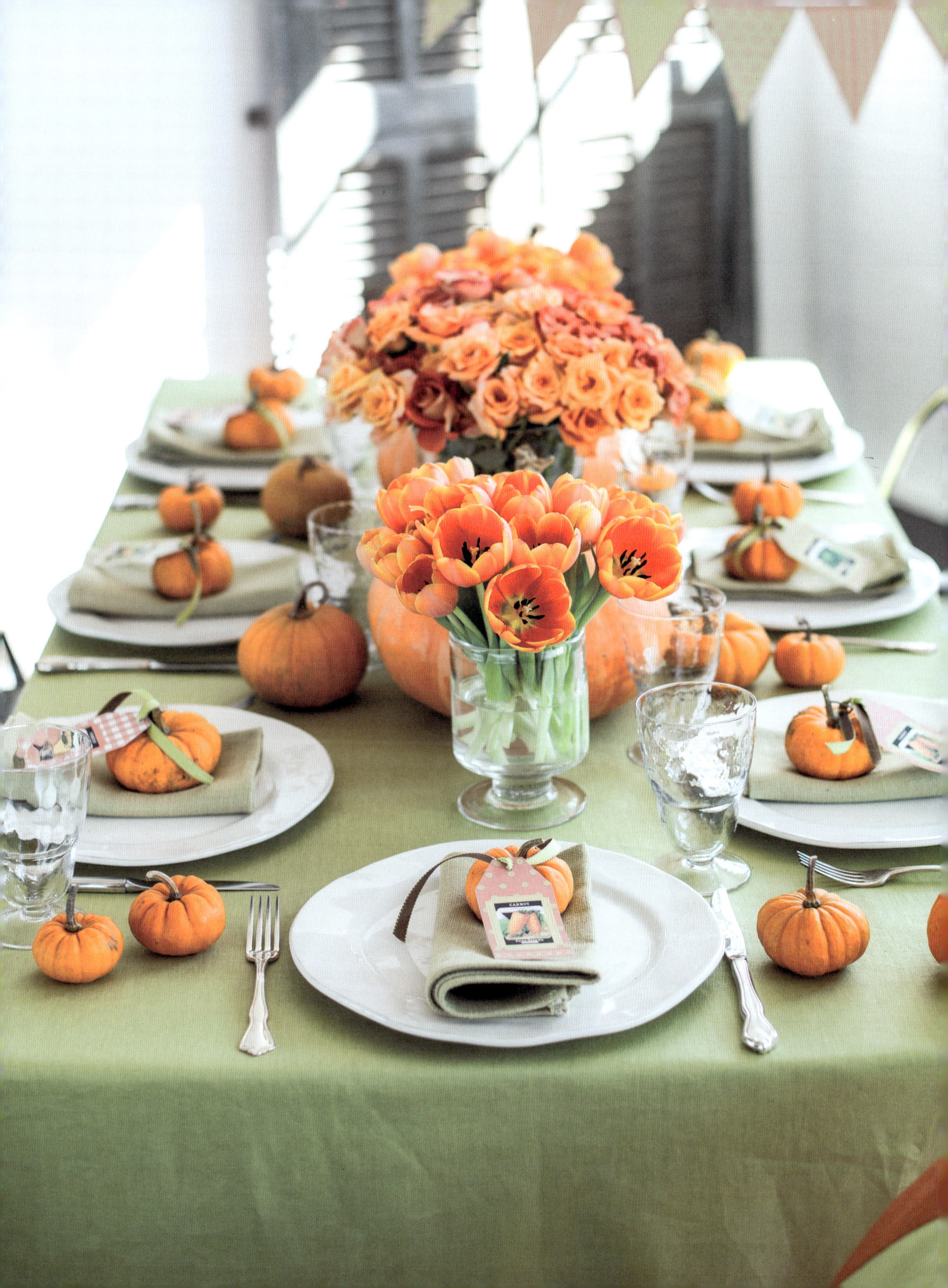

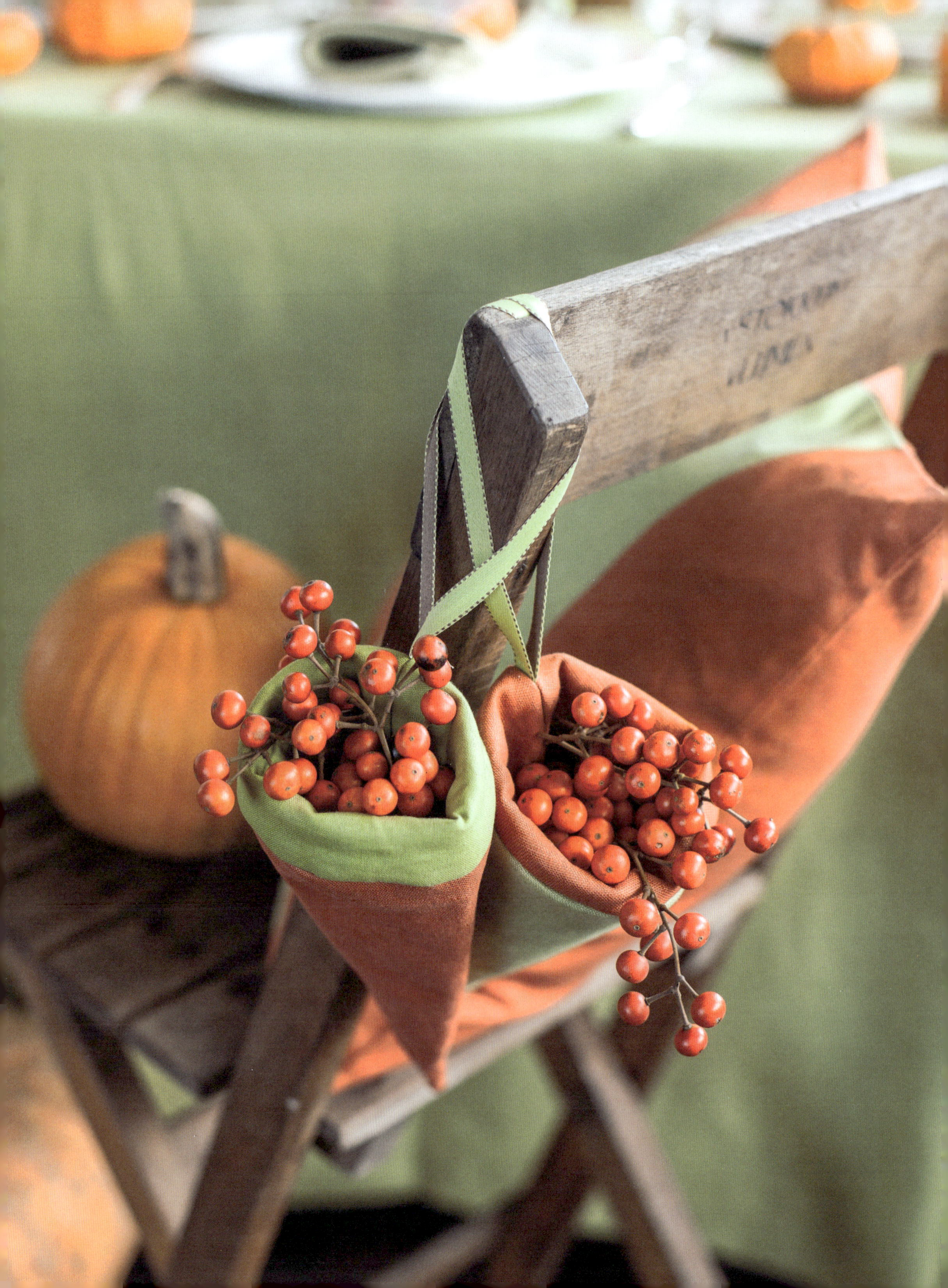

Another bonus that comes with autumn is the abundance of glorious foliage and berries all around us. Using these, we can achieve some truly stunning floral effects for the table or maybe just for fun.

By following nature's palette it's impossible to go wrong so let your instincts and creativity work together to add colourful touches to an autumn banquet or even an informal barbecue, such as bunches of berries spilling out of these easy-to-make cones (left). This is the time to use your thick table linen, chunky plates and bowls and anything else with a rustic look and feel.

Throughout much of this chapter there's rather a special emphasis on pumpkins. Interestingly, according to the dictionary a pumpkin is a fruit – but whatever you want to call them don't overlook their decorative value.

I would rather sit on a pumpkin and have it all to myself, than be crowded on a velvet cushion.

Henry David Thoreau

On these and following pages russet-coloured tulips and roses in similar shades vie for attention against the cool green of the table linen.

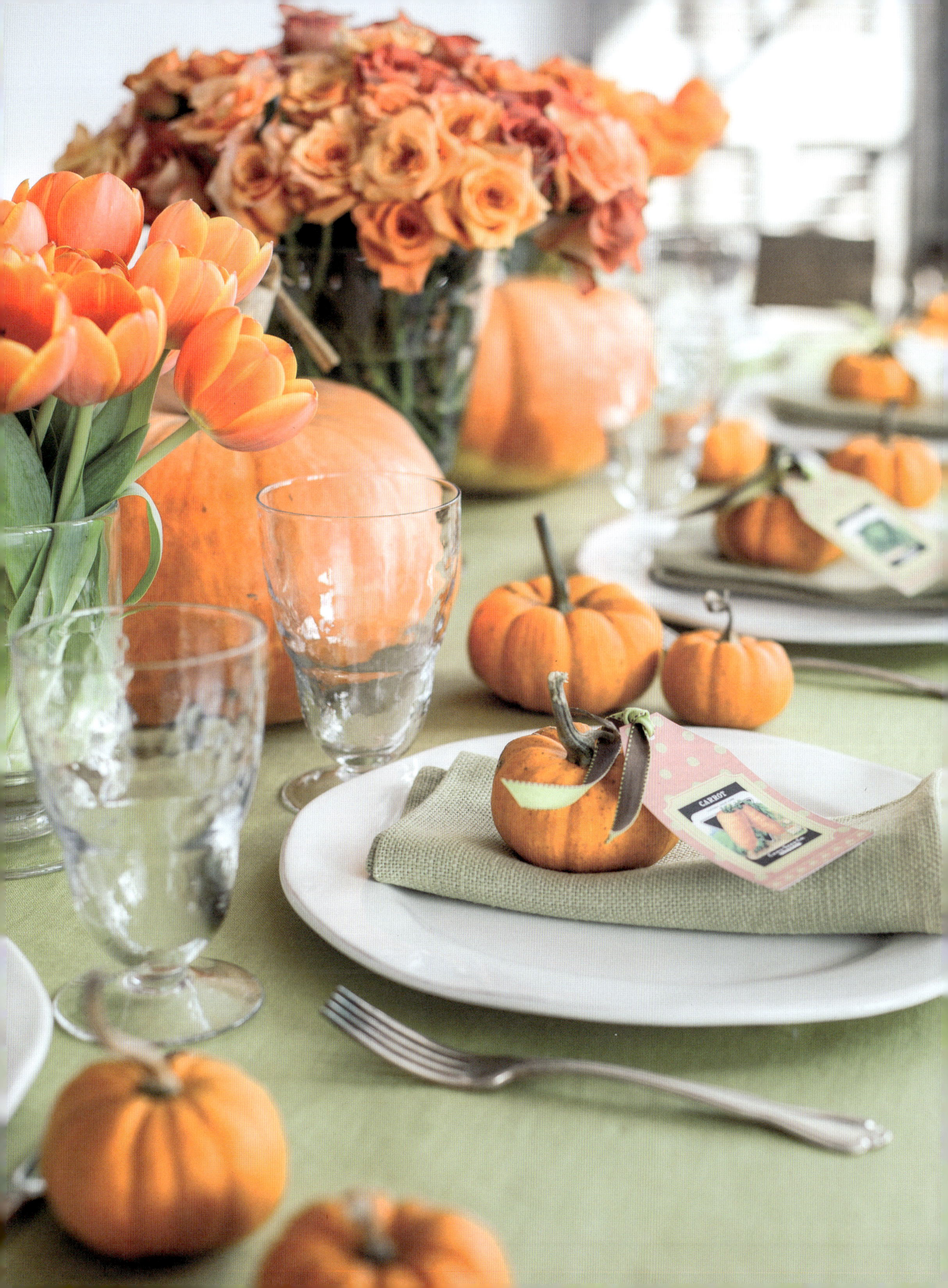
CARROT

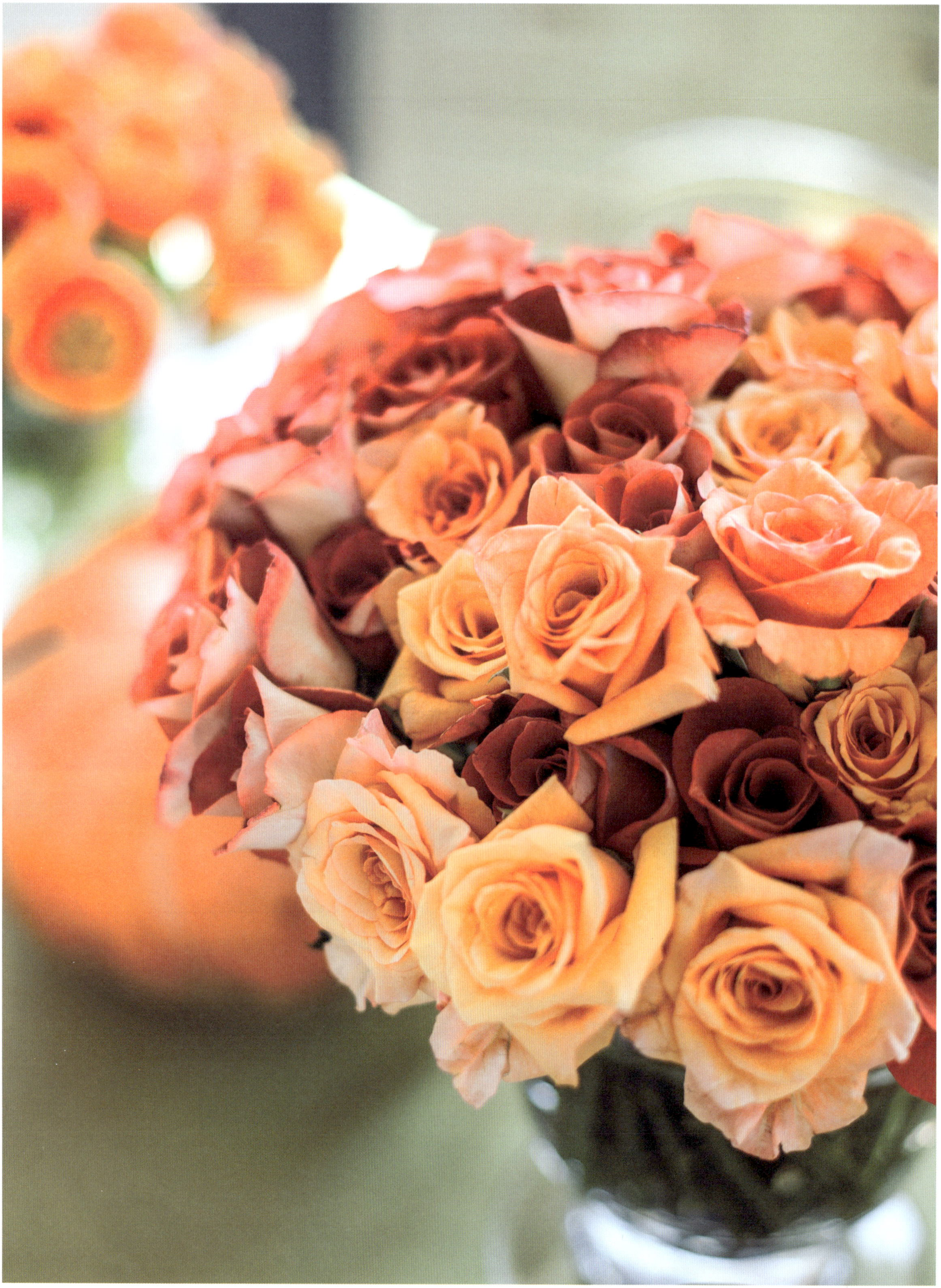

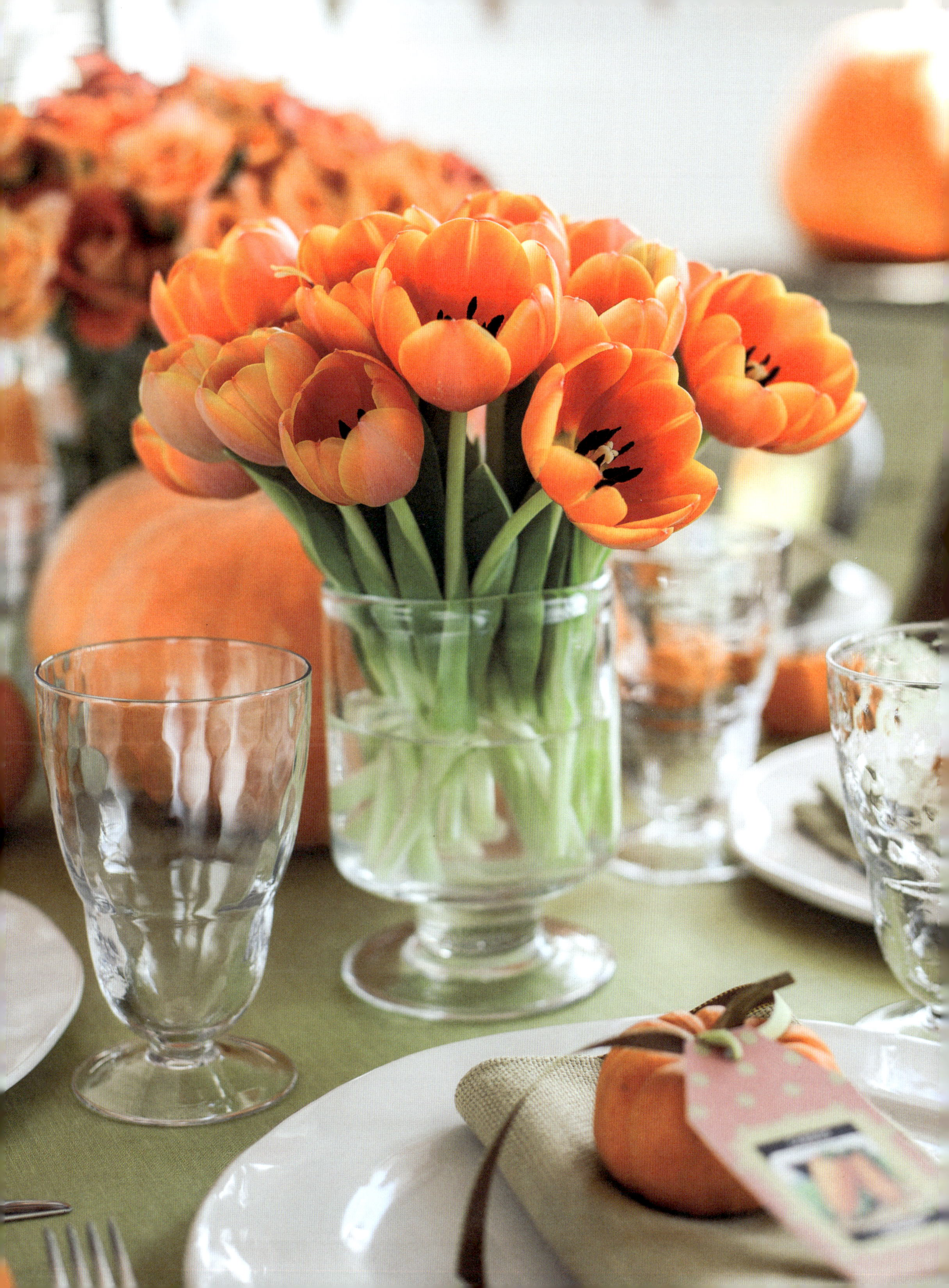

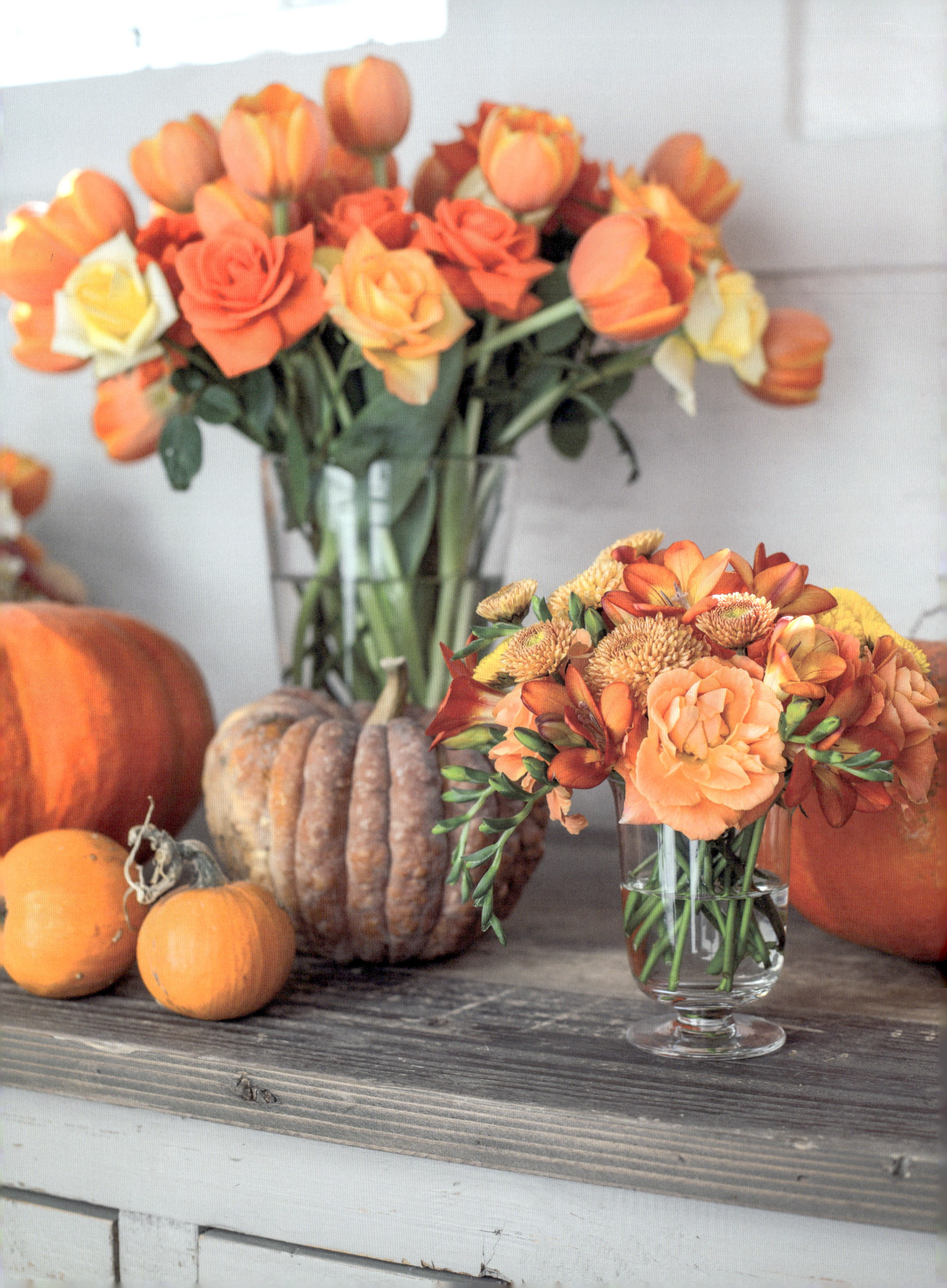

A touch of yellow in these casual bunches of freesias, roses, tulips and chrysanthemums highlights the rich colours of the ornamental pumpkins, used here to such dramatic effect.

In joy or sadness flowers are our constant friends.

Kakuzo Okakura

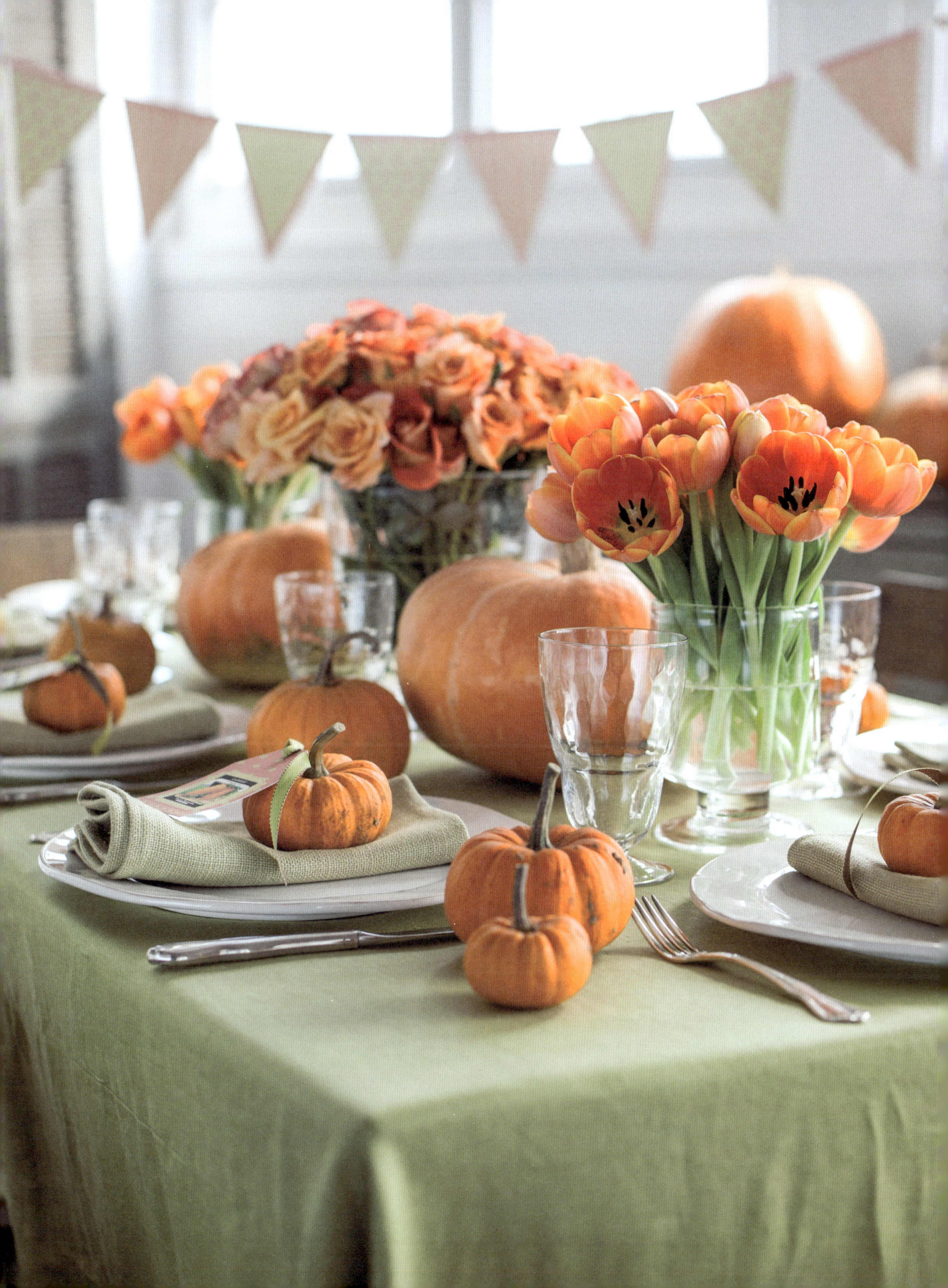

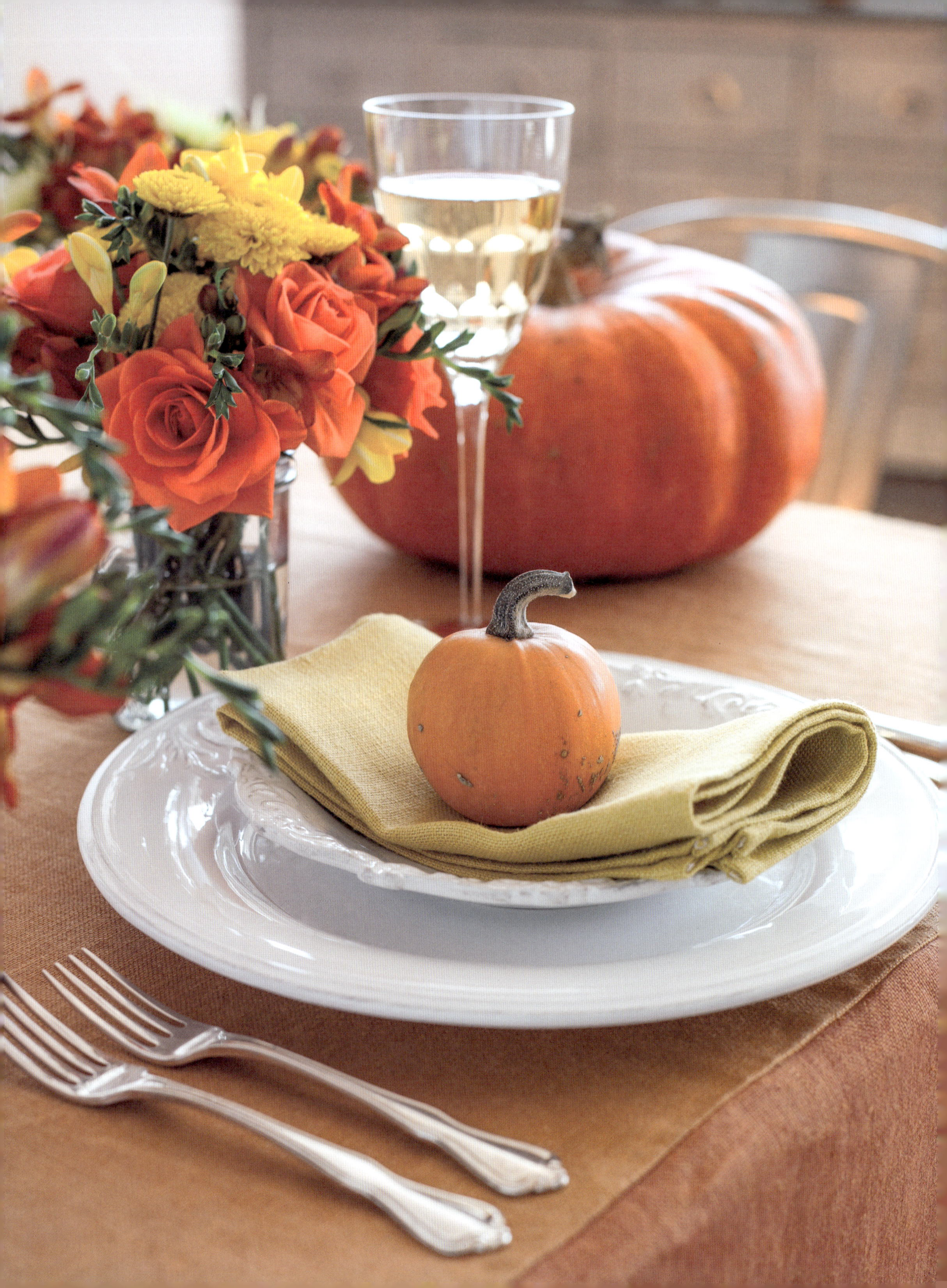

Once again, members of the gourd family are the stars of this attractive autumnal table setting. Plain table linen will always accentuate their rich tones and interesting textures.

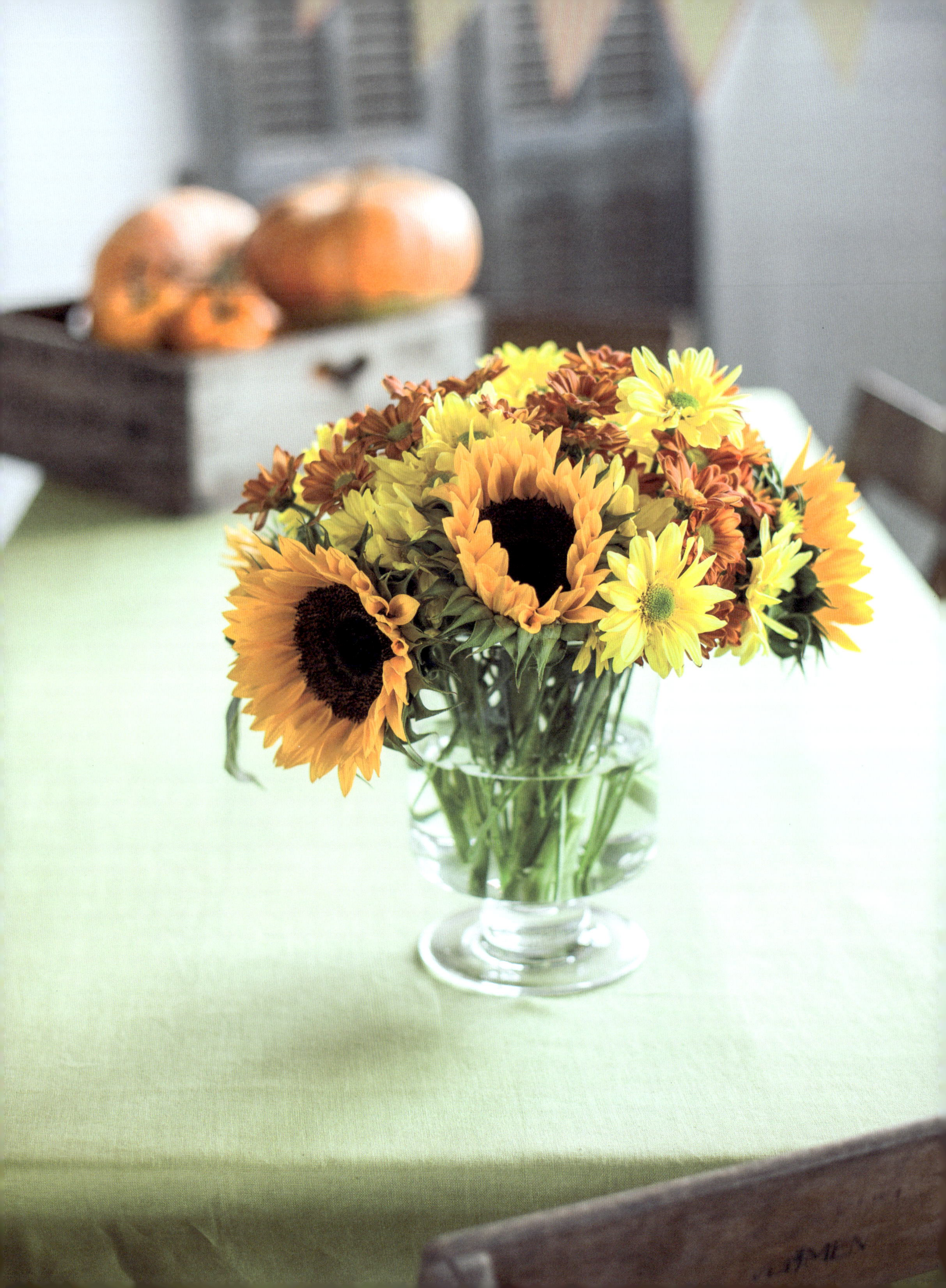

Make the most of the season's last sunflowers as it will be some time before their cheerful faces are seen again. Here they mix happily with the complementary colours of chrysanthemums and freesias.

Overleaf are two effective arrangements that bring the best of the season indoors; on the left are russet-coloured roses bunched in a plain glass vessel and on the right a simple but serene combination of hydrangeas, roses and kale.

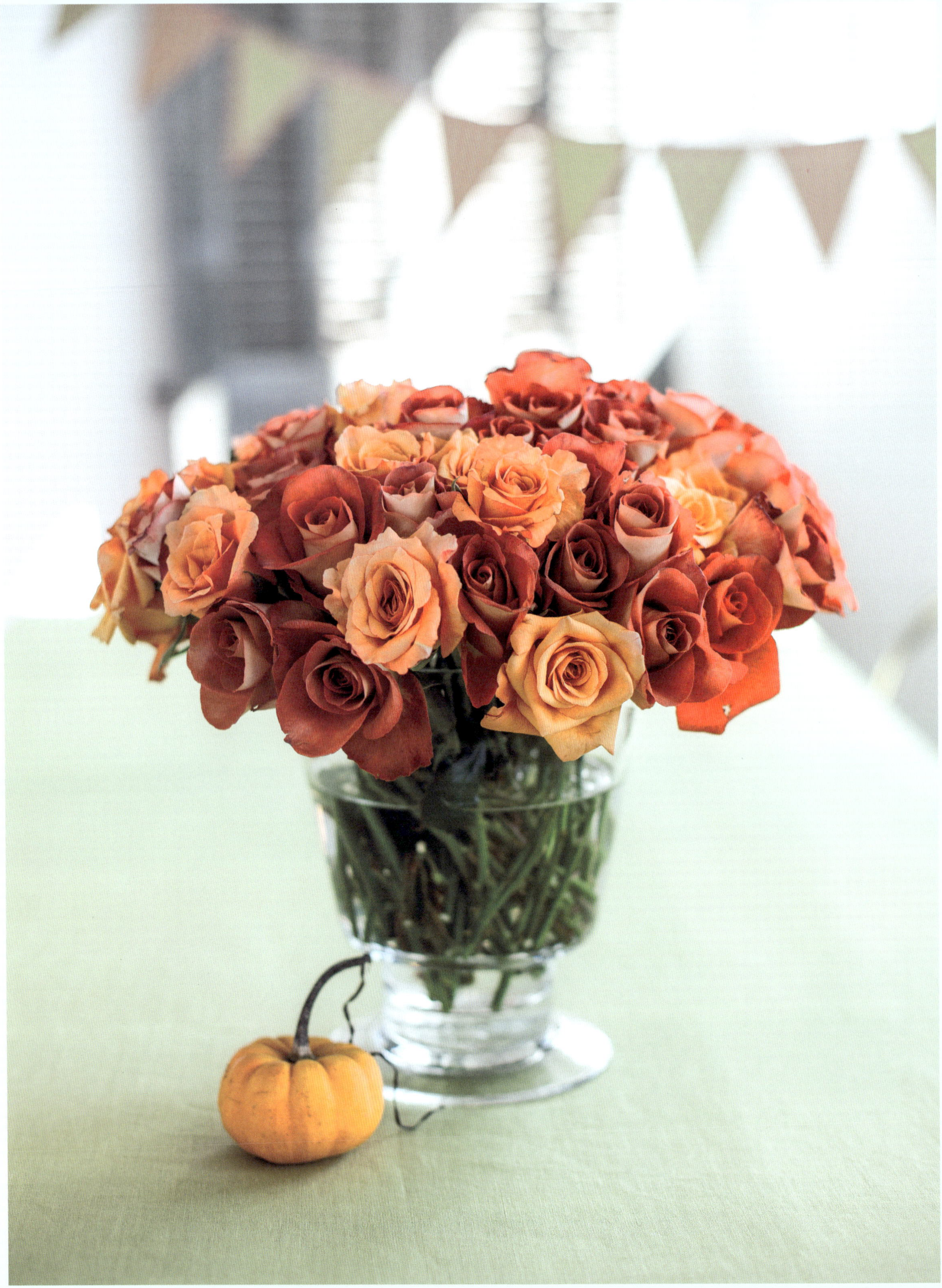

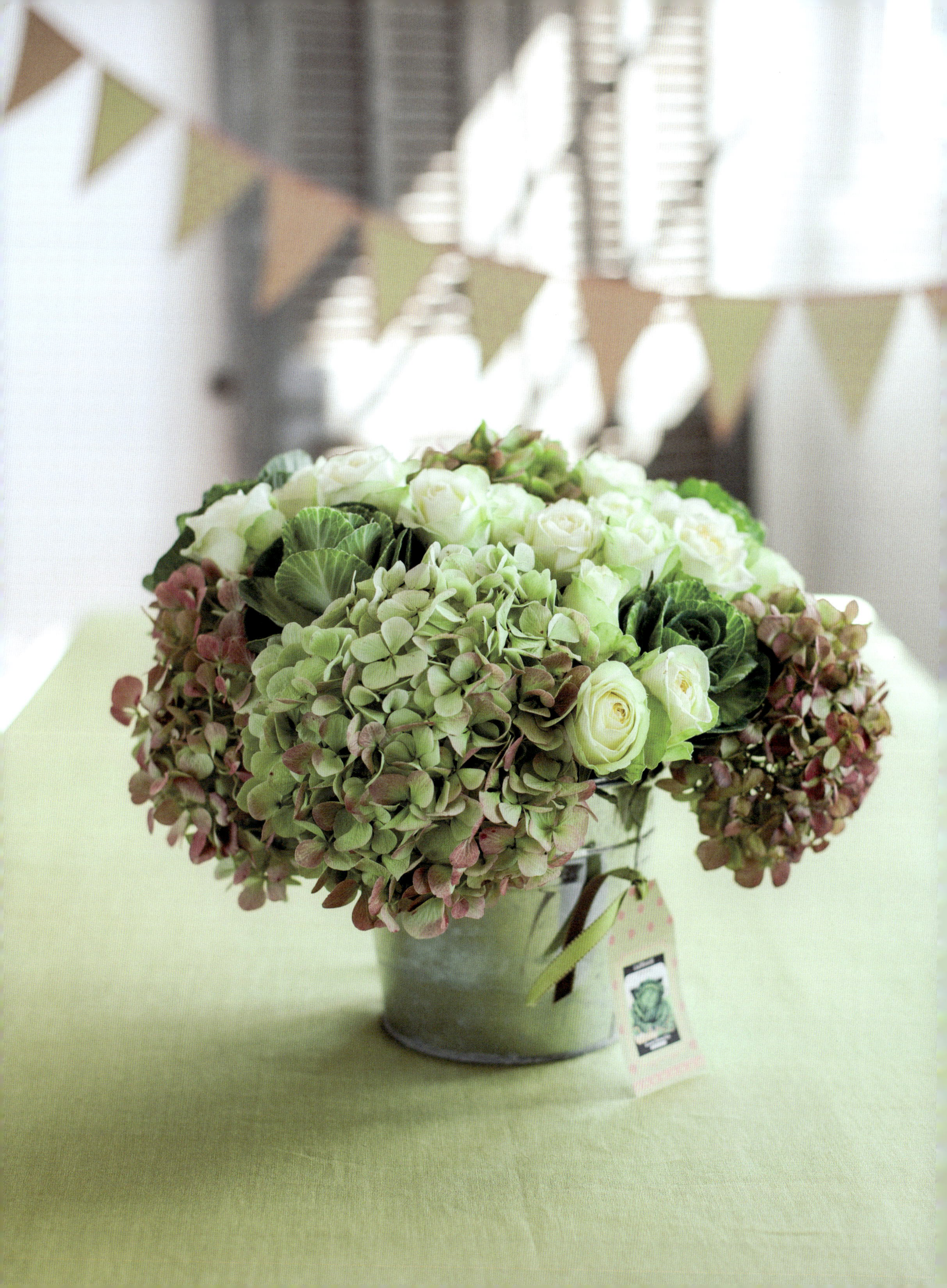

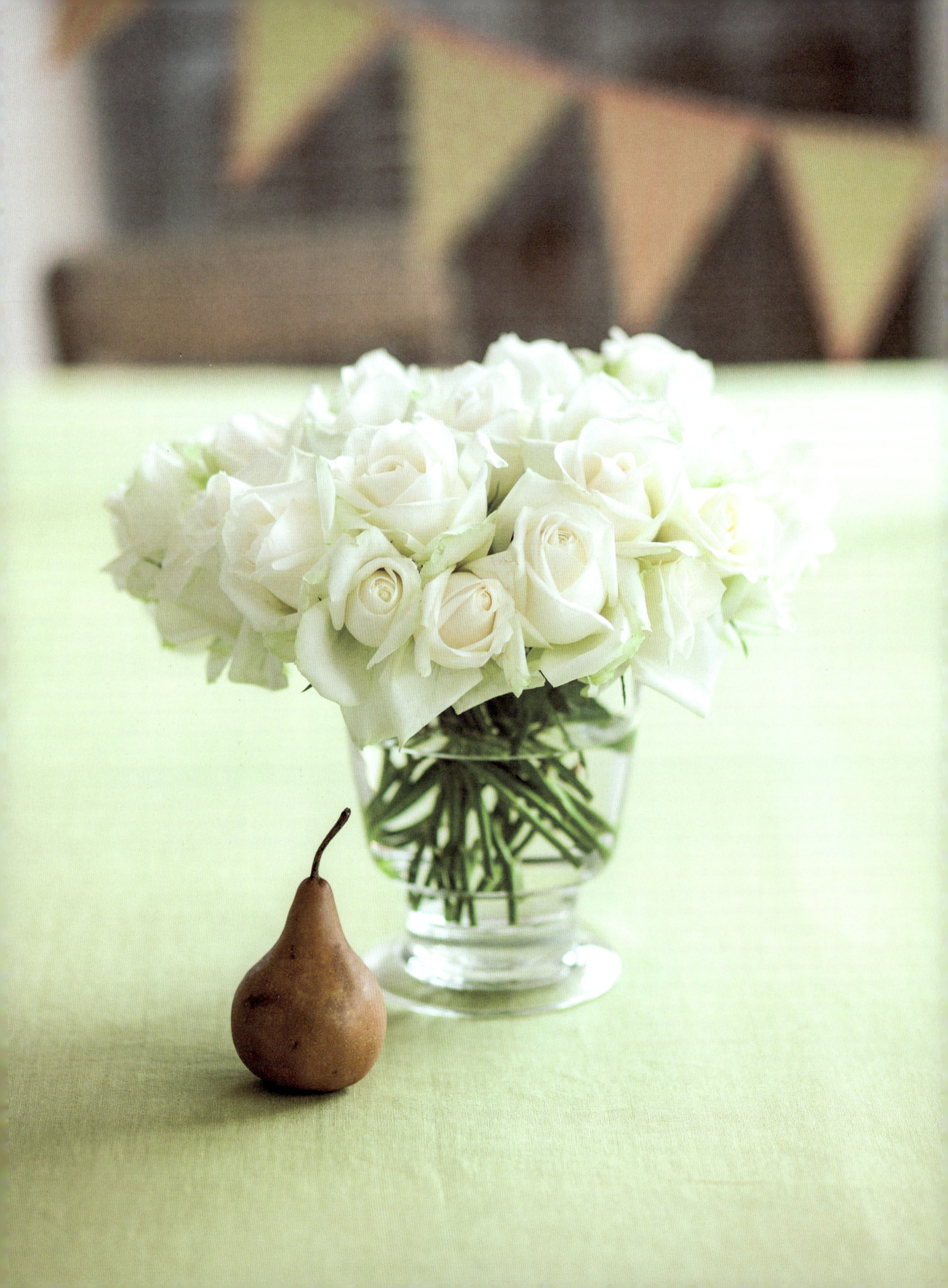

Although autumn will nearly always evoke earthy rich tones, there'll be times when more delicate colours are appropriate, such as these tightly furled white Vendella roses (left) and dainty dahlias enhanced by a few sprigs of flowering mint (right).

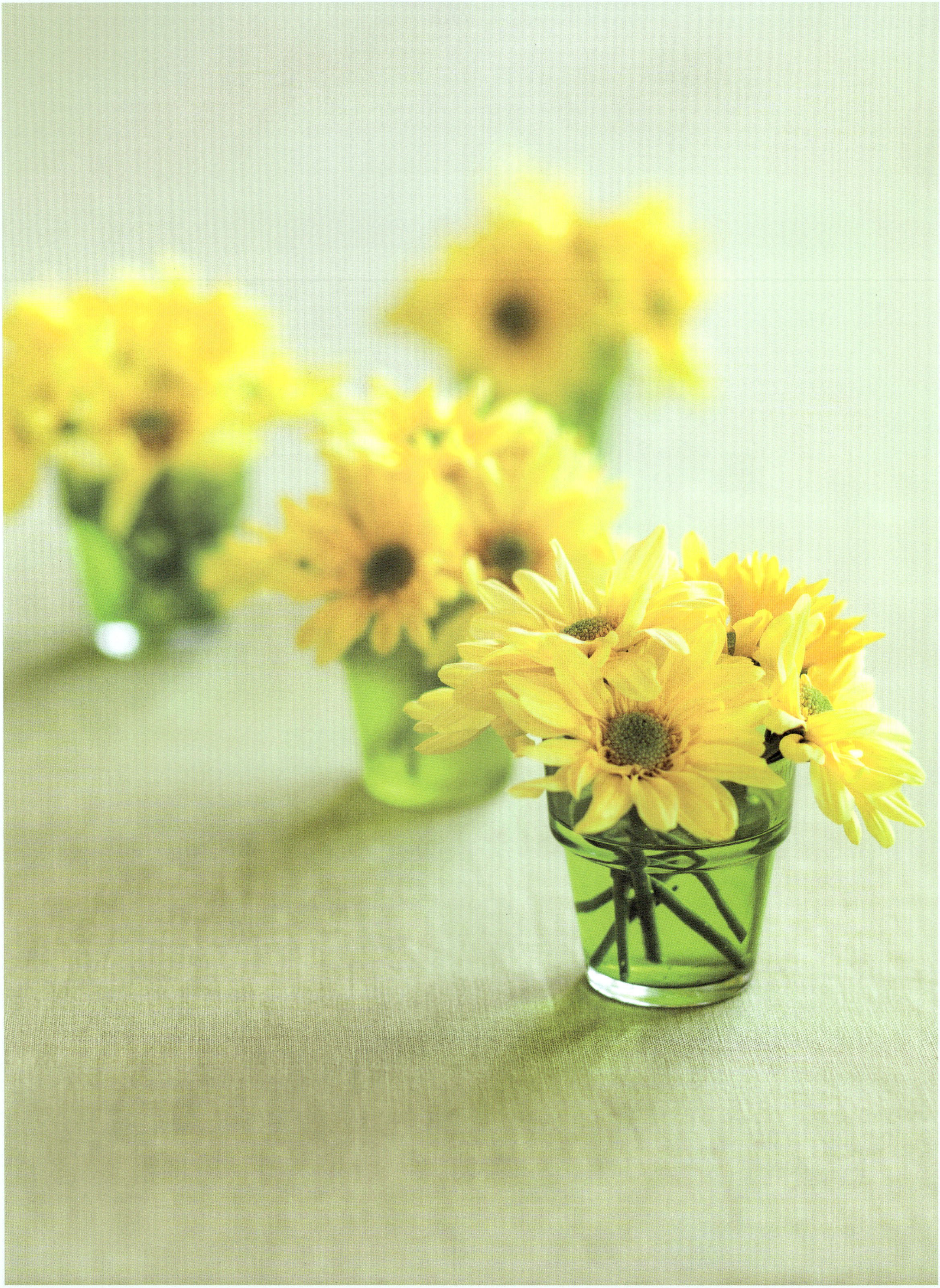

The Cs have it – let's hear it for the chrysanthemums, carnations and cosmos on these and the following pages. Pretty jars, glasses and perhaps a simple ribbon are all that's needed to set off these little beauties.

Flowers always make people better, happier, and more helpful; they are sunshine, food and medicine for the soul.

Luther Burbank

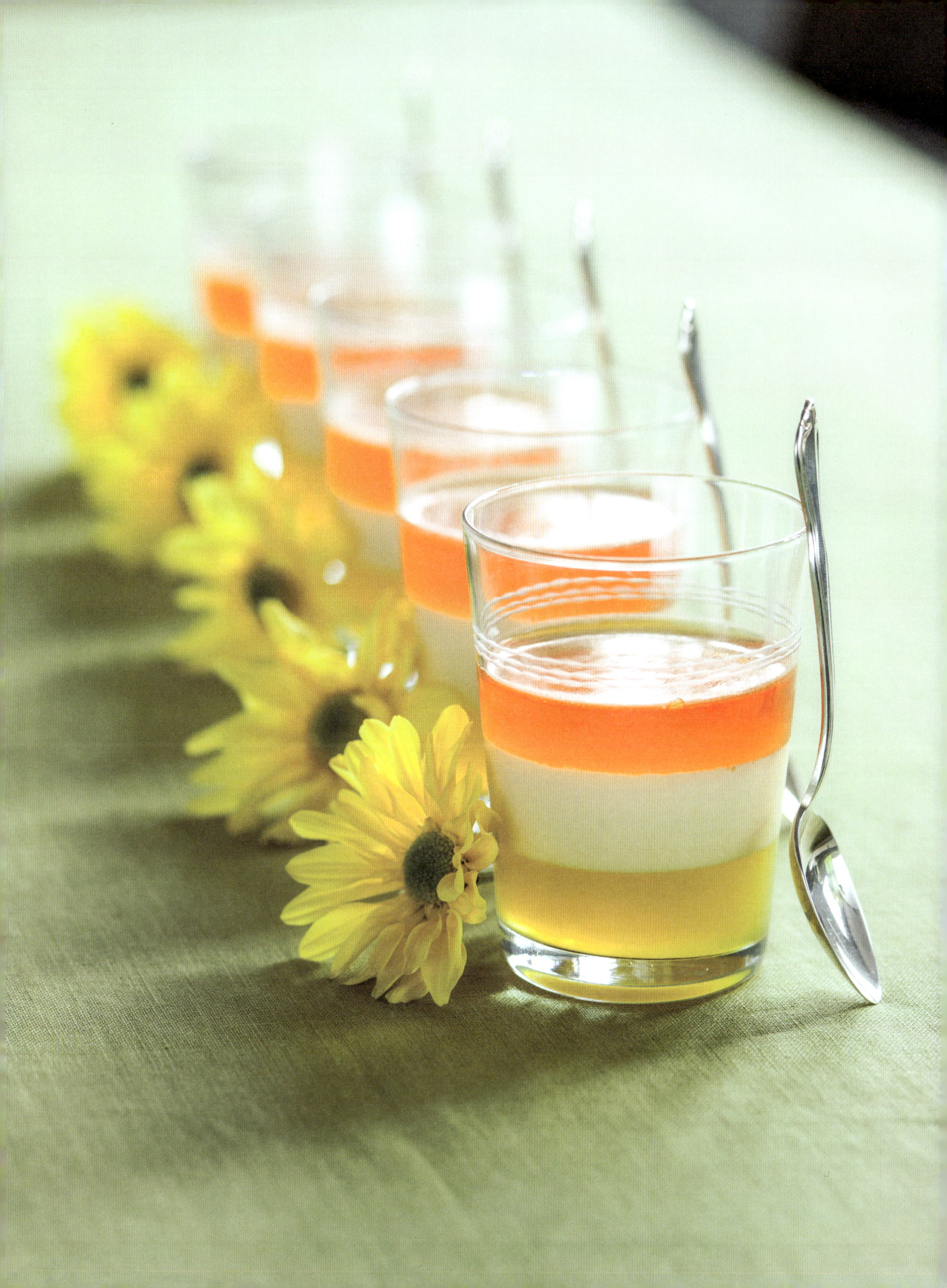

The purest and most
thoughtful minds
are those which love
colour the most.

John Ruskin

As well as all those gorgeous earthy tones, autumn also offers a gentler palette that is faintly reminiscent of a field crammed with blueberry bushes and blackberry vines. Even the ornamental kale used here – along with freesias, roses, hydrangeas, stock, carnations and lisianthus – has a soft purplish tinge.

Like the earthy tones earlier in this chapter these rich sensual colours are glamorous enough in themselves in that they need very little in the way of accessories. Keep table linen simple and when you're mixing colours such as in the setting shown on the right use plain plates and napkins.

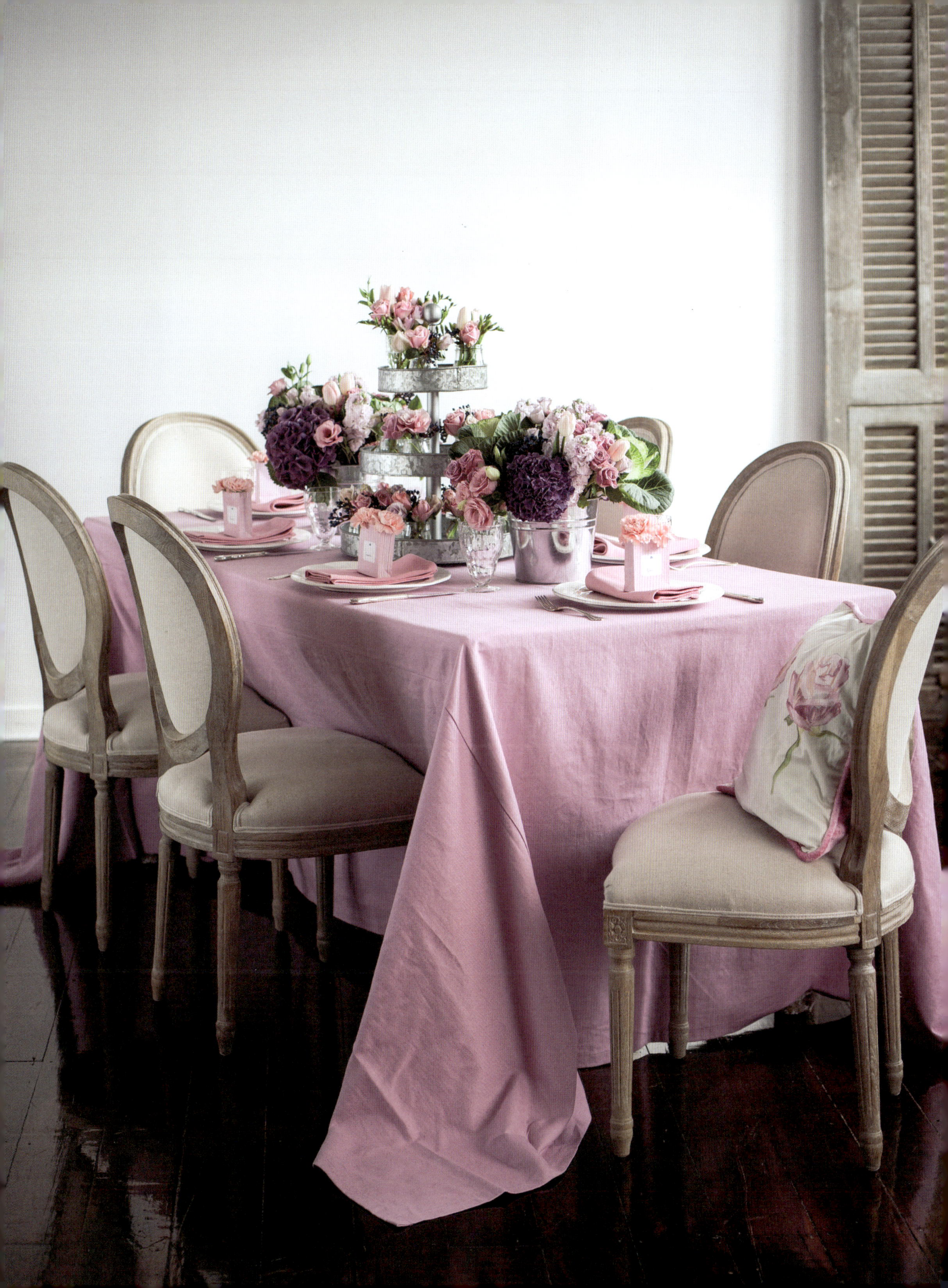

Joan

Dainty pinks are part of that gentler palette and these pretty carnations sit so well against the lush darkness of the purple hydrangeas.

Autumn 171

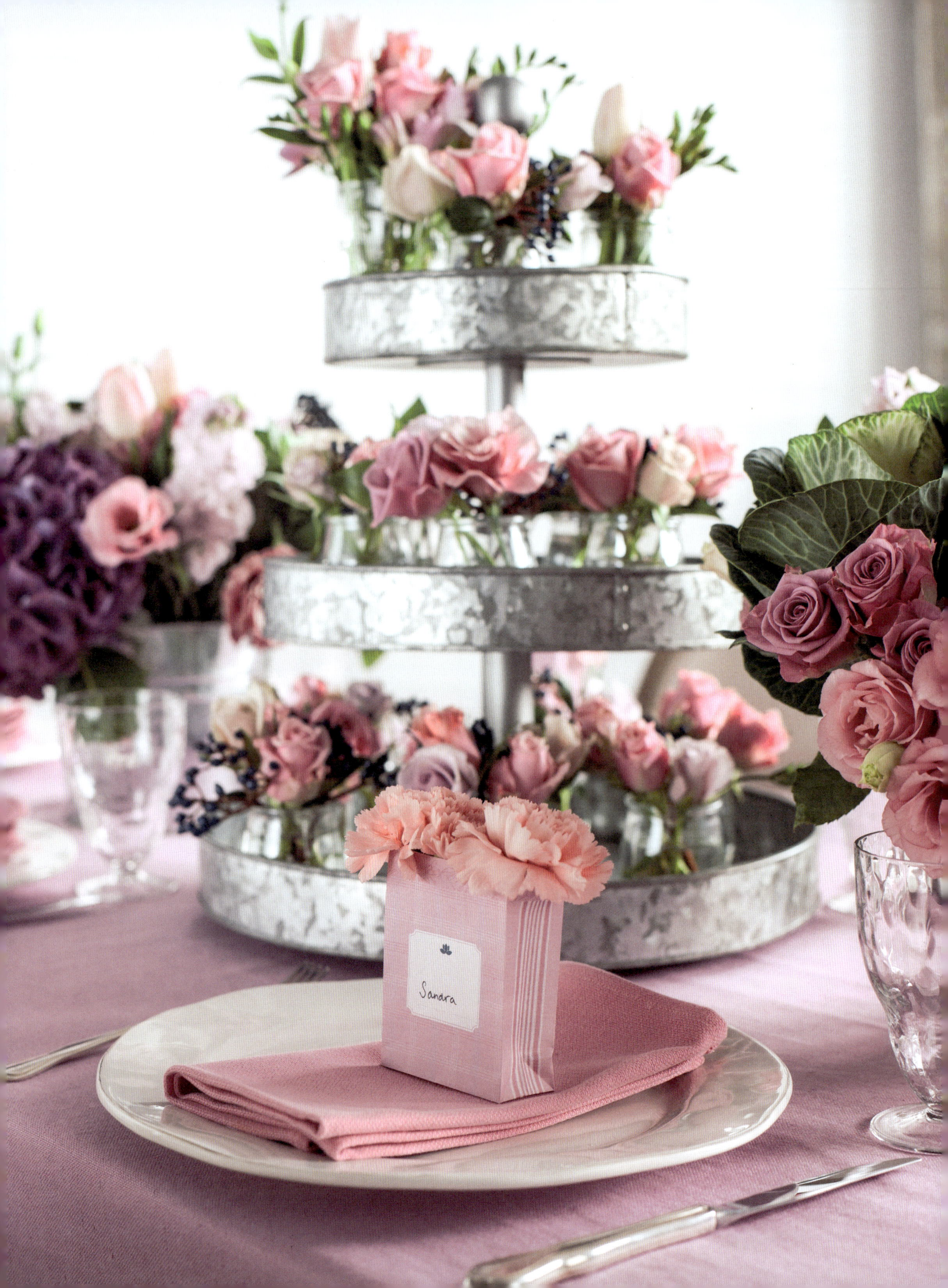
Sandra

The masses of pink roses, hydrangeas and freesias on these pages are enhanced by textured kale leaves and delicate purple berries.

The simple perfection of anemones is followed, overleaf, by the beauty of a single white Avalanche rose contrasted against a profusion of velvety deep red rose petals.

Autumn 175

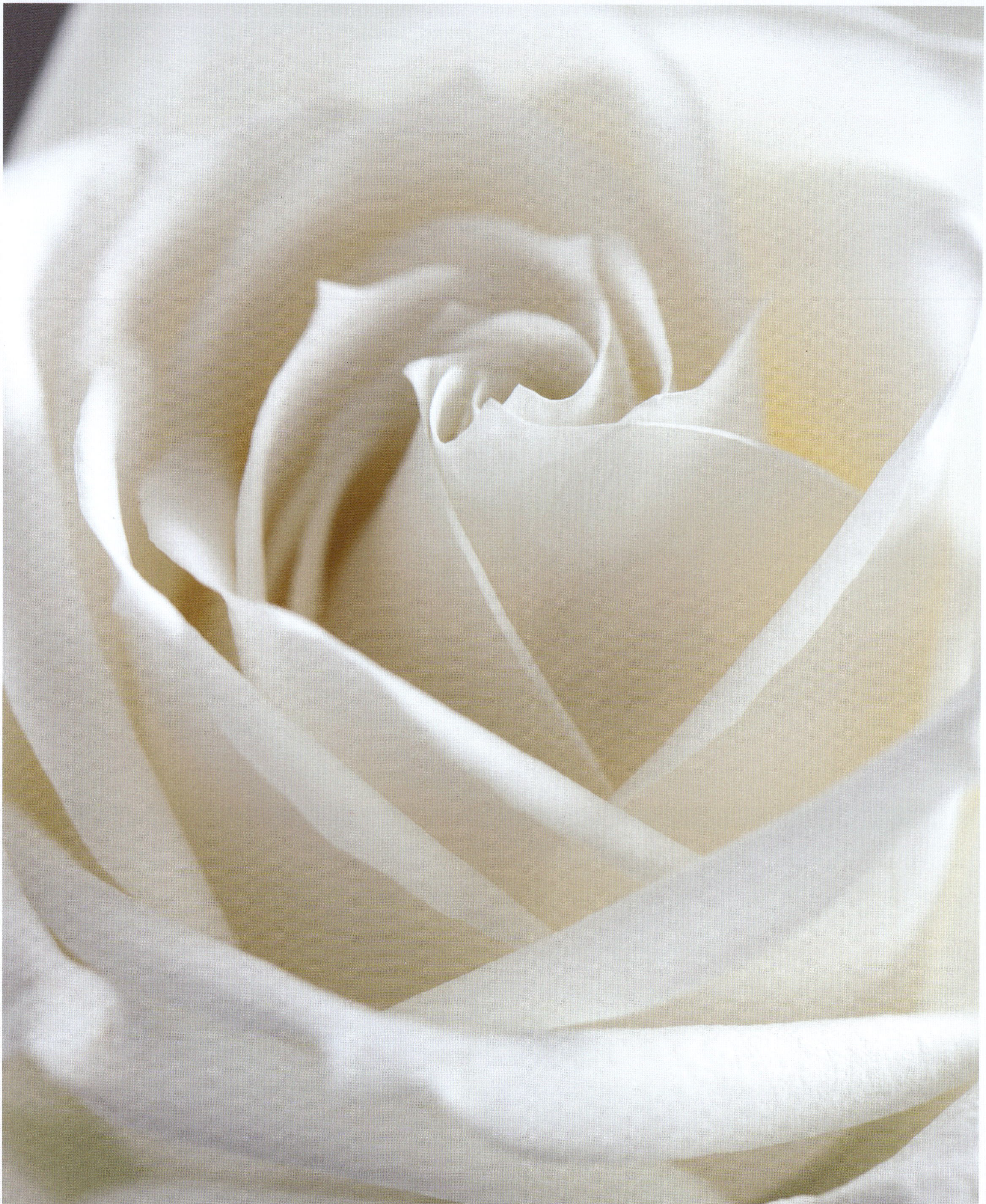

Autumn

Mere colour, unspoiled by meaning, and unallied with definite form, can speak to the soul in a thousand different ways.

Oscar Wilde

Large balls of scrunched-up tissue paper that can be suspended overhead are an effective way to reflect the colours and theme of a table setting. This one utilises a palette of delicate pink and lilac roses and sweet peas offset by lushly deep purple anemones.

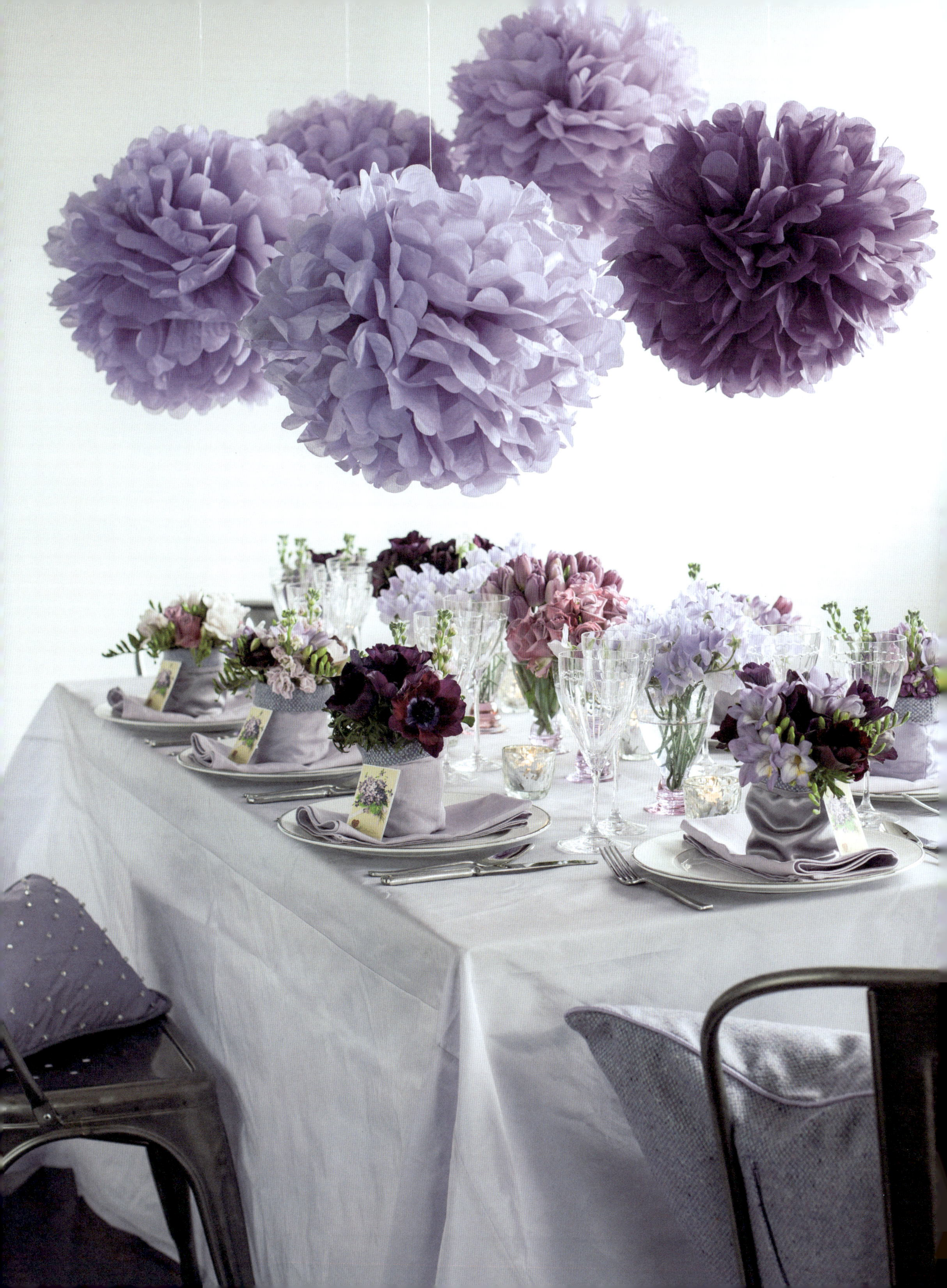

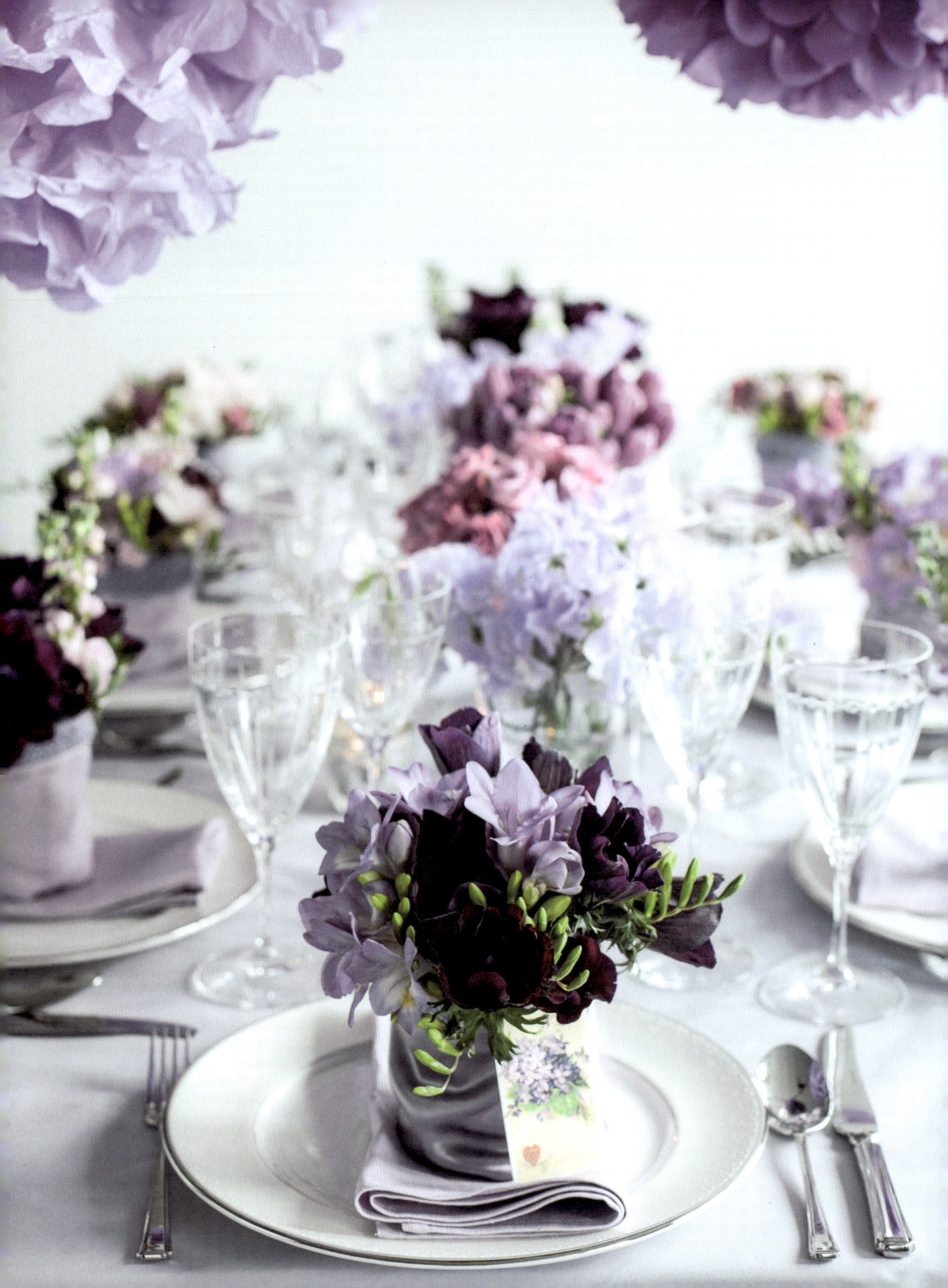

Although the stems of these exquisite bunches of roses, sweet peas and anemones are not in sight, the green of the plump freesia buds provides a natural contrast.

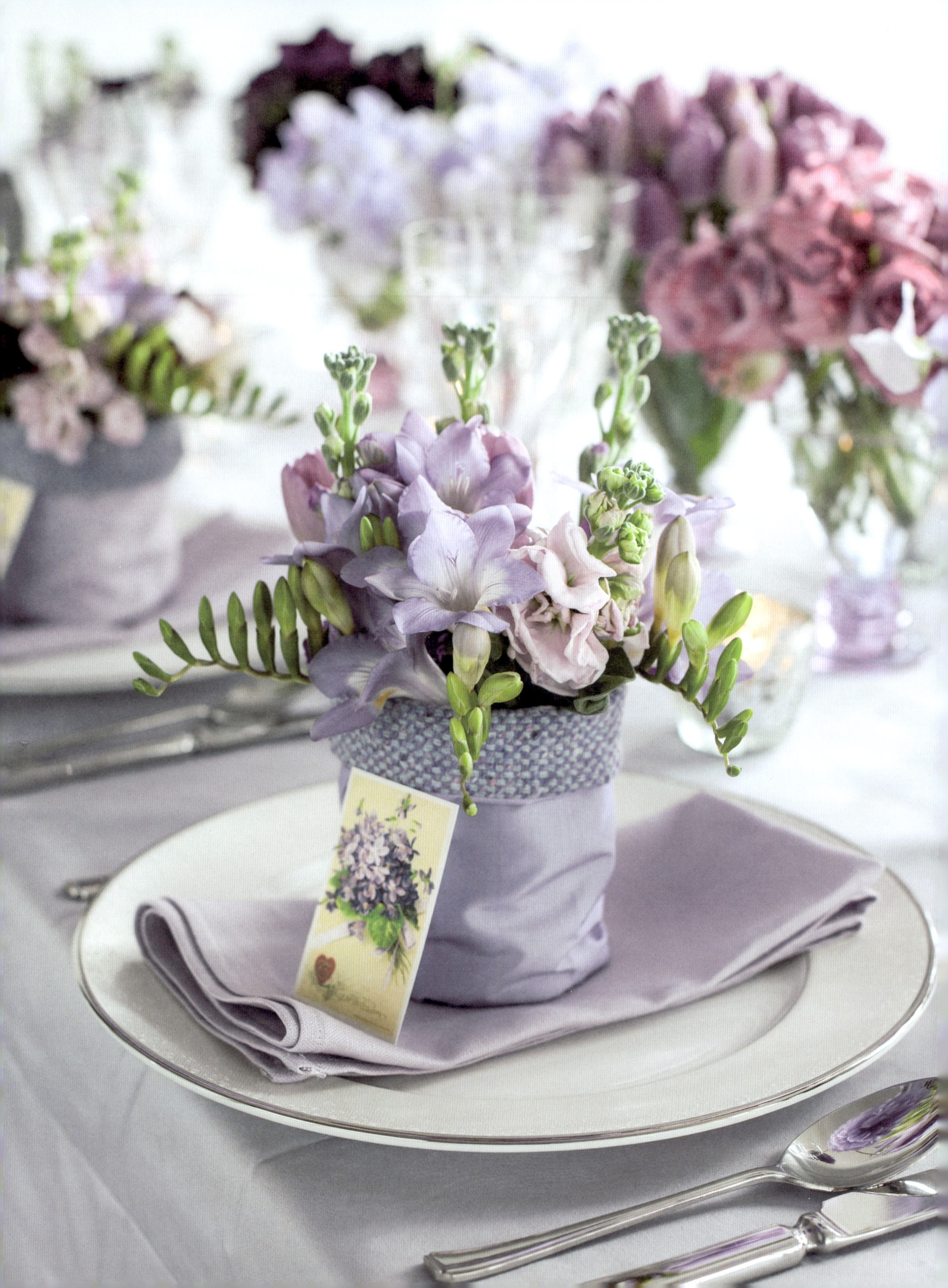

Why do two colours, put one next to the other, sing? Can one really explain this? No. Just as one can never learn how to paint.

Pablo Picasso

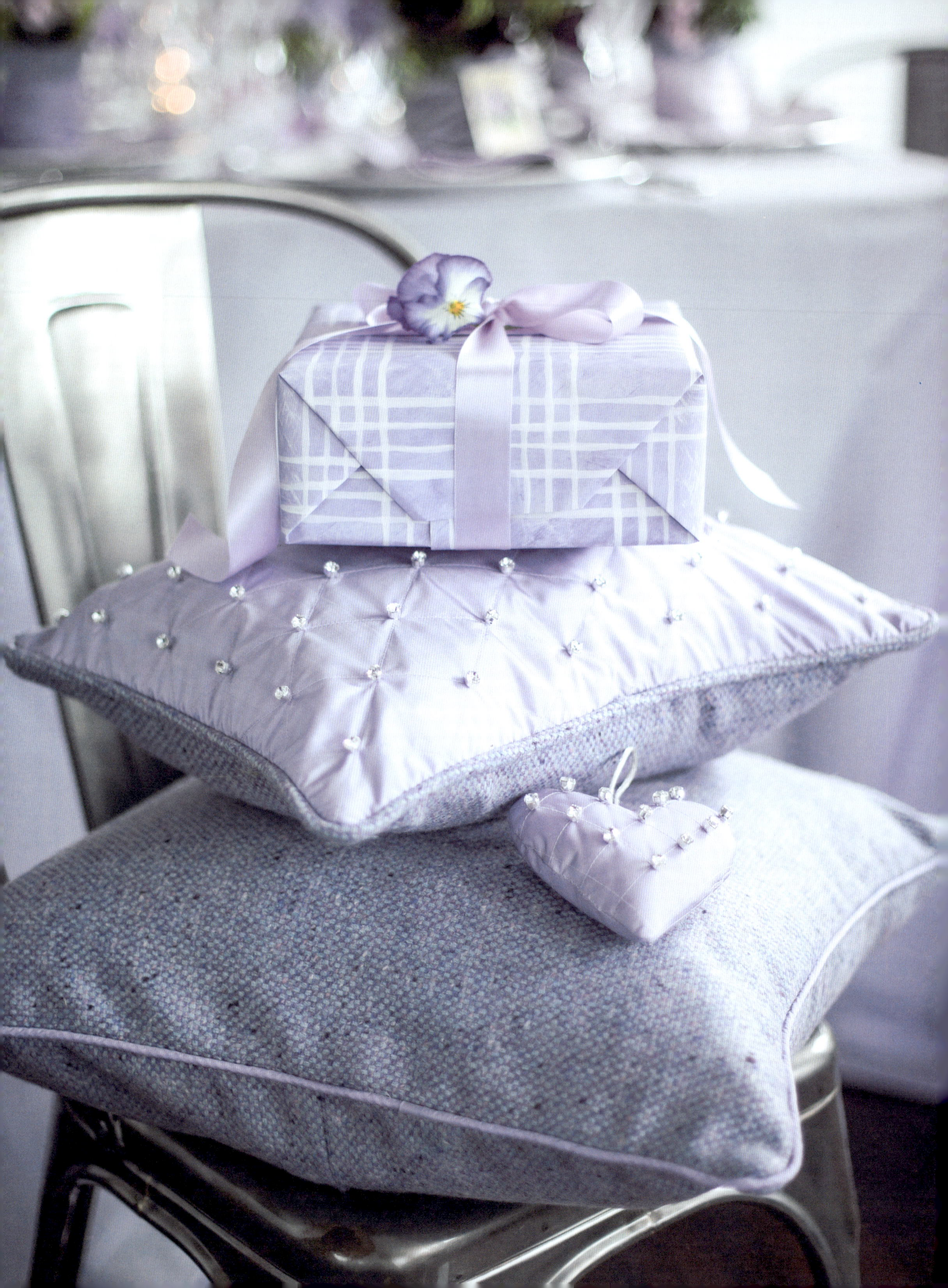

The fragrance and delicate structure of sweet peas and pansies (overleaf) make them a favourite for those times when a light feminine touch is required. They're perfect for embellishing food, too.

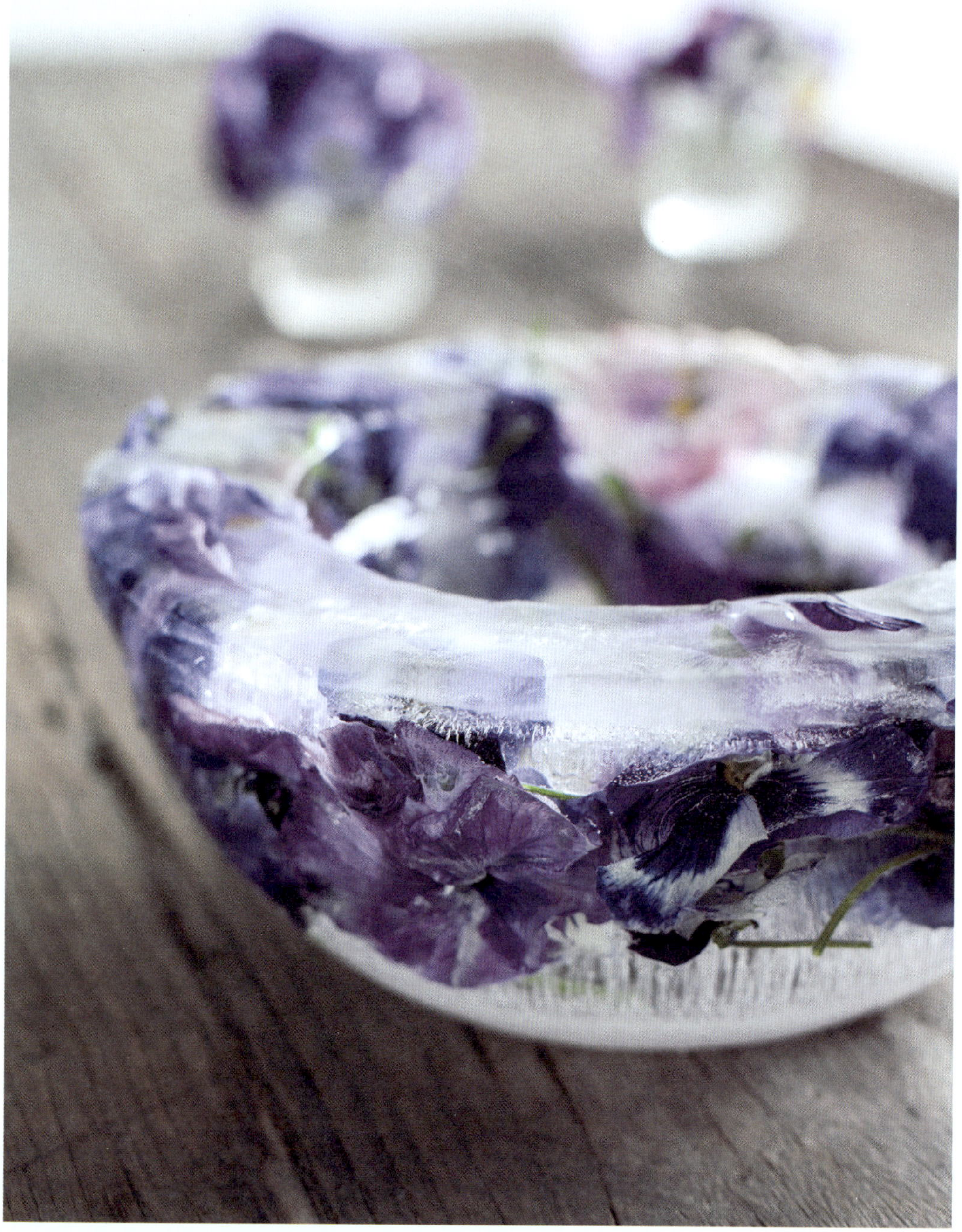

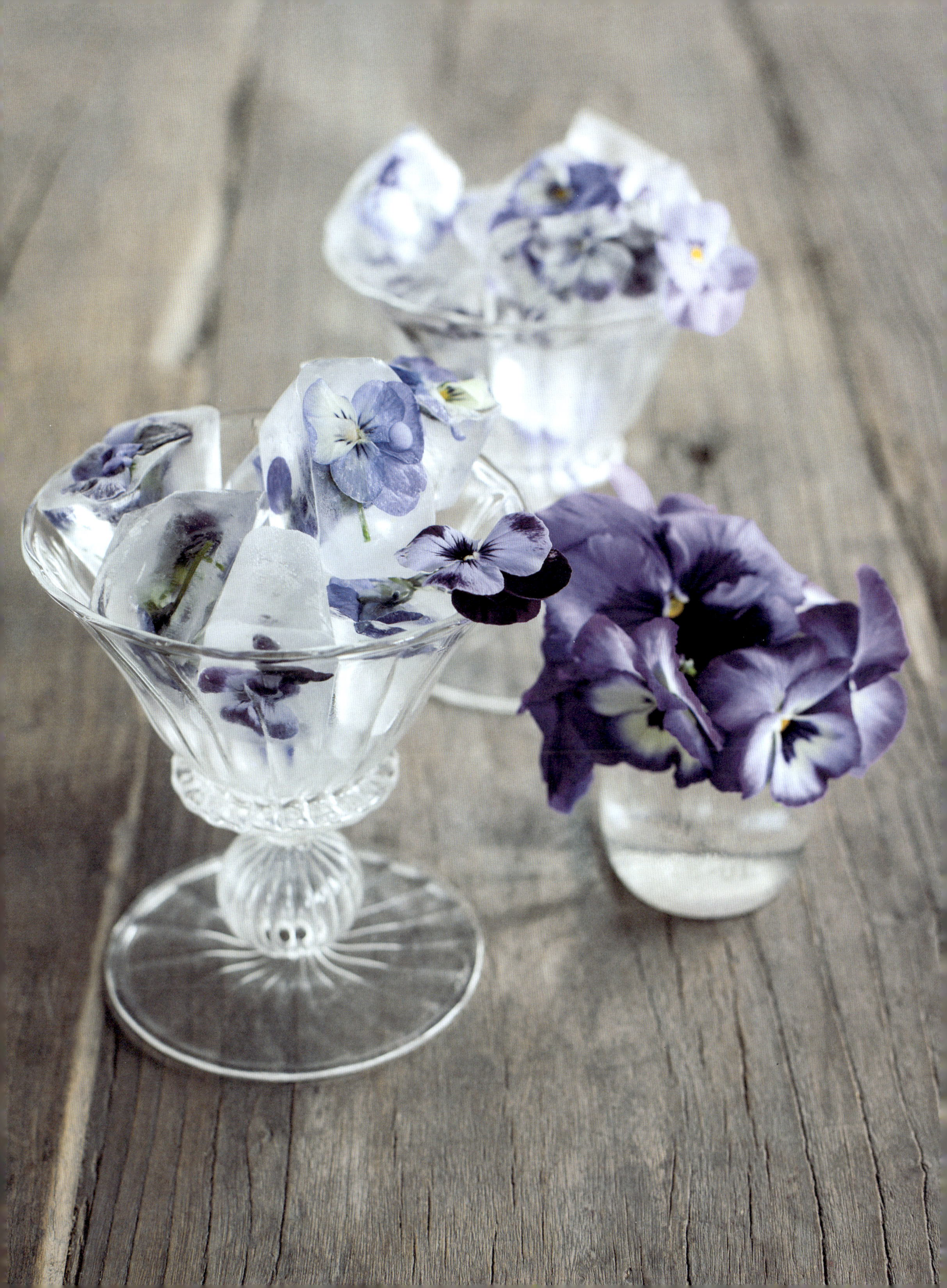

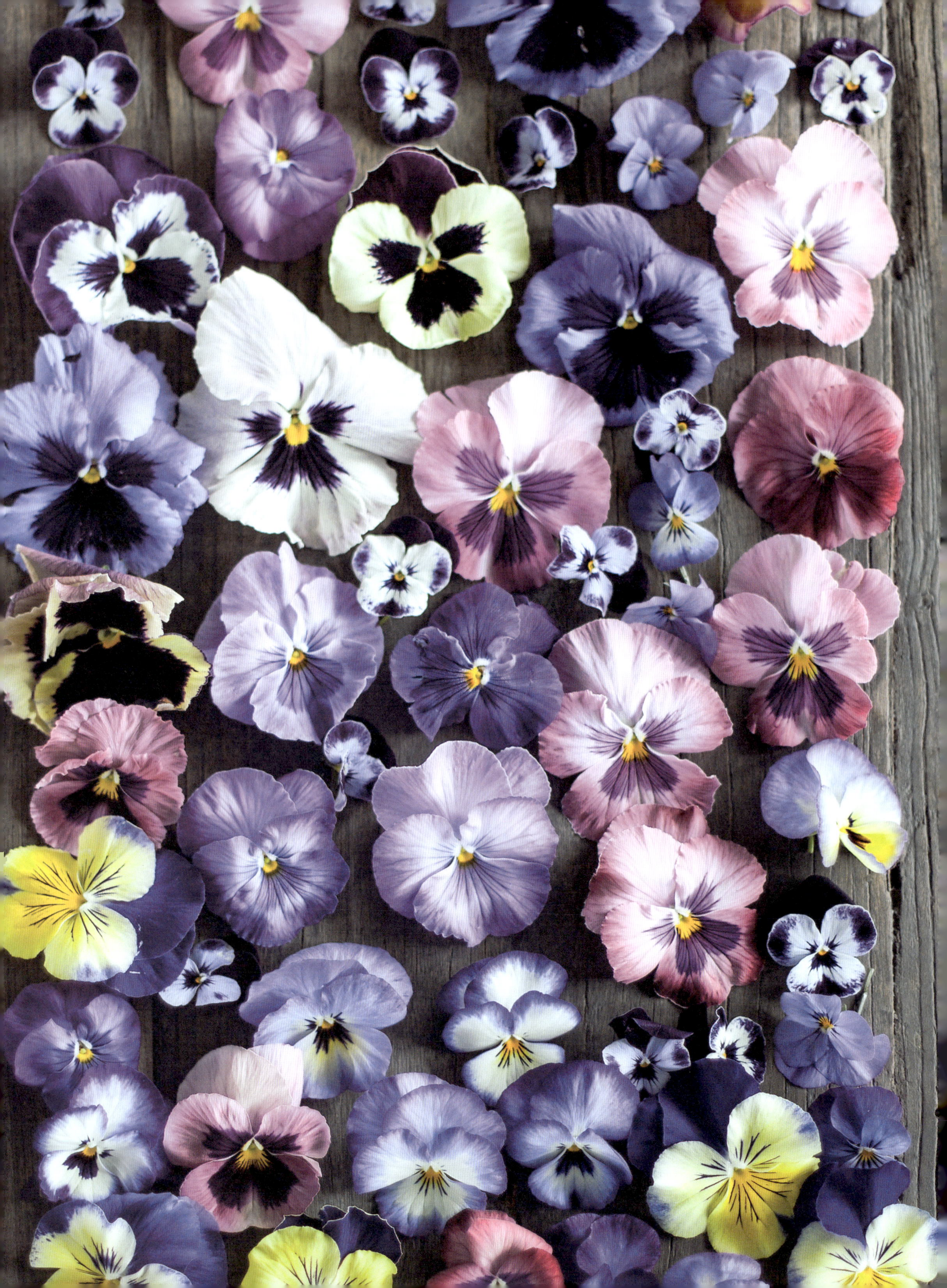

The beauteous pansies rise
In purple, gold, and blue,
With tints of rainbow hue
Mocking the sunset skies.

Thomas John Ouseley

Combining bright reds and crisp greens is another of nature's fabulous party tricks at this time of year. Perhaps it's her way of reminding us that winter is now just around the corner so this gorgeous splash of colour is a great note on which to end the lushness of autumn.

Here I've used roses, tulips, freesias and ranunculus to create a rustic indoor-outdoor effect. These colours demand your attention so don't be shy about using big bold patterns to complement them.

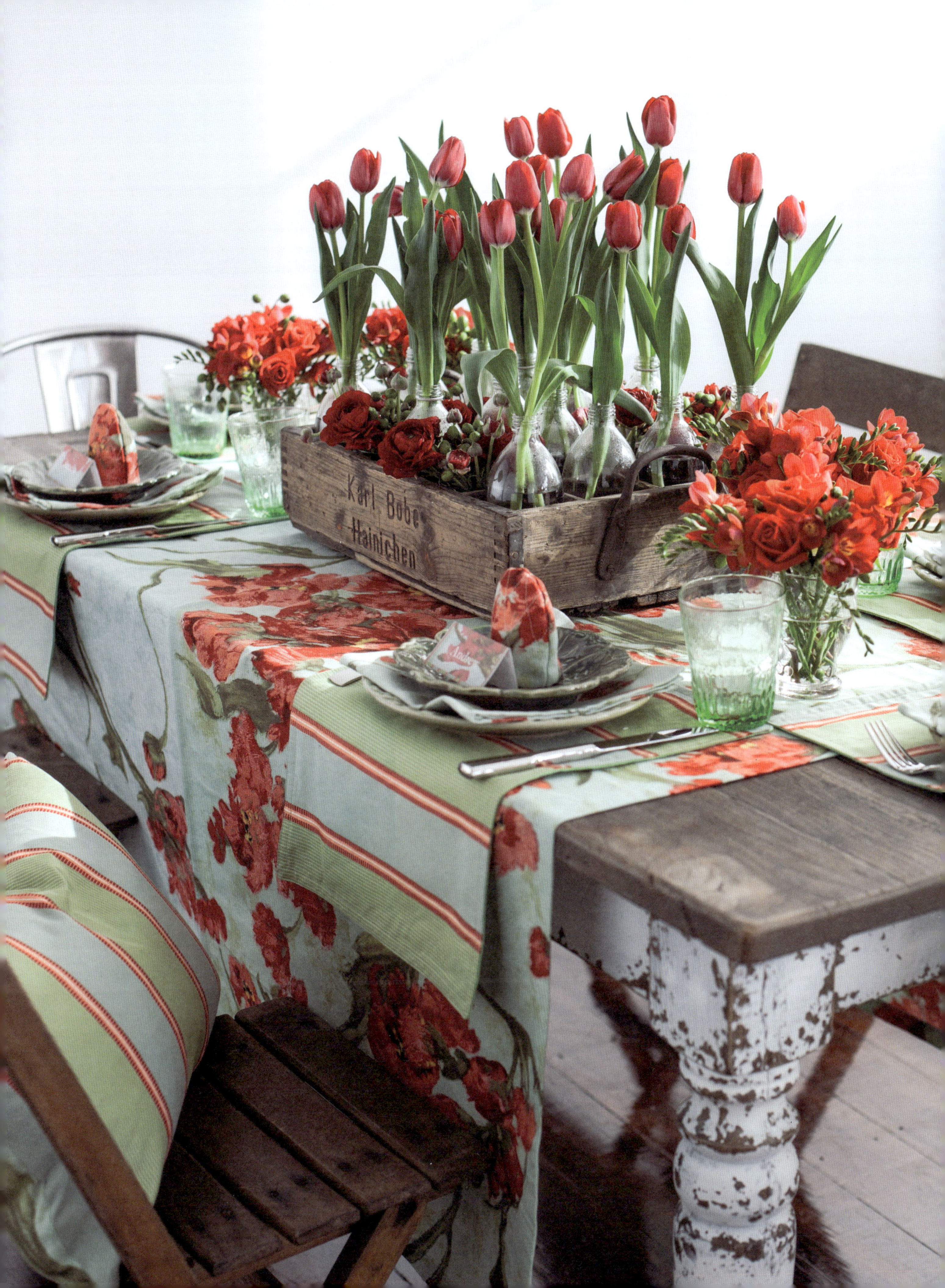
Karl Bobe
Hainichen

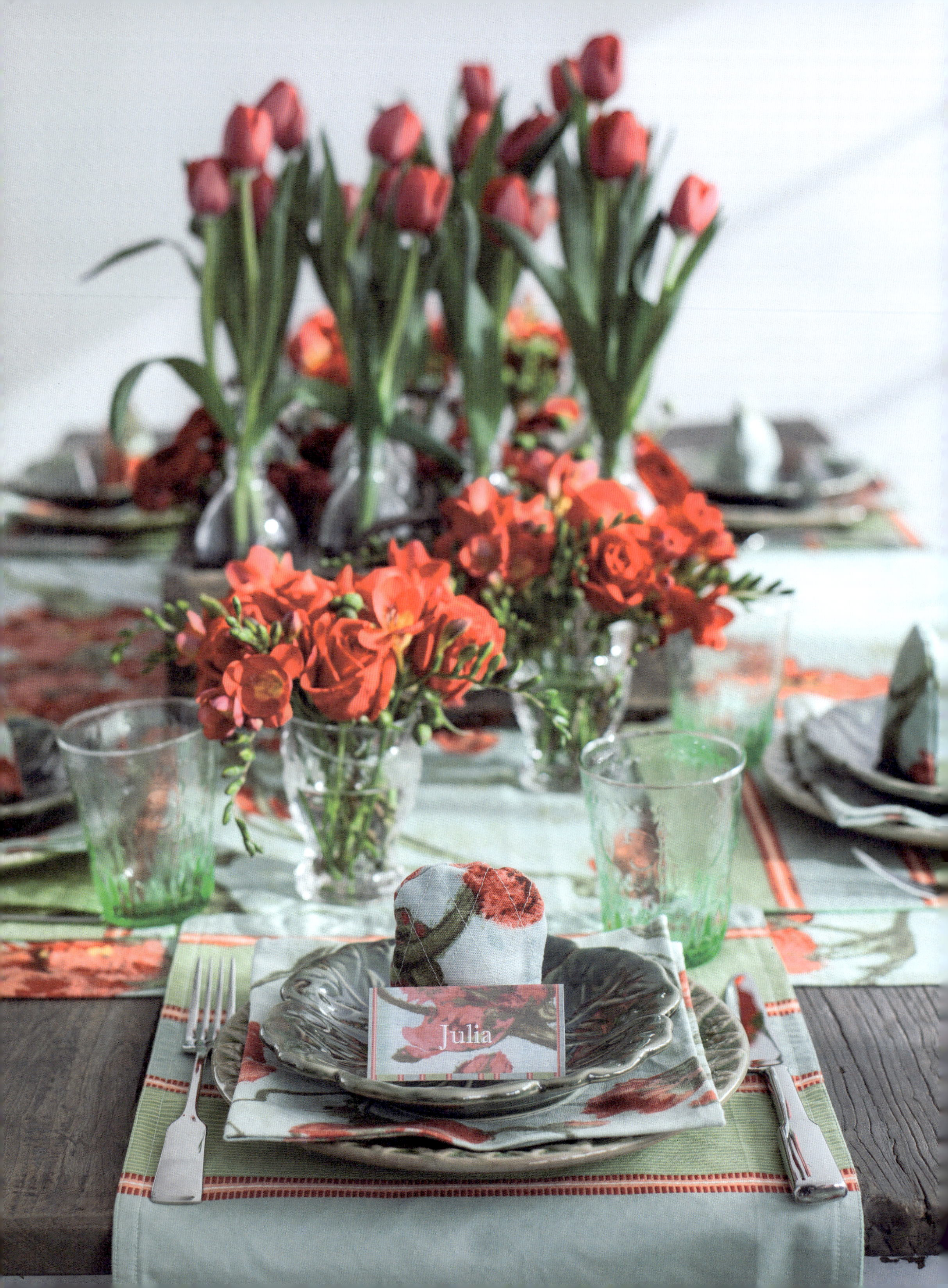
Julia

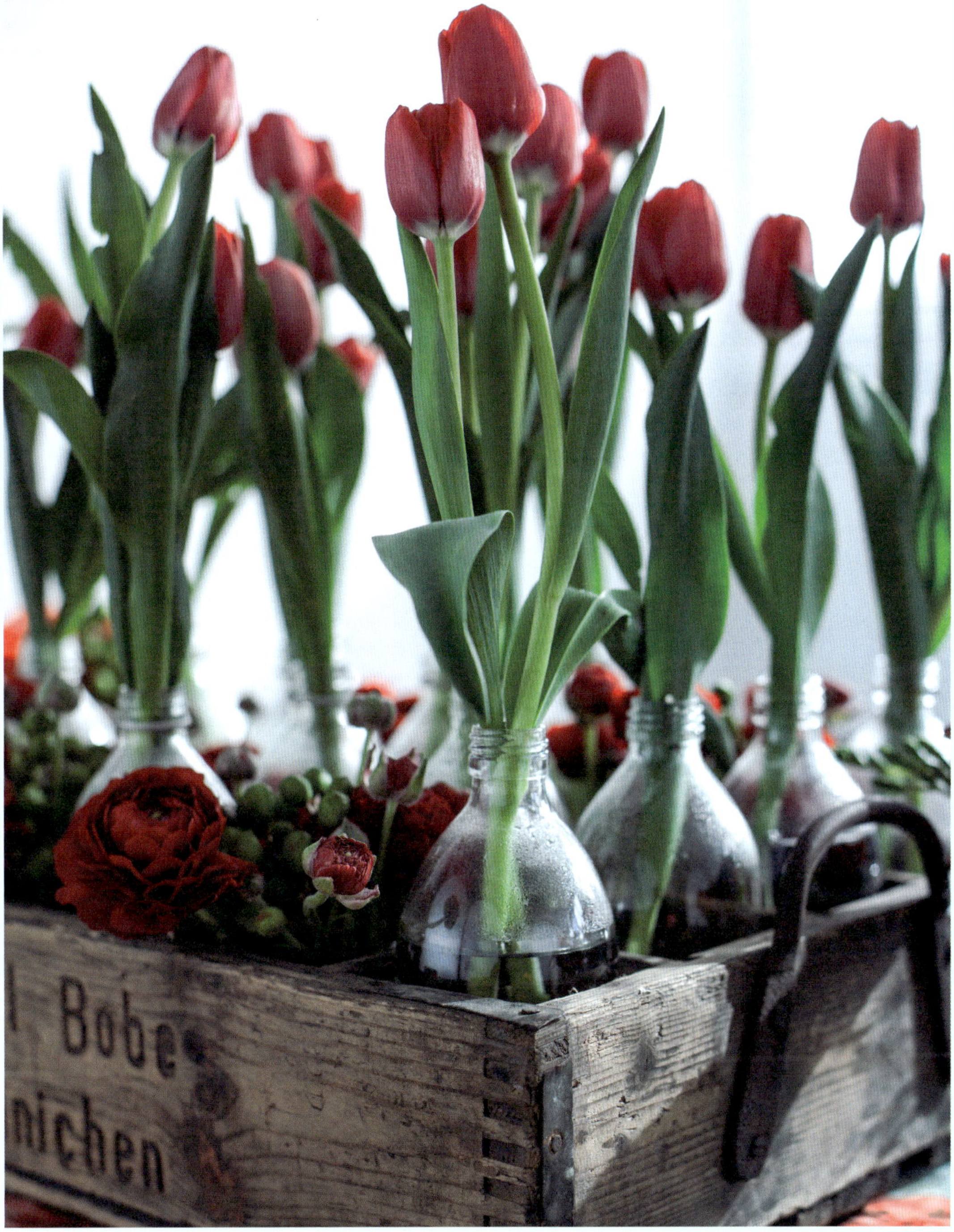

A cake for the eyes, rather than for the mouth, can make a dramatic centrepiece. This one, crafted from carnations, miniature roses and chrysanthemums, and mounted on a stark white cake stand, needs little else.

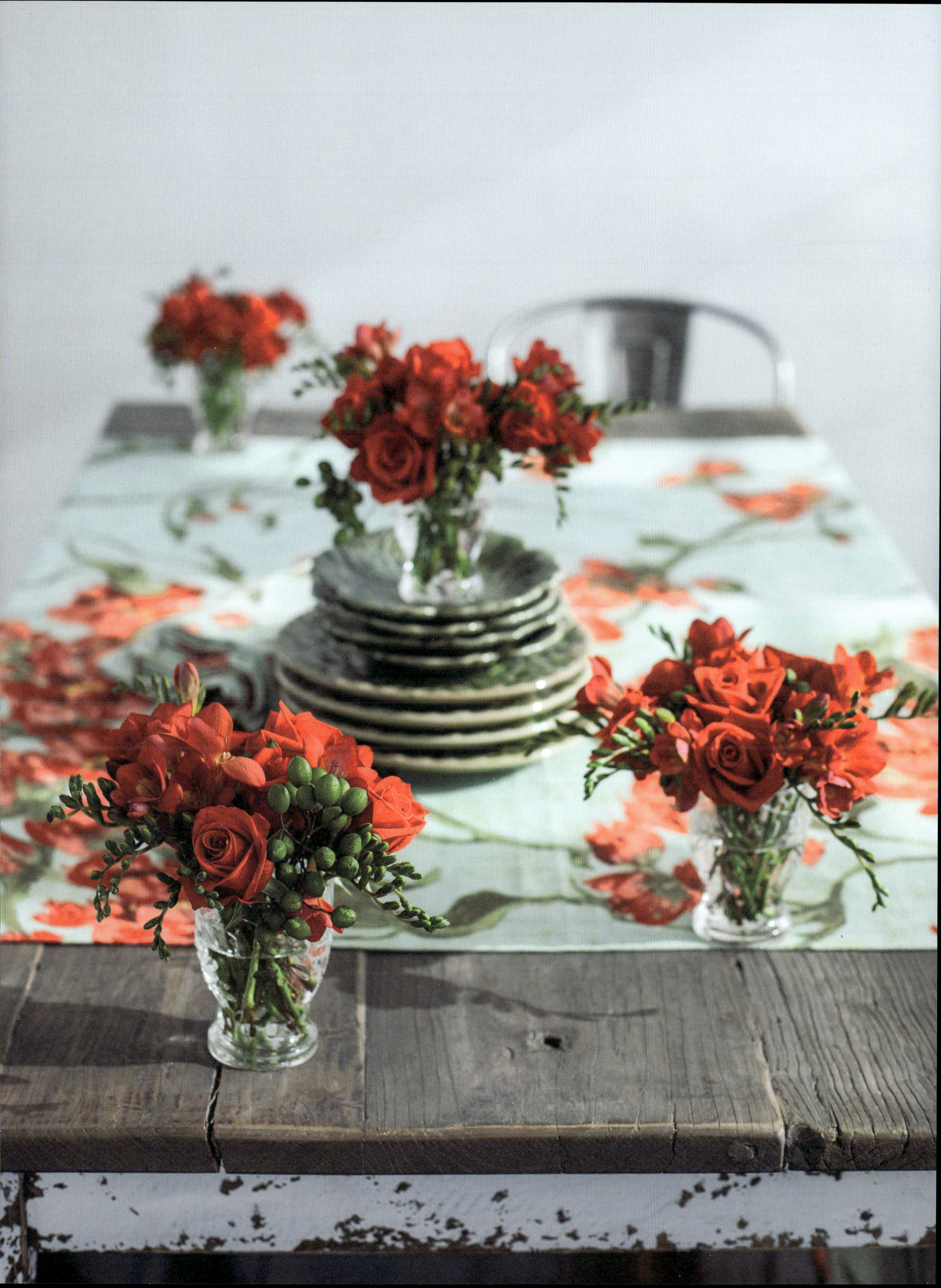

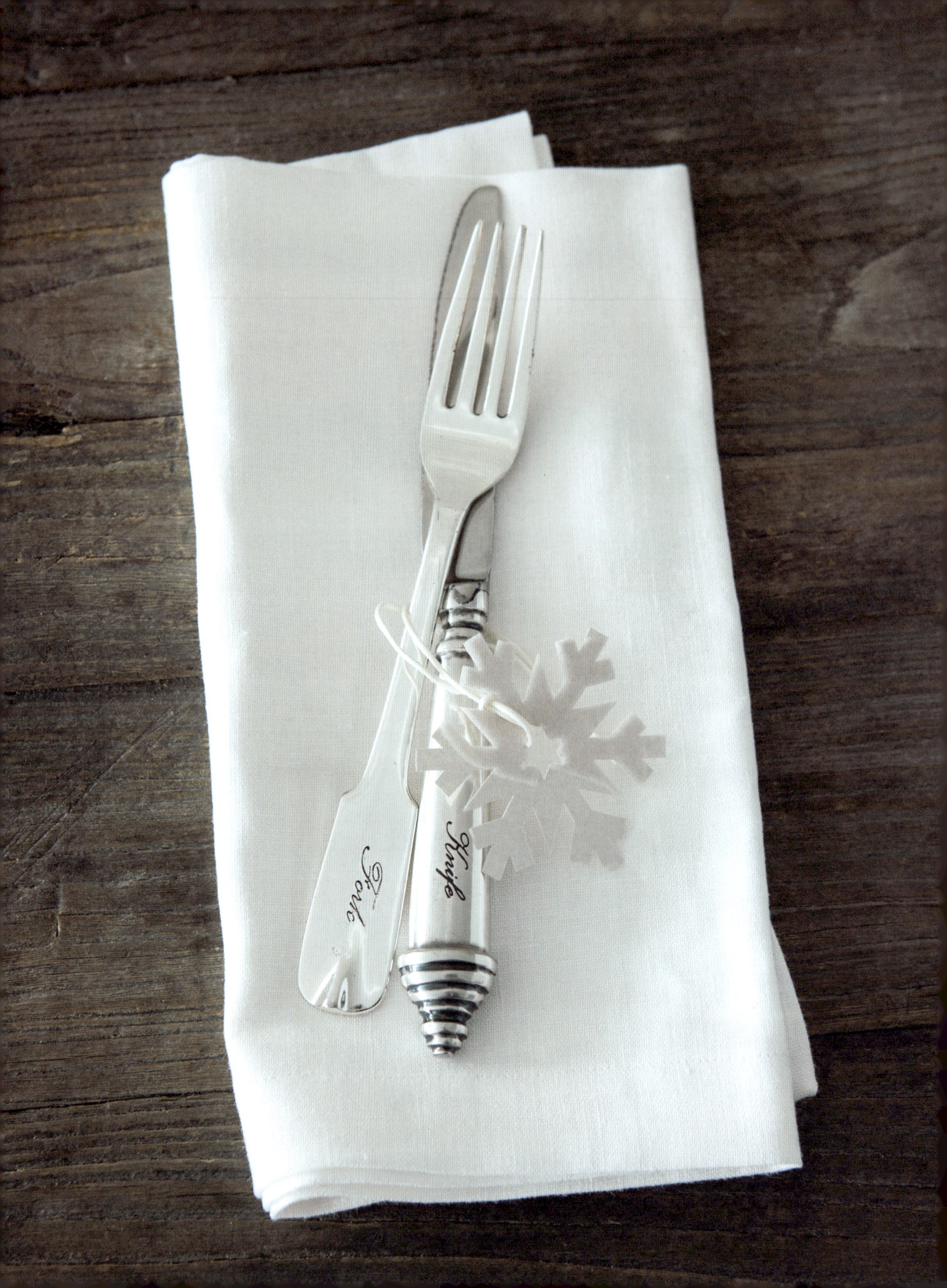
Fork
Knife

WINTER

When you have only
two pennies left in the
world, buy a loaf of
bread with one, and a
lily with the other.

Chinese proverb

Once winter has us in its grip we are forced to spend more time indoors, using fresh flowers to help make our immediate environment as cheerful and bright and as visually stimulating as possible makes good sense. Most of the flowers that you buy – even at this time of year – will have felt the warmth of the sun on them and when you bring them home with you some of that warmth will come with them. Quite possibly they'll add some fragrance to your home, too.

There are so many ways to do this, including making the most of found objects such as the festive-looking birch log that features in the next few pages. Hollowed out and filled with Oasis (wet floral foam), it now serves as a magnificent centrepiece. All the other decorative touches on the table reflect the purity of the white freesias, lilies, roses, stock, ranunculus and tulips crammed into the log – the overall combination suggesting an icy winter starkness that good food and good company will soon overcome.

Although I would find it hard to go past white for this winter table, there's no reason why you couldn't use another colour. Just remember that the overall effect is achieved by keeping your colour palette as simple as possible.

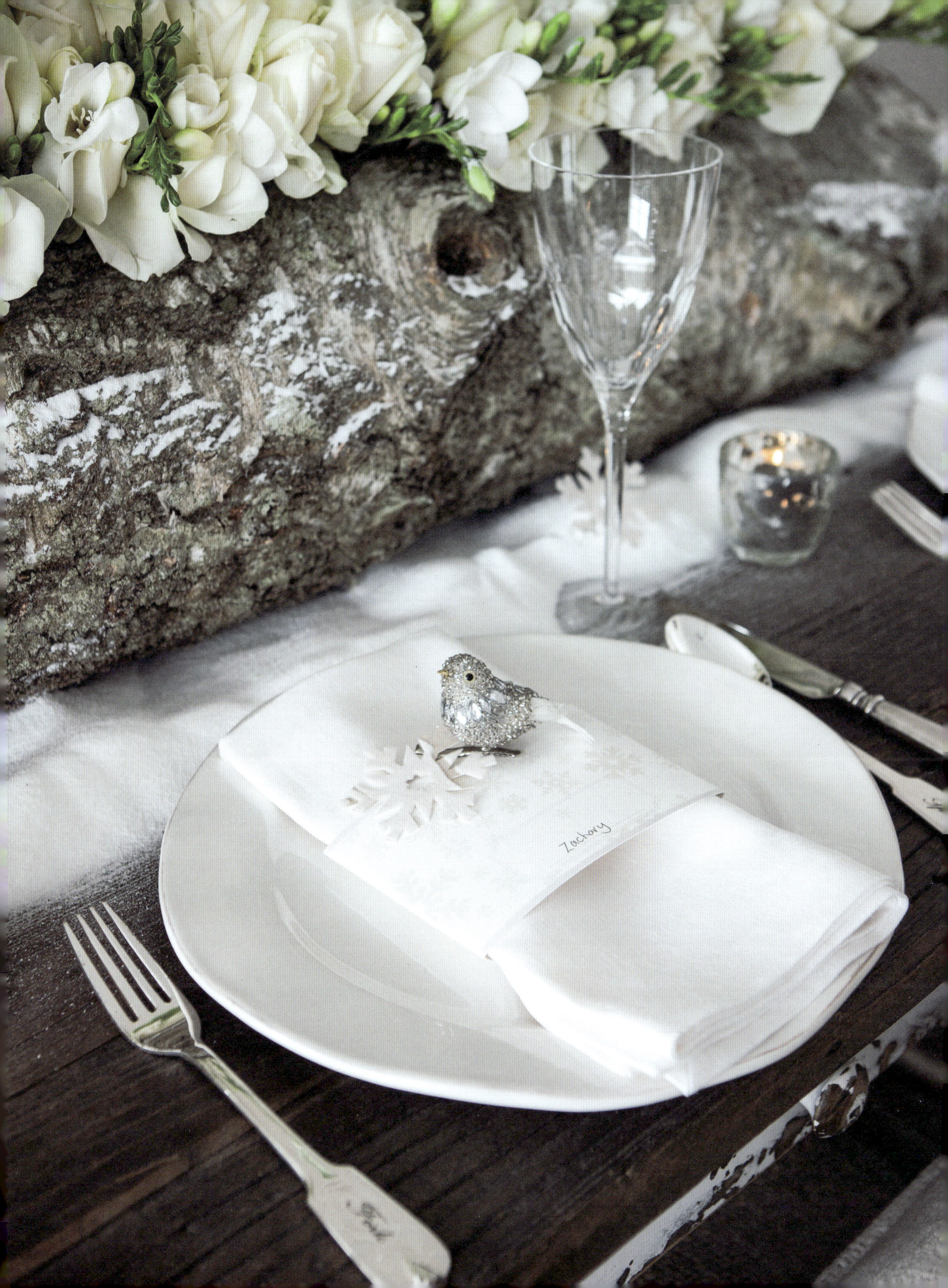
Zachary

Ben

Little touches that personalise table settings are always appreciated by both young and old. Such touches can be as simple as a few colourful berries bunched attractively on a napkin or a more sophisticated approach that uses a white-on-white effect as seen here; the result to strive for is one that is visually stimulating.

Winter arrangements really suit a crisp look – it's a look that reminds you of what it's like to be outside at this time of year when your breath condenses and everything is quite stark, yet manages to have a certain serenity about it. A little faux snow here and there indoors will enhance this effect, such as can be seen on the log centrepiece on the previous and subsequent pages.

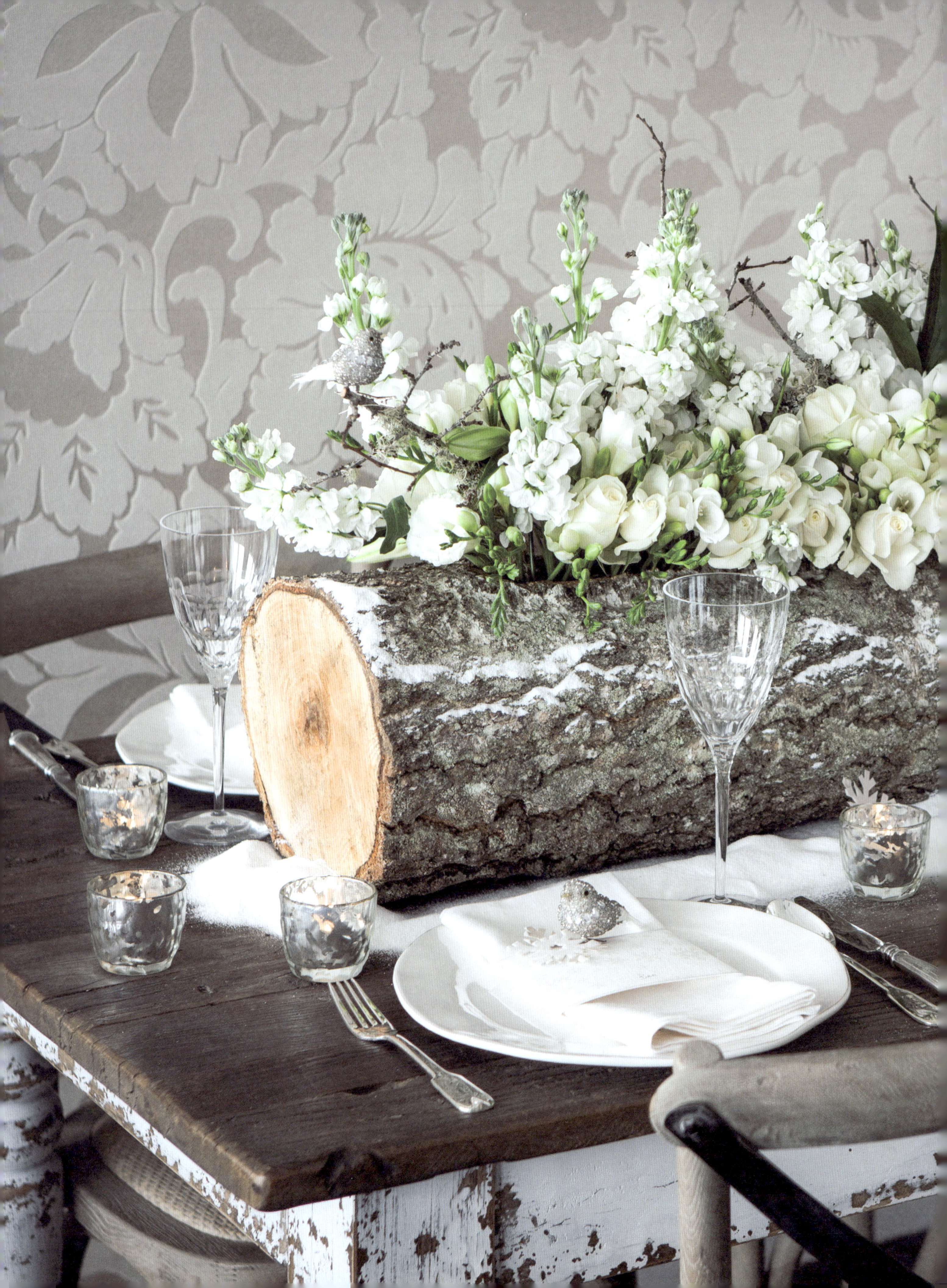

Nature looks dead in winter because her life is gathered into her heart. She withers the plant down to the root that she may grow it up again fairer and stronger. She calls her family together within her inmost home to prepare them for being scattered abroad upon the face of the earth.

Hugh Macmillan

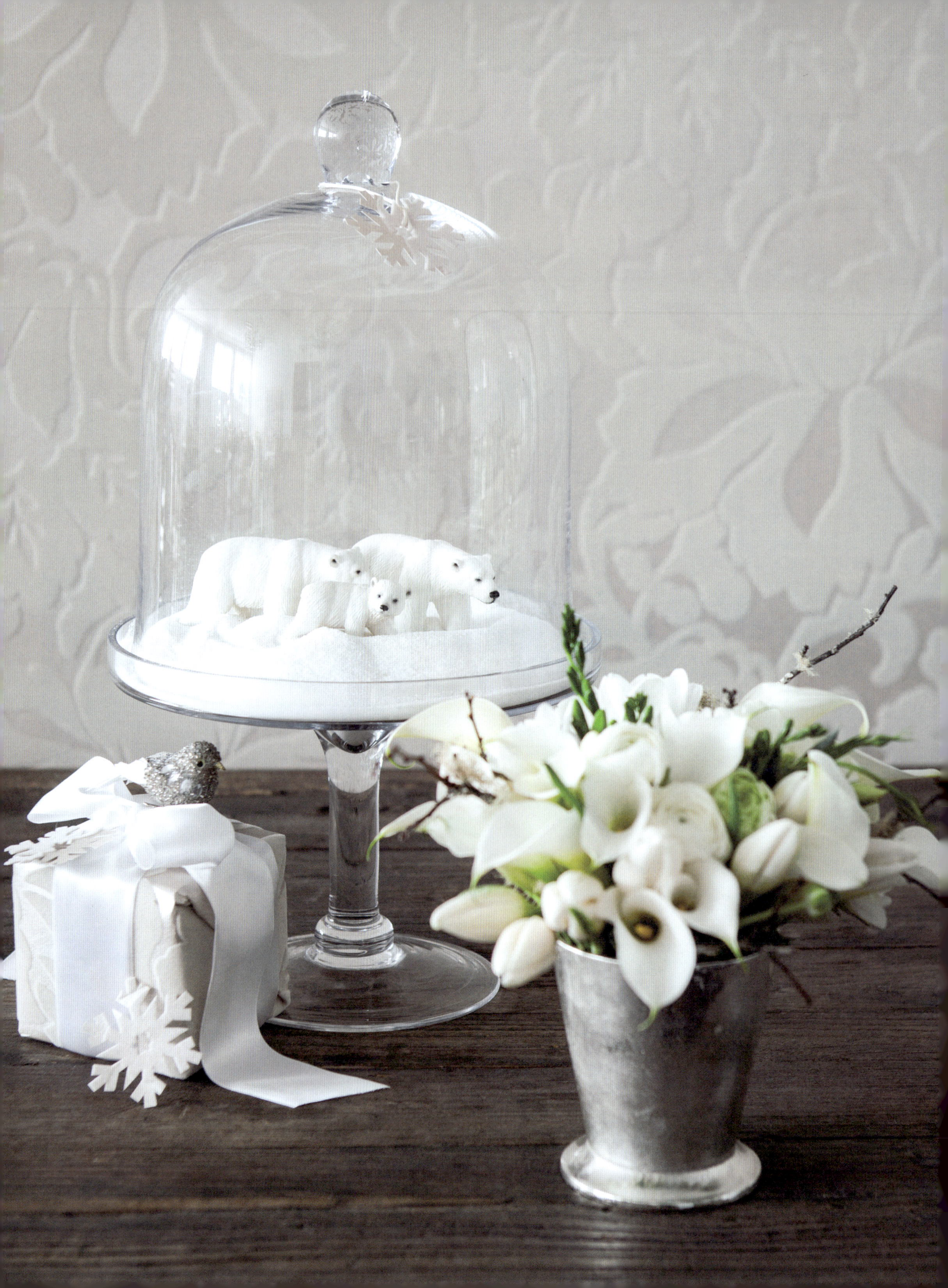

The stark white of the simple arrangements on the left and right featuring roses, lilies, freesias and tulips is offset by the soft green of the plump freesia buds.

Of winter's lifeless world each tree now seems a perfect part; Yet each one holds summer's secret deep down within its heart.

Charles G. Stater

A collection of bone china cups can also serve as decorative candle-holders. If you make the candles yourself, consider adding a few drops of essential oil to imbue the immediate surroundings with a delicate fragrance.

Overleaf soft blues and taupe provide an understated background to informally bunched erlicheer, miniature roses, bay and eucalyptus on the left and a rustic mass of roses and stock surrounded by lamb's ear on the right.

Winter 207

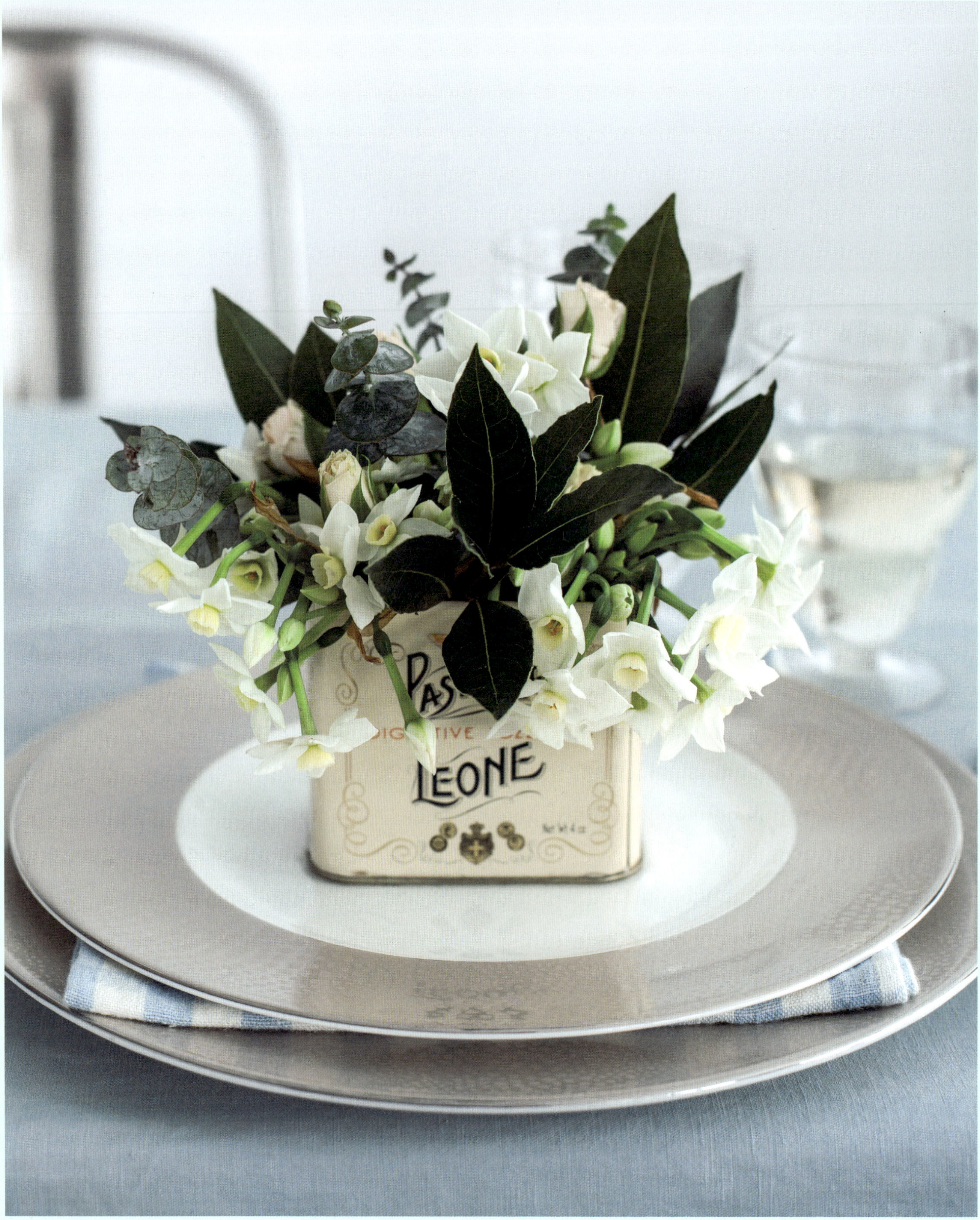
LEONE

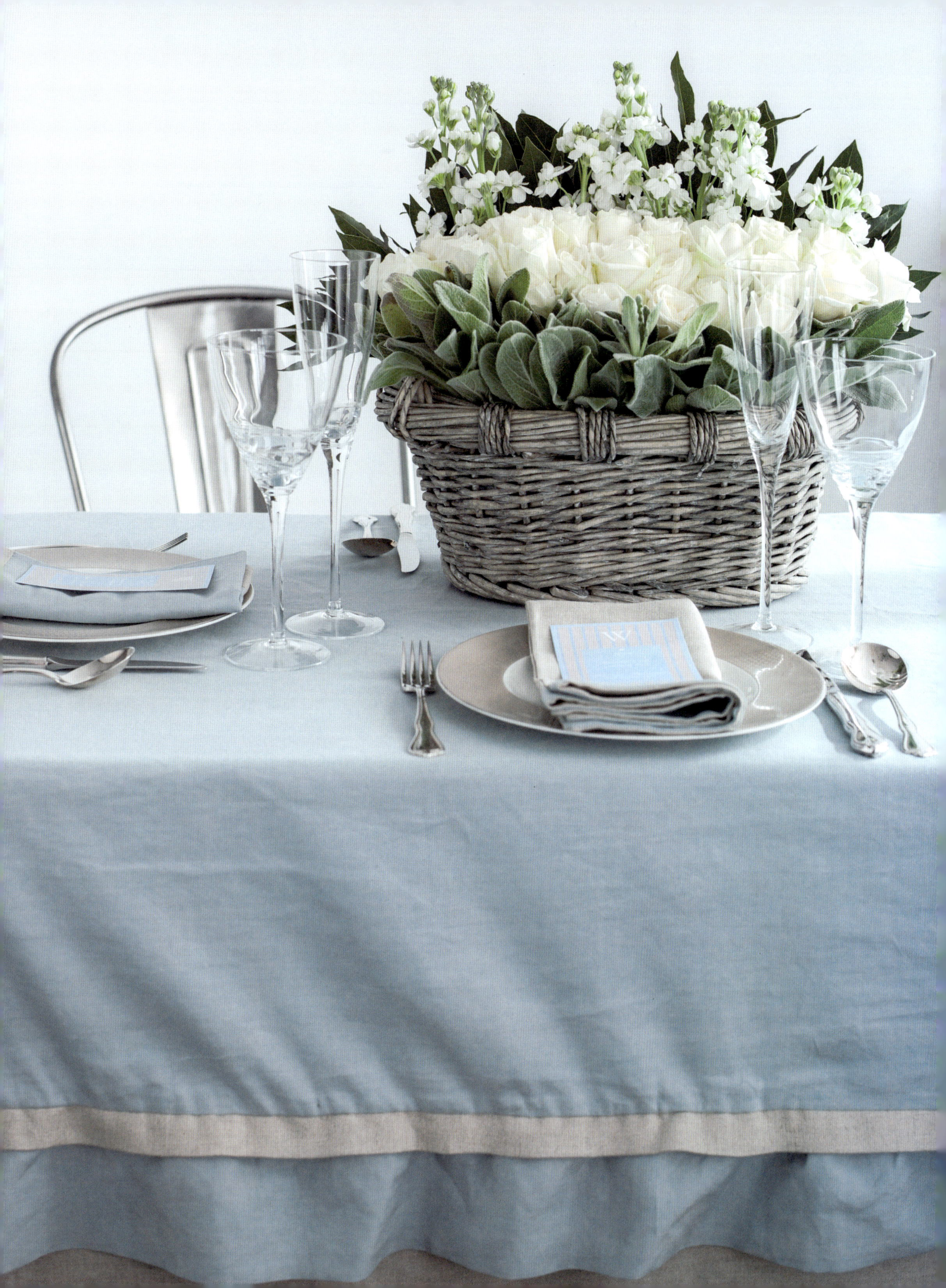

Brighten up the table with small posies of erlicheer, each marked with a place name (above). If you wish, you could give these posies to your guests as a souvenir of a special occasion. This attractive centrepiece (right) features chrysanthemums, stock, lilies and kale.

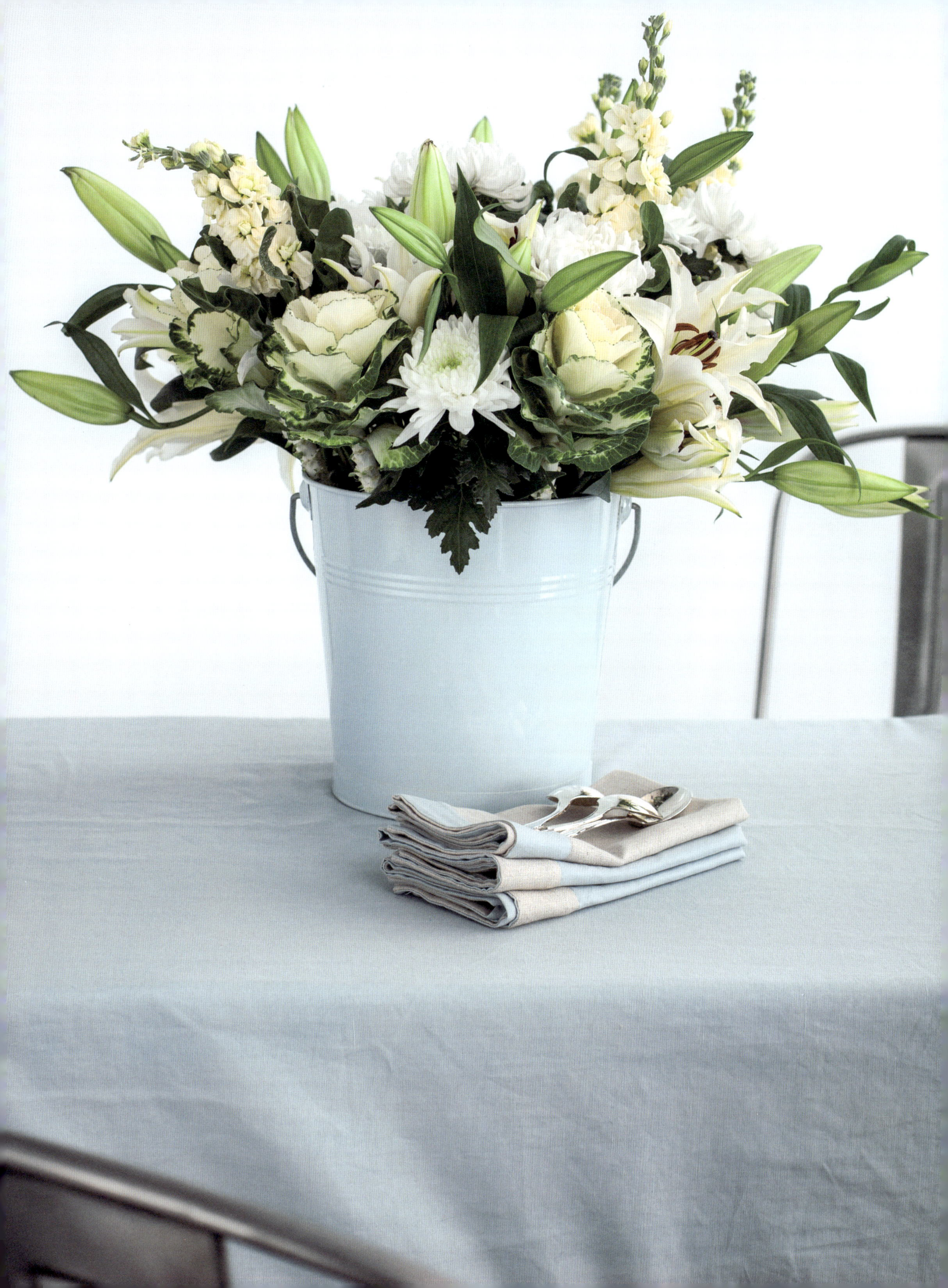

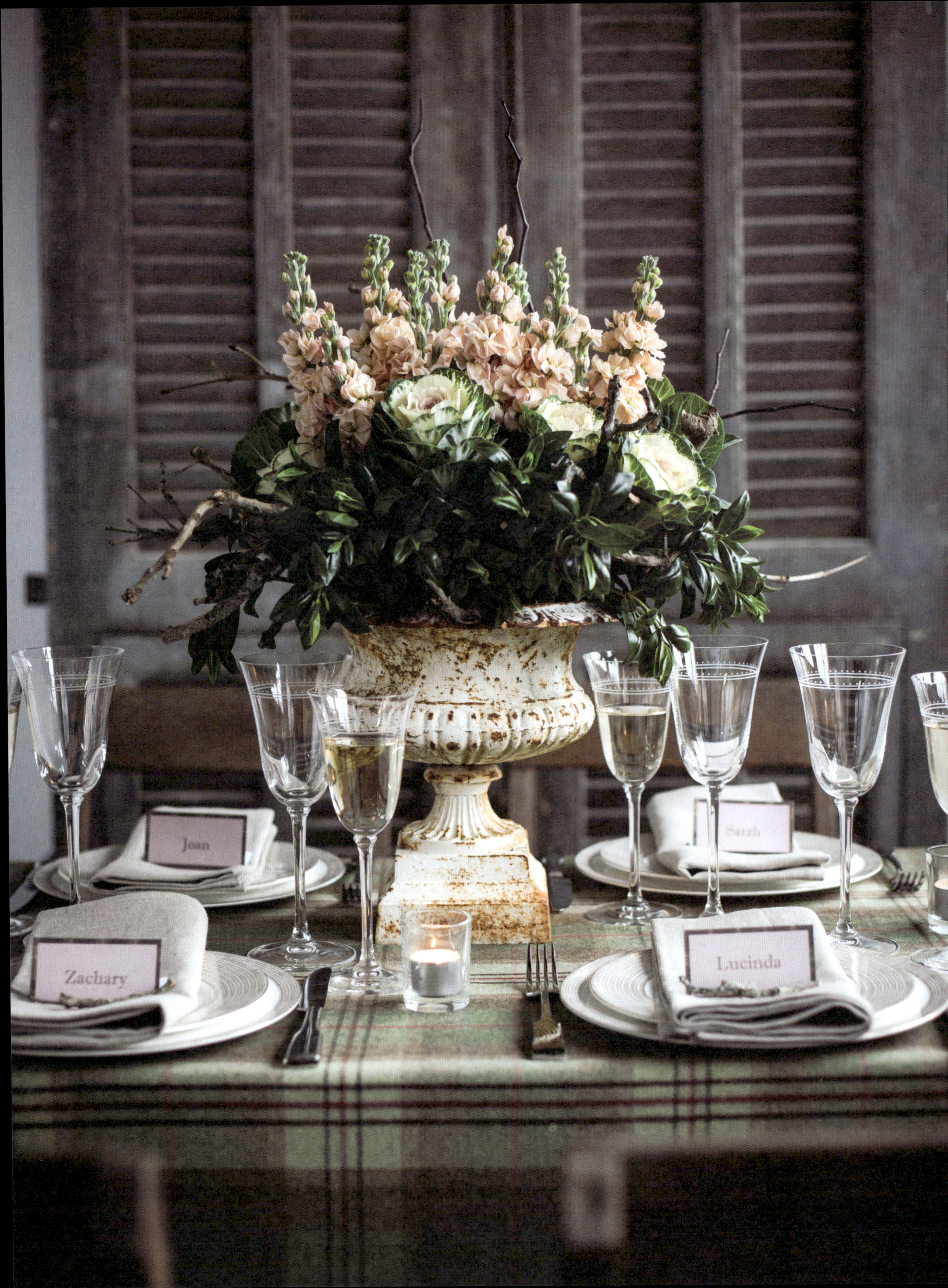
Joan
Sarah
Zachary
Lucinda

Although there might not be much happening in the garden at this time of year, it's always easy to find plenty of green foliage to set off some sweetly scented stock as seen in this rustic arrangement that also includes some decorative kale. The plaid tablecloth adds a hint of nostalgia, which for many of us is the essence of winter, while each place setting features a moss-covered twiglet, a reminder of the season.

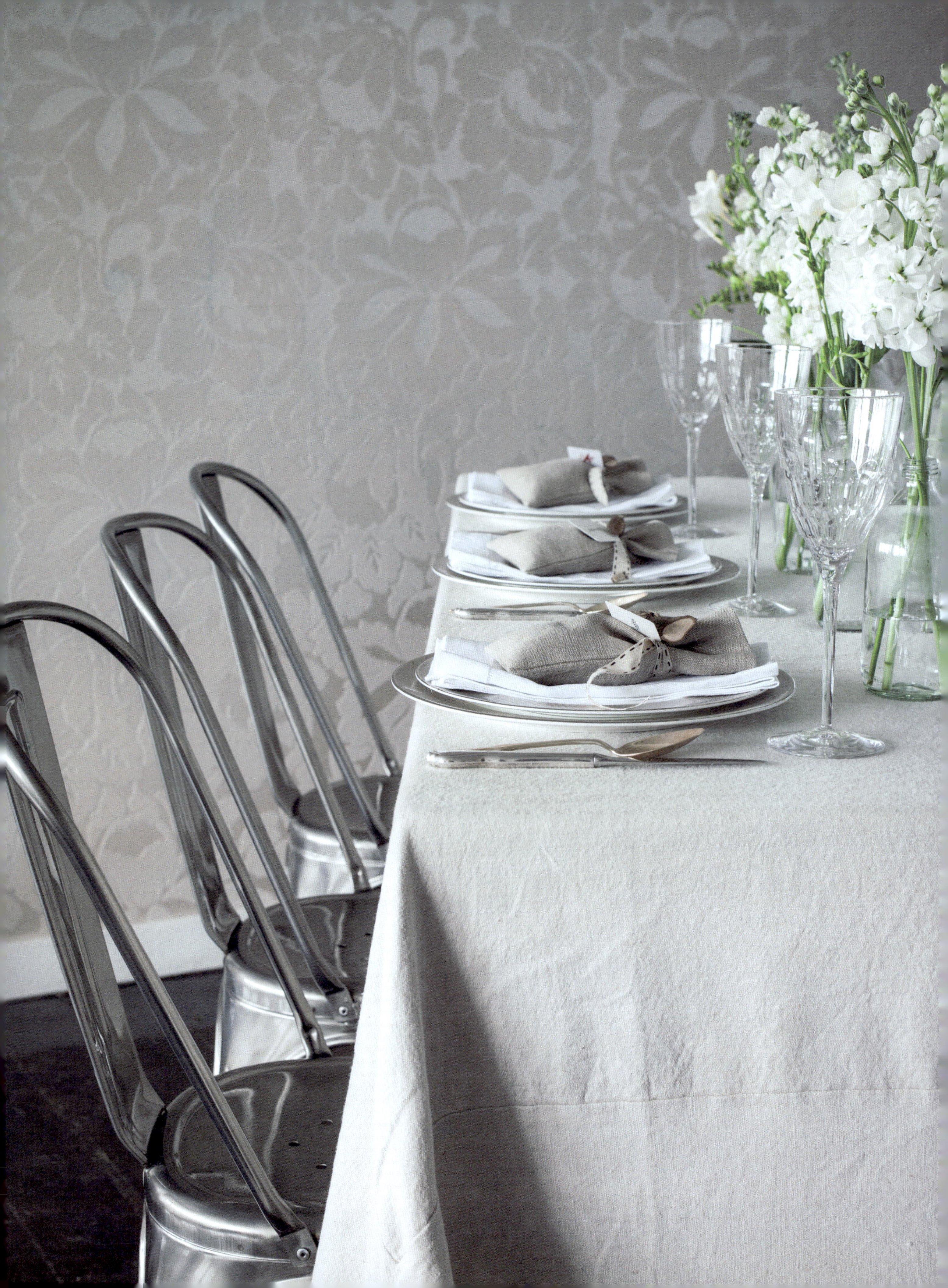

The flowers of late winter and early spring occupy places in our hearts well out of proportion to their size.

Gertrude S. Wister

It's hard to improve on the simplicity of freesias and stock as displayed here in plain glass bottles down the length of the table.

Once again tea cups, this time of a delicate design, set off these pretty white ornithogalum to best effect.

Winter 217

One kind word can warm three winter months.

Japanese proverb

Make these fragrant freesias complemented by icy white roses and the season's first erlicheer really stand out by putting them in pristine glass bottles and enhancing each bunch with a little green foliage.

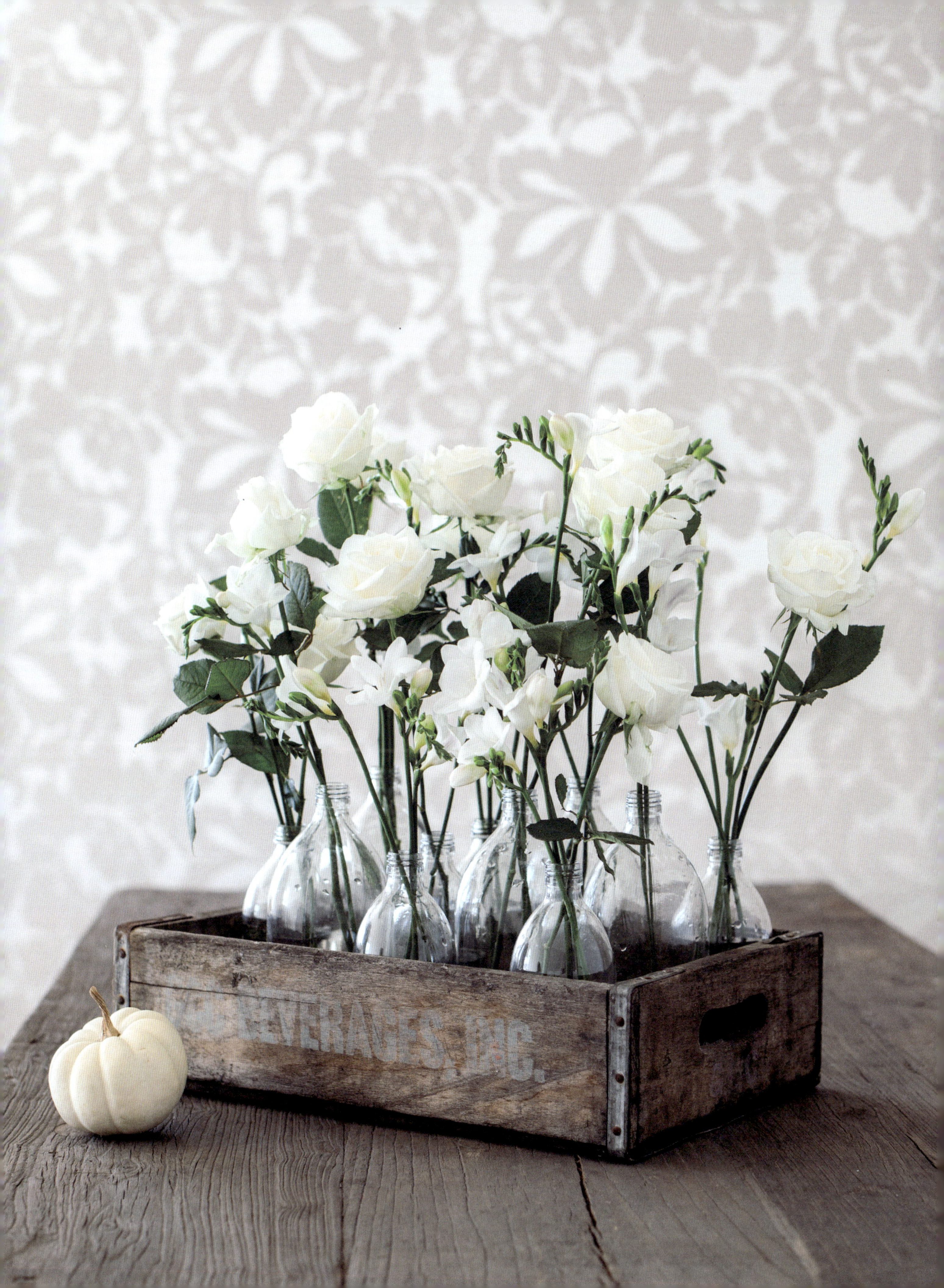
BEVERAGES, INC.

Autumn might be just a memory but there should be no shortage of pumpkins and squashes to add a rustic touch to exquisite little posies of erlicheer.

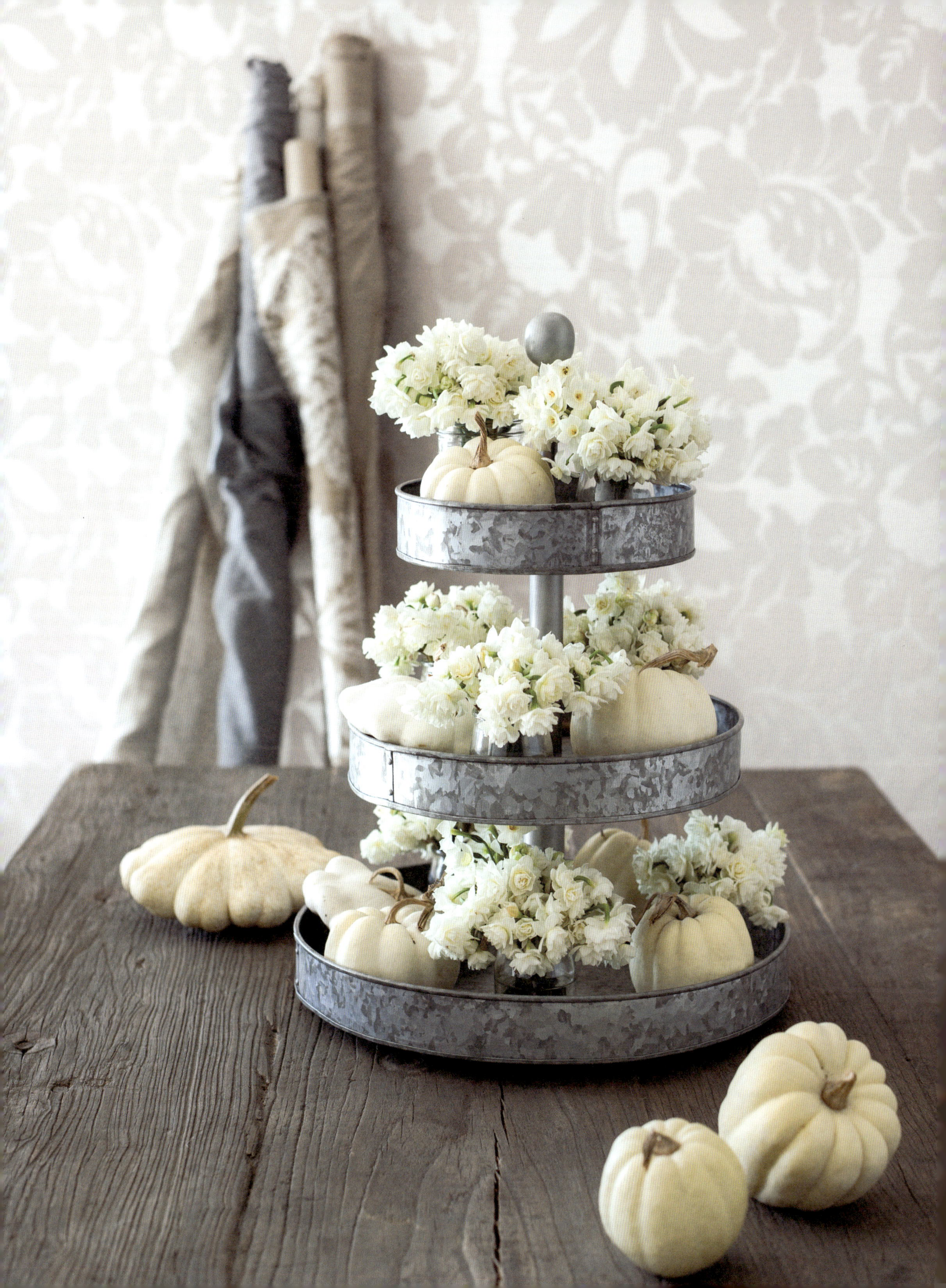

If one daffodil is worth a thousand pleasures, then one is too few.

William Wordsworth

When those very first daffodils become available, whether in your own garden or from your local flower seller, they deserve our undivided attention so keep distractions in terms of containers as simple as possible.

From now on there'll be more colour available, reminding us that the golden warmth of the sun is not too far away.

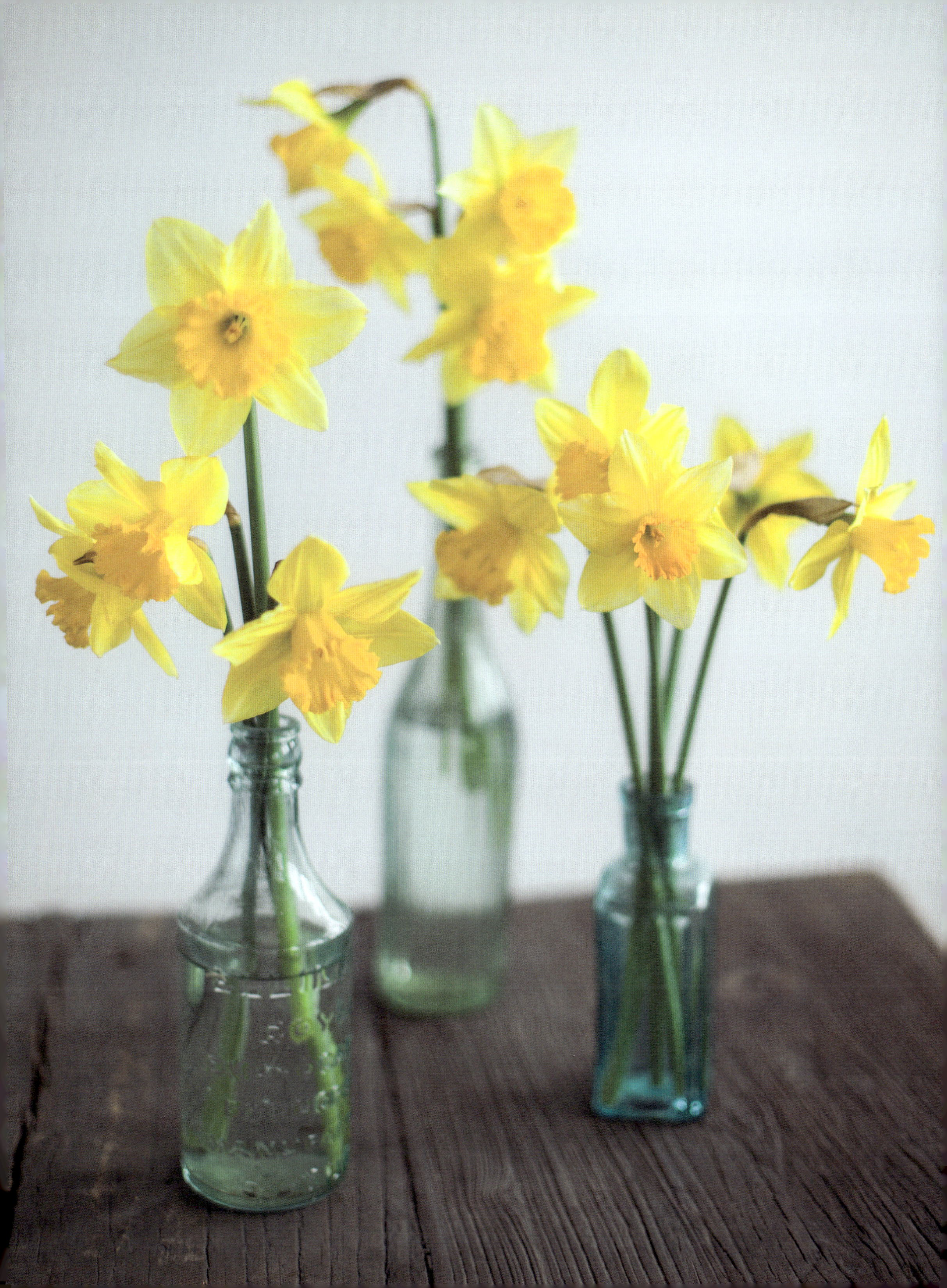

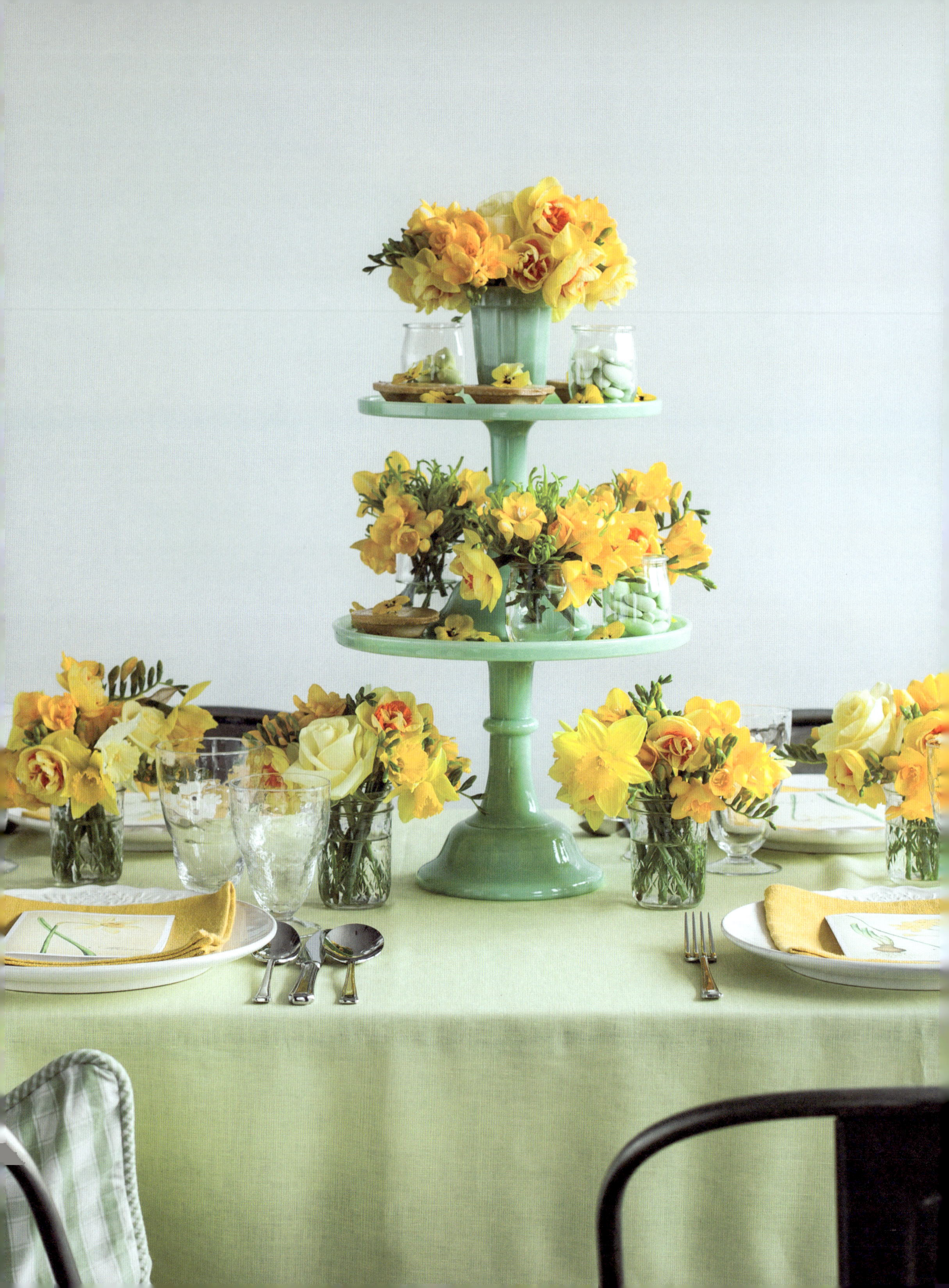

If you've got something to celebrate at this time of year, then make the most of these glorious blooms. As long as you keep your overall theme simple and confined to just one main colour – as seen on the left through the use of massed daffodils, roses and freesias – more is definitely better.

Yellow pansies add a cheerful note to the rustic bread sticks (above right) while a mustard tin right) sets off the perfection of these golden daffodils.

Now that winter is on its way out, it's time to splash some colour around. The sheer vibrancy of nature's combination of yellow and green will give a lift to any setting, whether it's the delicacy of fresh pansies above and left or the exuberance of the massed freesias and daffodils on the right.

Overleaf a combination of carnations, roses and chrysanthemums are used to great effect in this dramatic flower cake. The unifying theme here is colour and simple glassware.

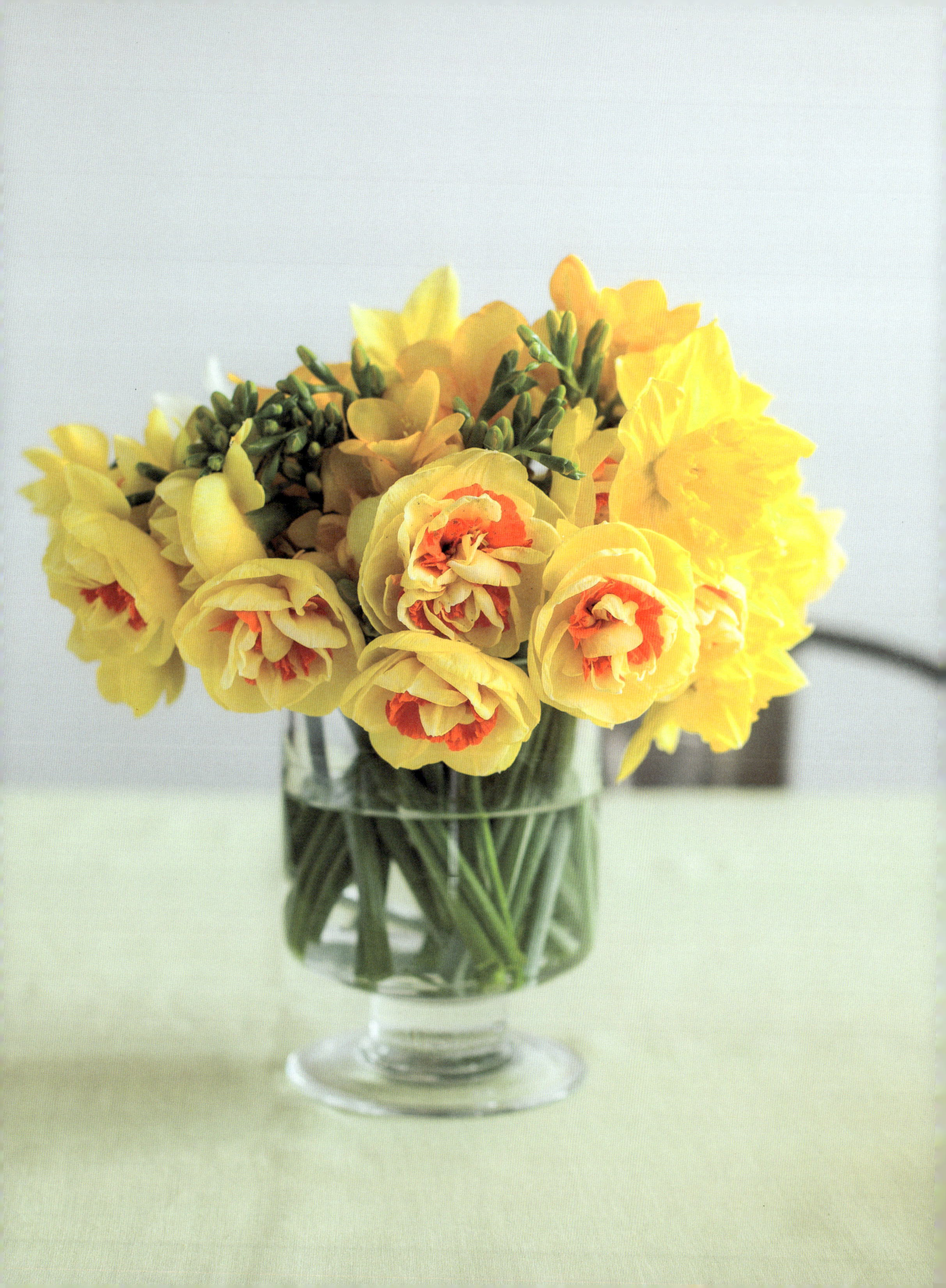

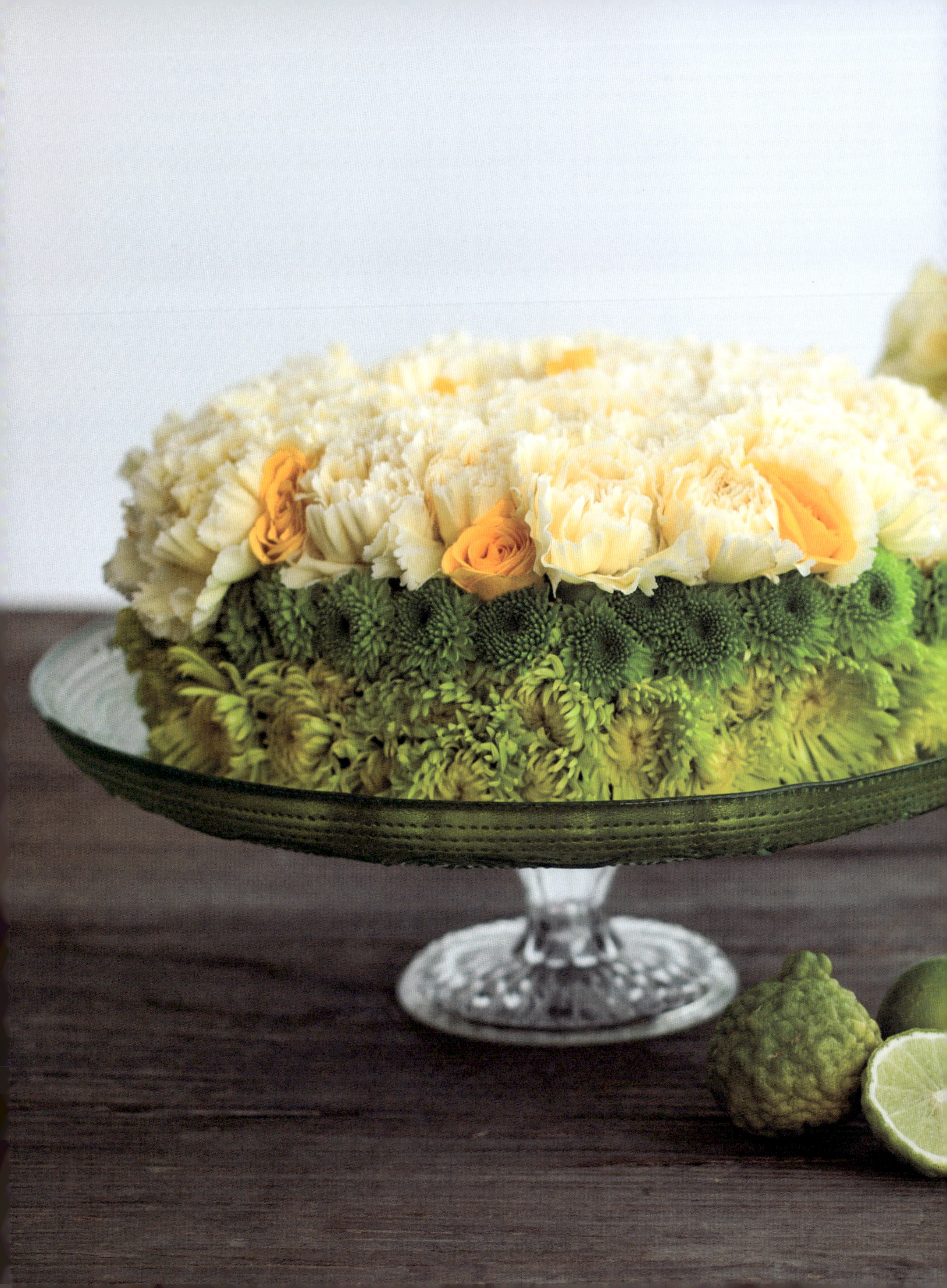

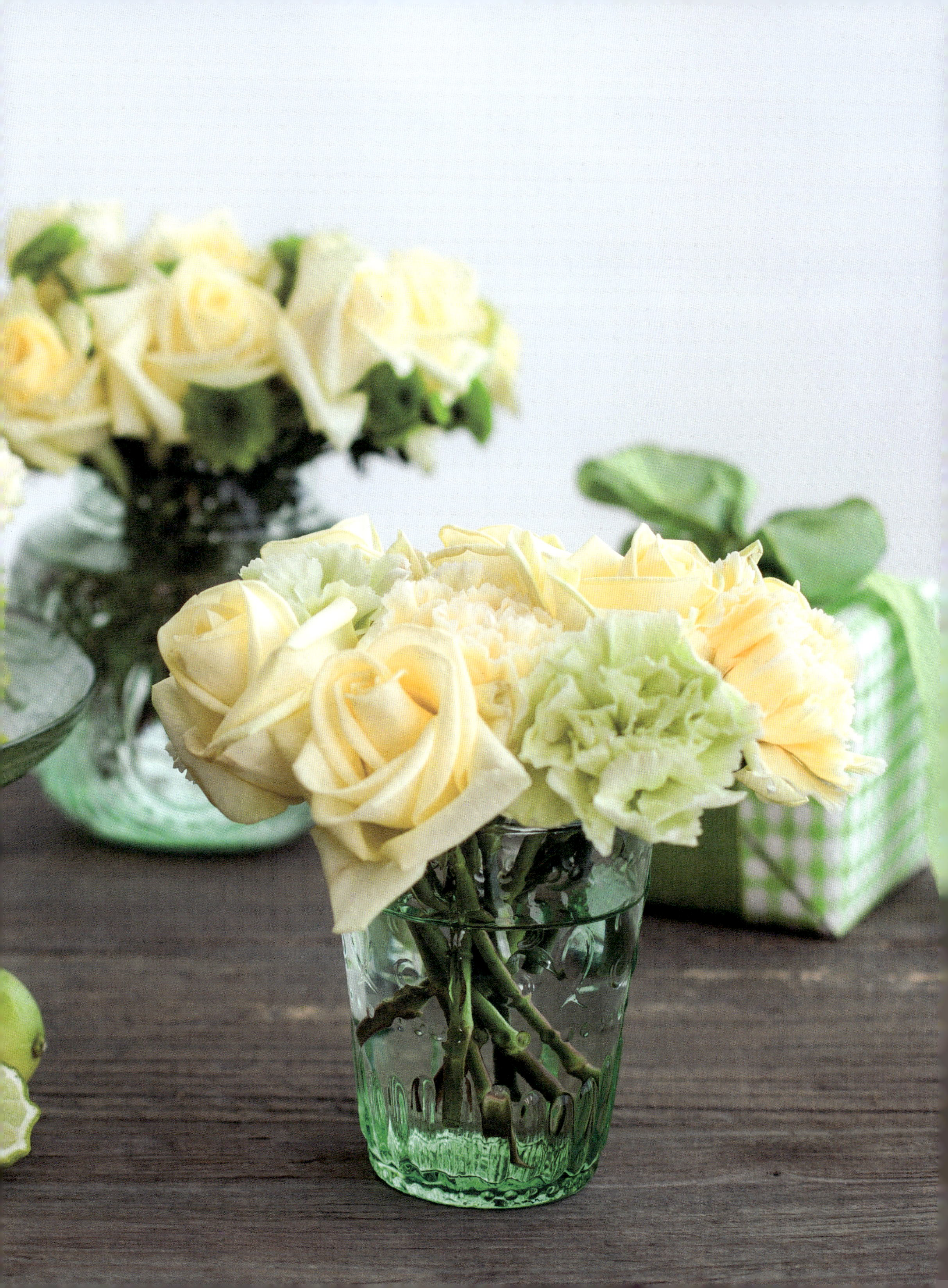

As well as colour, it's a great time of year to introduce a little romance into our lives. It really is time to start smelling the roses – and the sweet peas that tell us spring is now just around the corner. Sitting pretty in decorated tins, these fragrant posies with their spray of green berries on these pages and overleaf are a great way to spread the love.

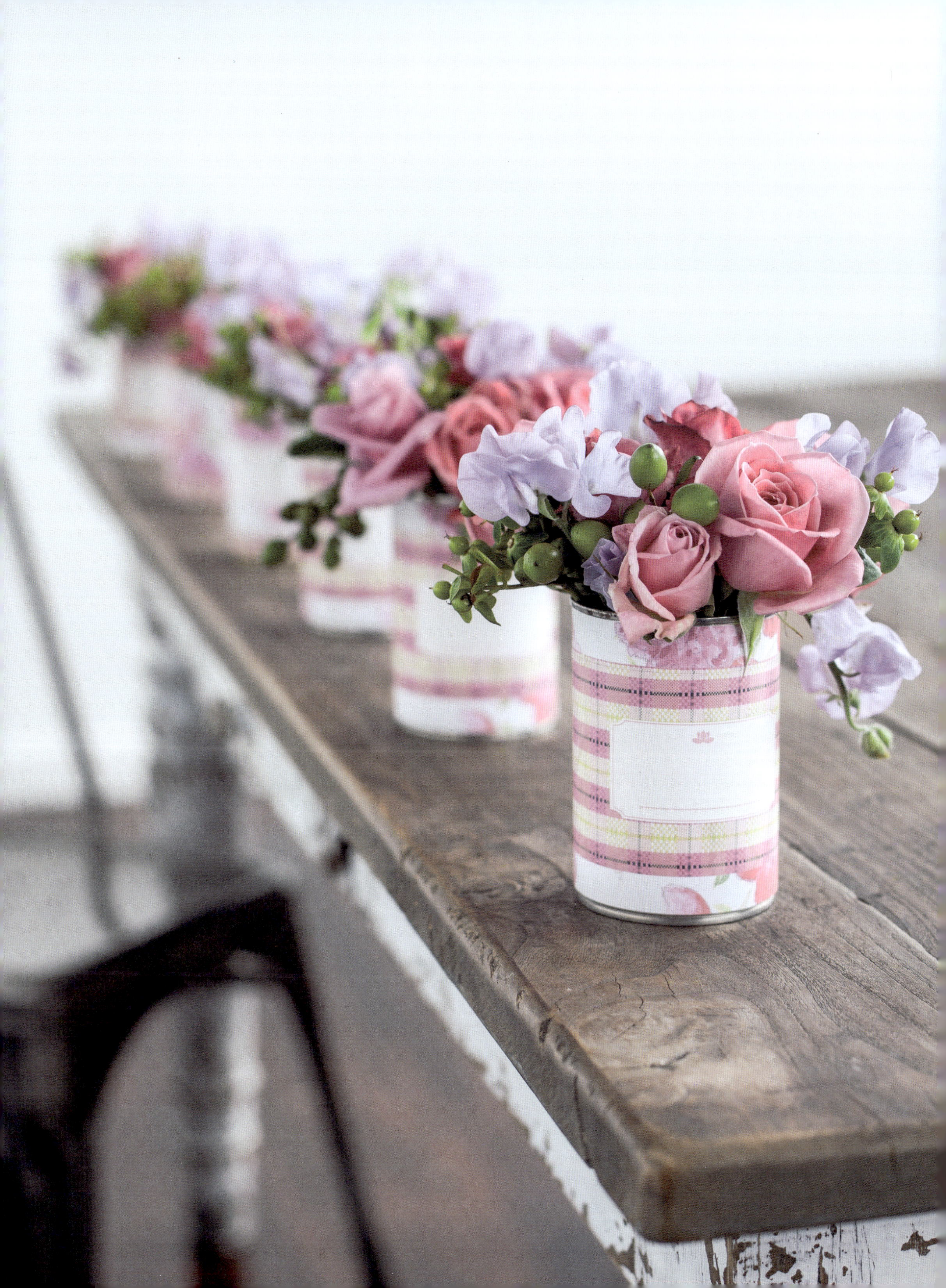

Another sure sign that winter is nearly done is the arrival of tulips; whether still tightly furled like the pink beauties here or drooping romantically, the perfection of their petals will have your guests gasping in pleasure.

Winter 233

The tulip's petals shine in dew,
All beautiful, but none alike.

James Montgomery

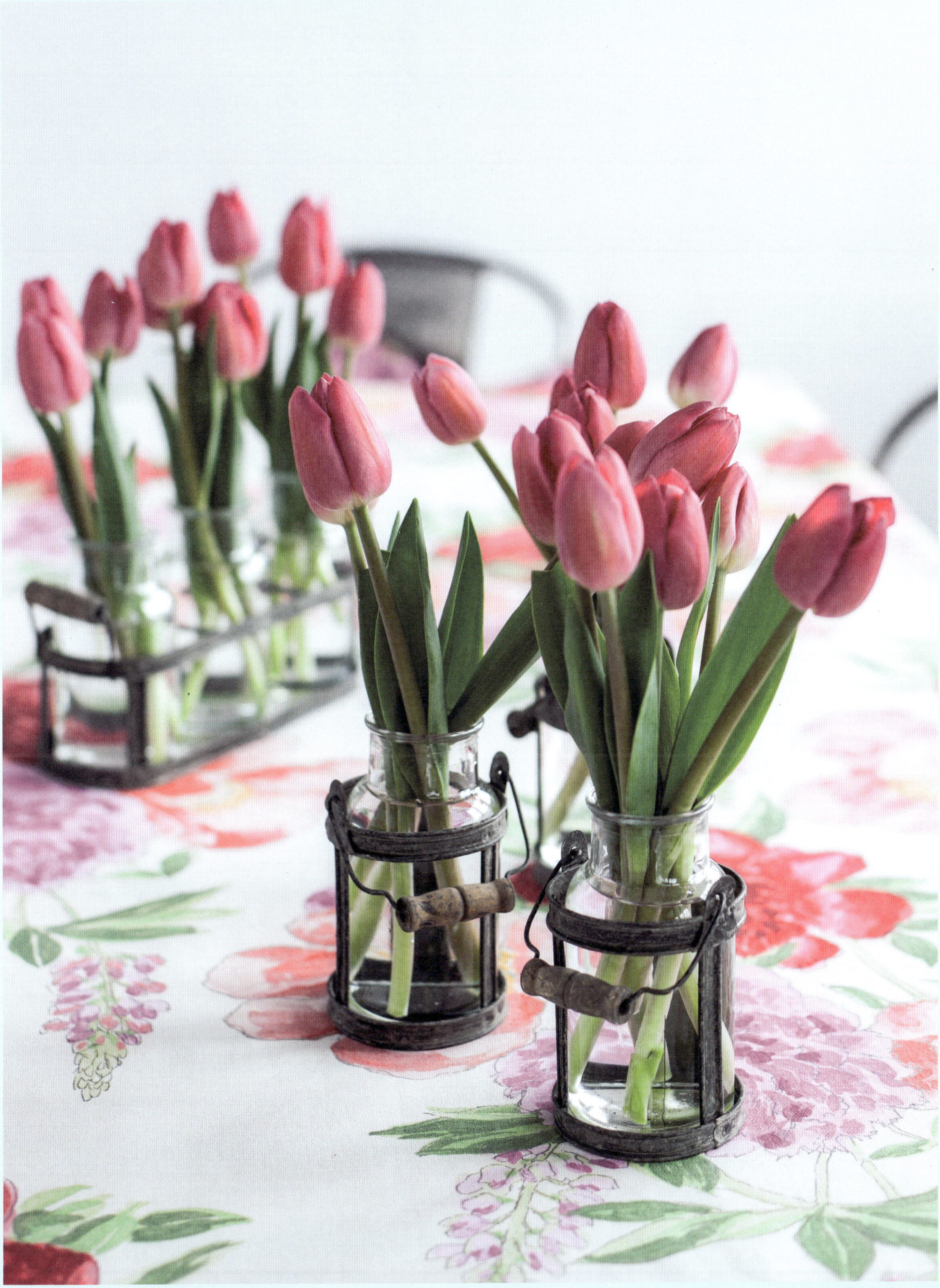

No recipe is required to make these flower cakes, each of which looks more than good enough to eat. Such arrangements are better elevated, making these pretty pastel-coloured cake stands the ideal way to enjoy them from every aspect. Featuring carnations, roses, viburnum flowers and lamb's ear, each one only requires a base into which flower stems can be inserted.

Winter 237

Dream rose gateaux

A delicate rosebud and a personalised label make these party favours especially memorable, while the bone china tea cup and saucer set overleaf showcases the dainty perfection of roses and ranunculus in bud.

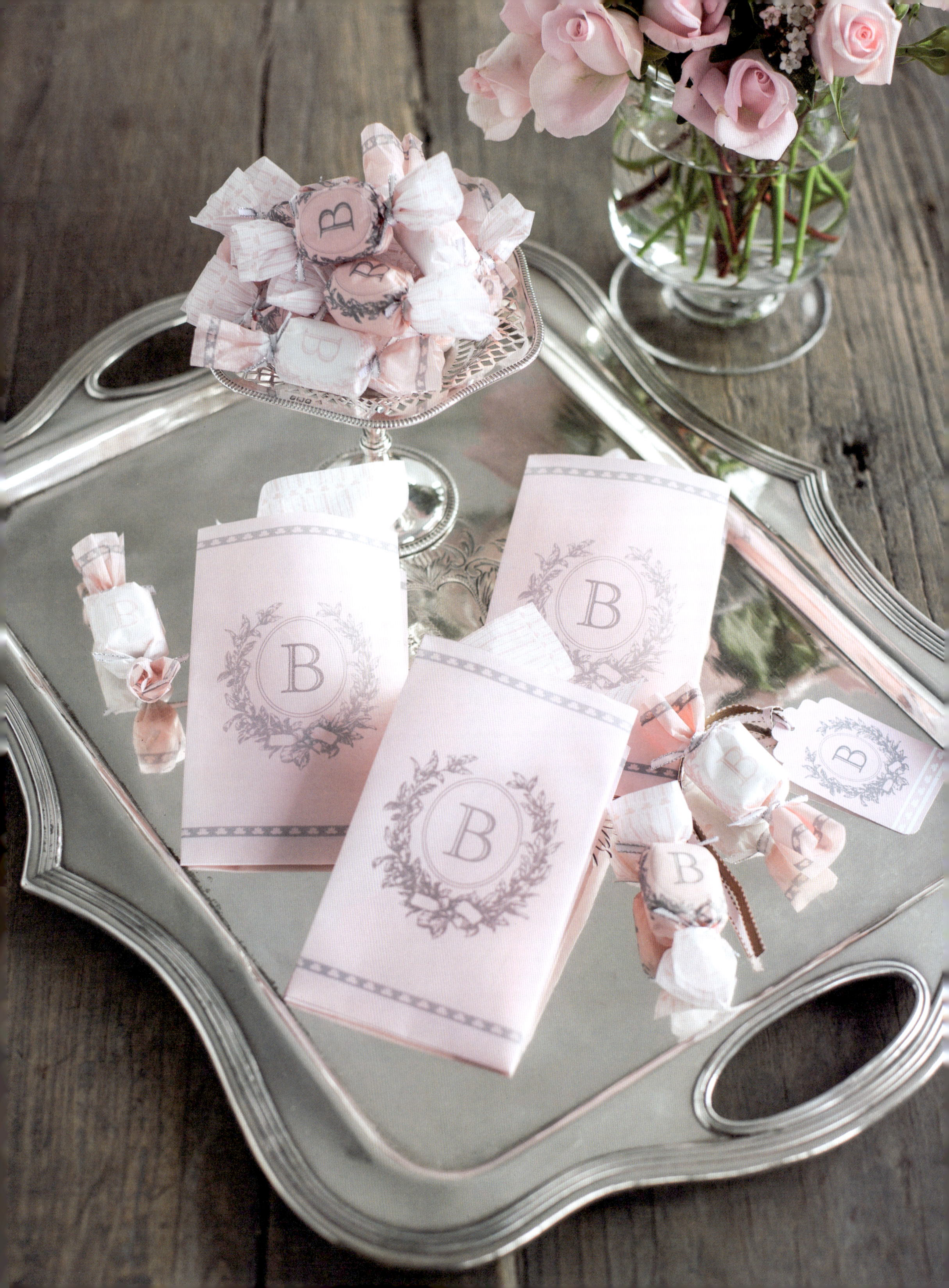
B
B
B
B

Winter 241

242 Winter

When you have an abundance of freesias, roses, stock or any other scented blooms, keep the arrangement as simple as possible so your guests can gain the utmost sensual pleasure from them.

God has sown his name on the heavens in glittering stars; but on earth he planteth his name by tender flowers.

Jean Paul Richter

What would a wedding or similarly joyous occasion be without flowers? Massed, in plain white jugs and glass vessels, the combination of gypsophila, tulips, sweet peas, roses and freesias seen here and overleaf bring elegance and serenity to any setting or venue.

Although white is the main theme here, the complementary green foliage and berries add a touch of freshness to the big picture that is further enhanced by the casual scattering of some green succulents around and near the bases of some of the containers.

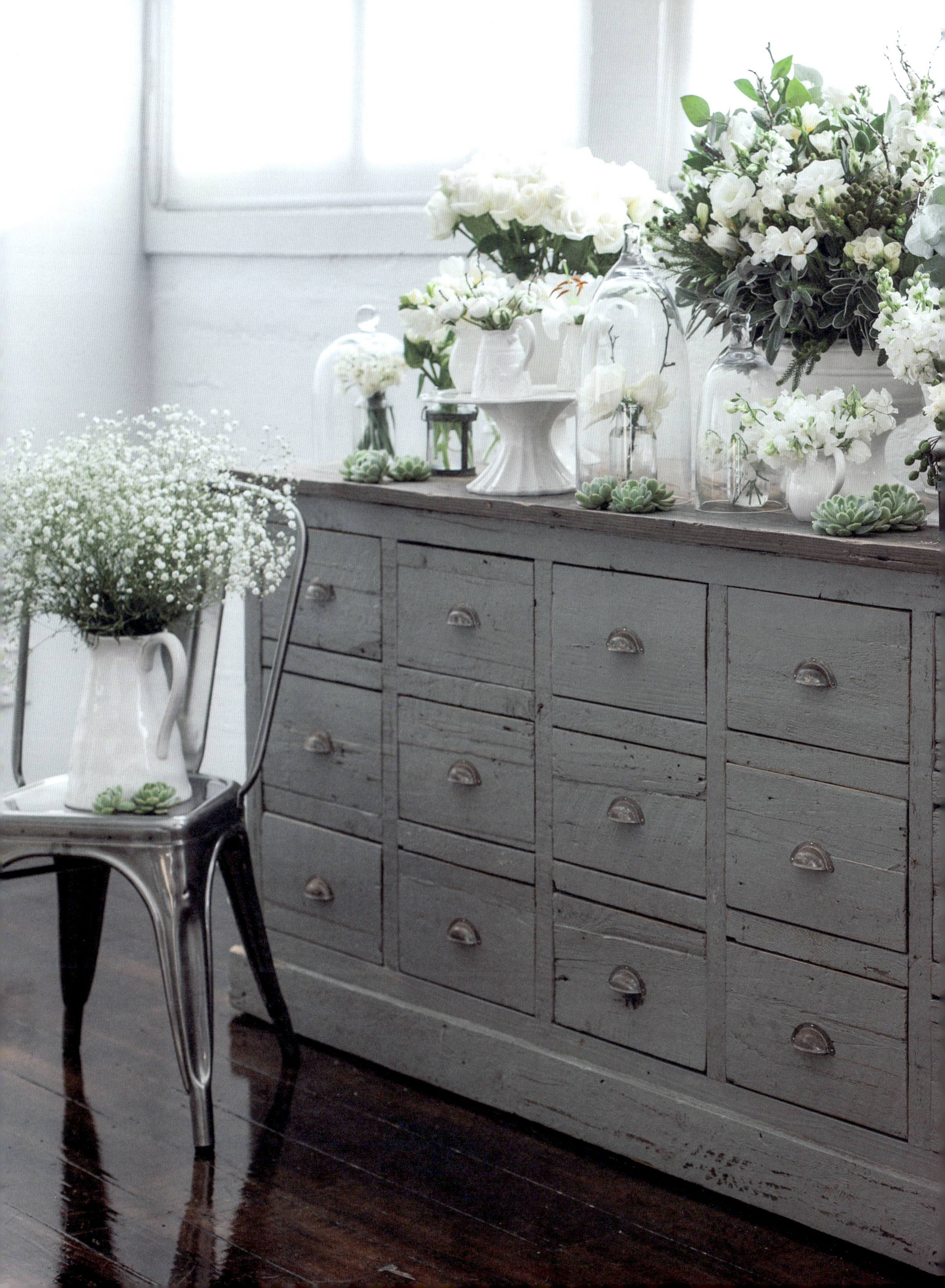

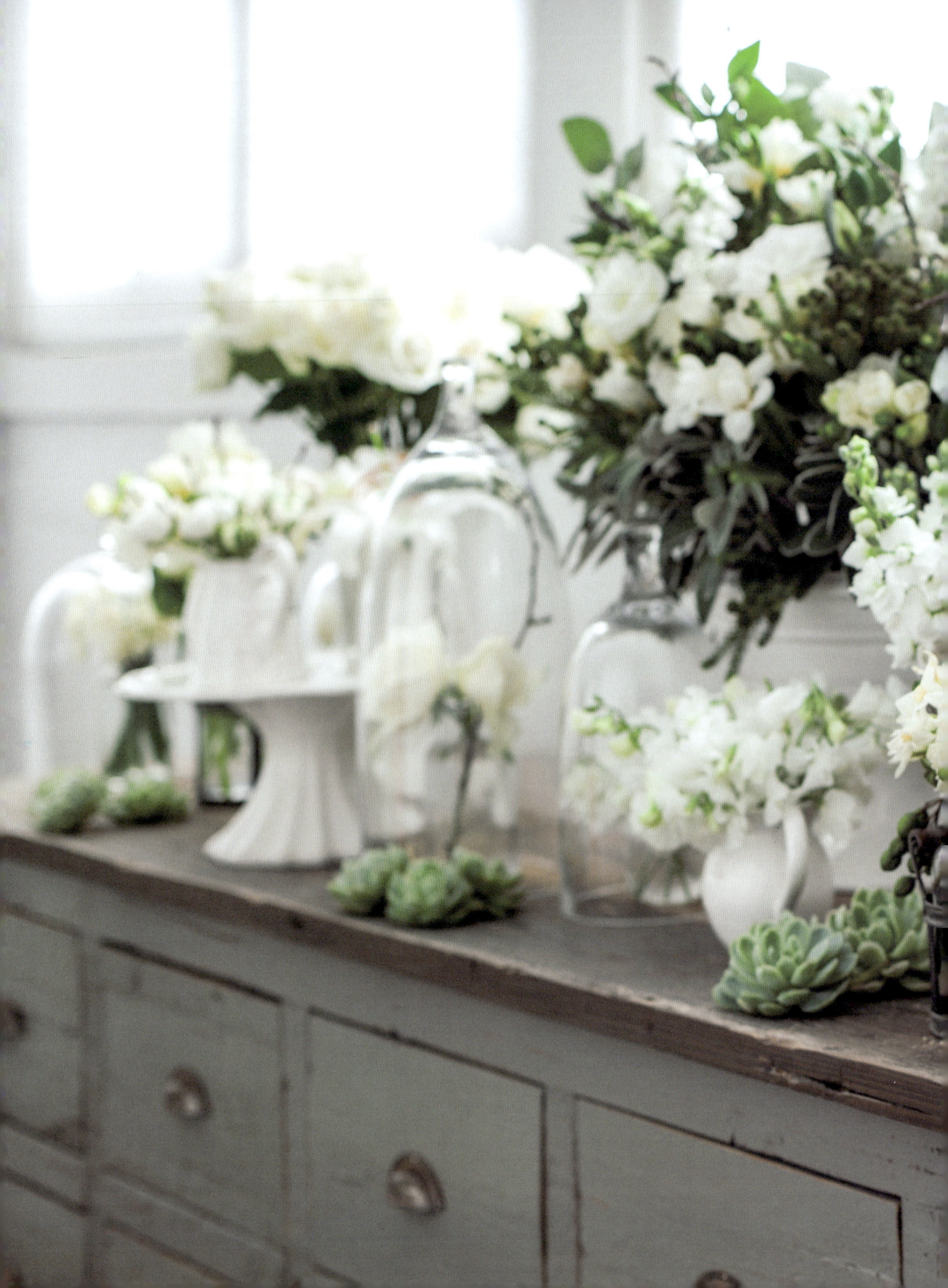

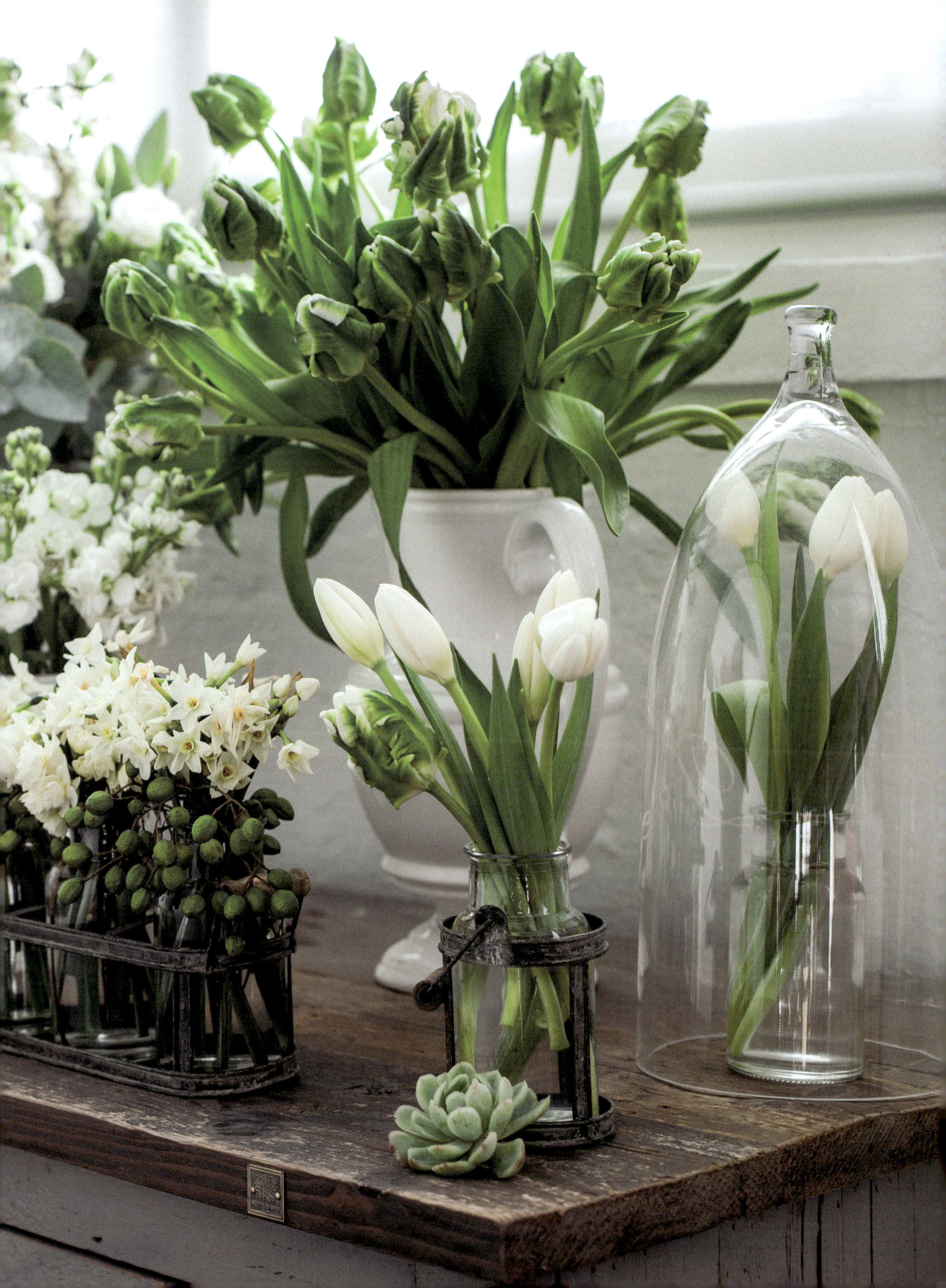

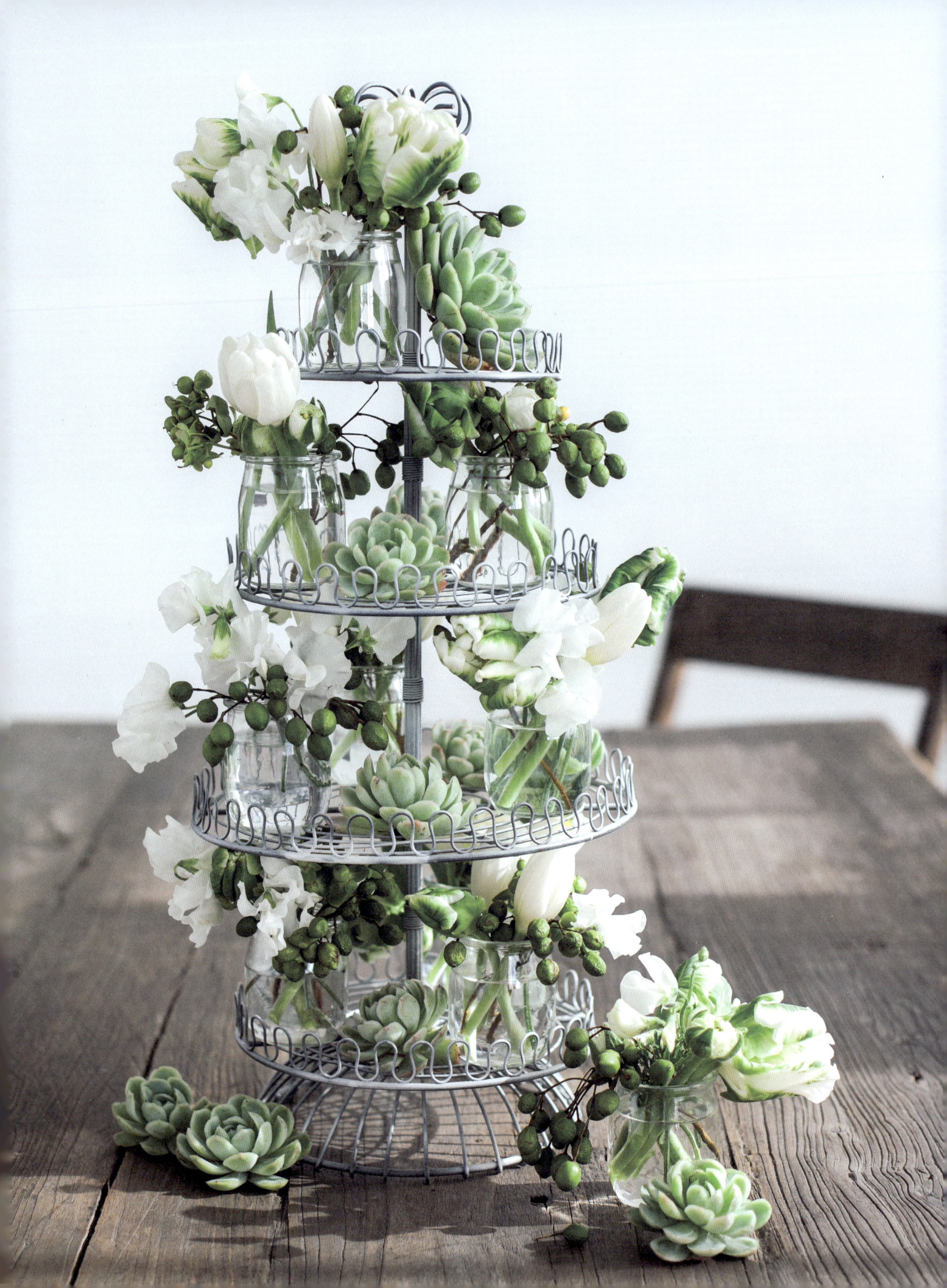

Succulents also feature on this striking tiered arrangement of freesias, sweet peas and berries (left), while a selection of dainty jugs of stock and ranunculus (right) can enhance the plainest background.

Freesias, freesias and more freesias – the simple perfection of these late winter blooms with their exquisite scent make any occasion a special one. And although there is a striking variety of textures used in the setting on the right, the colour green is clearly the unifying feature.

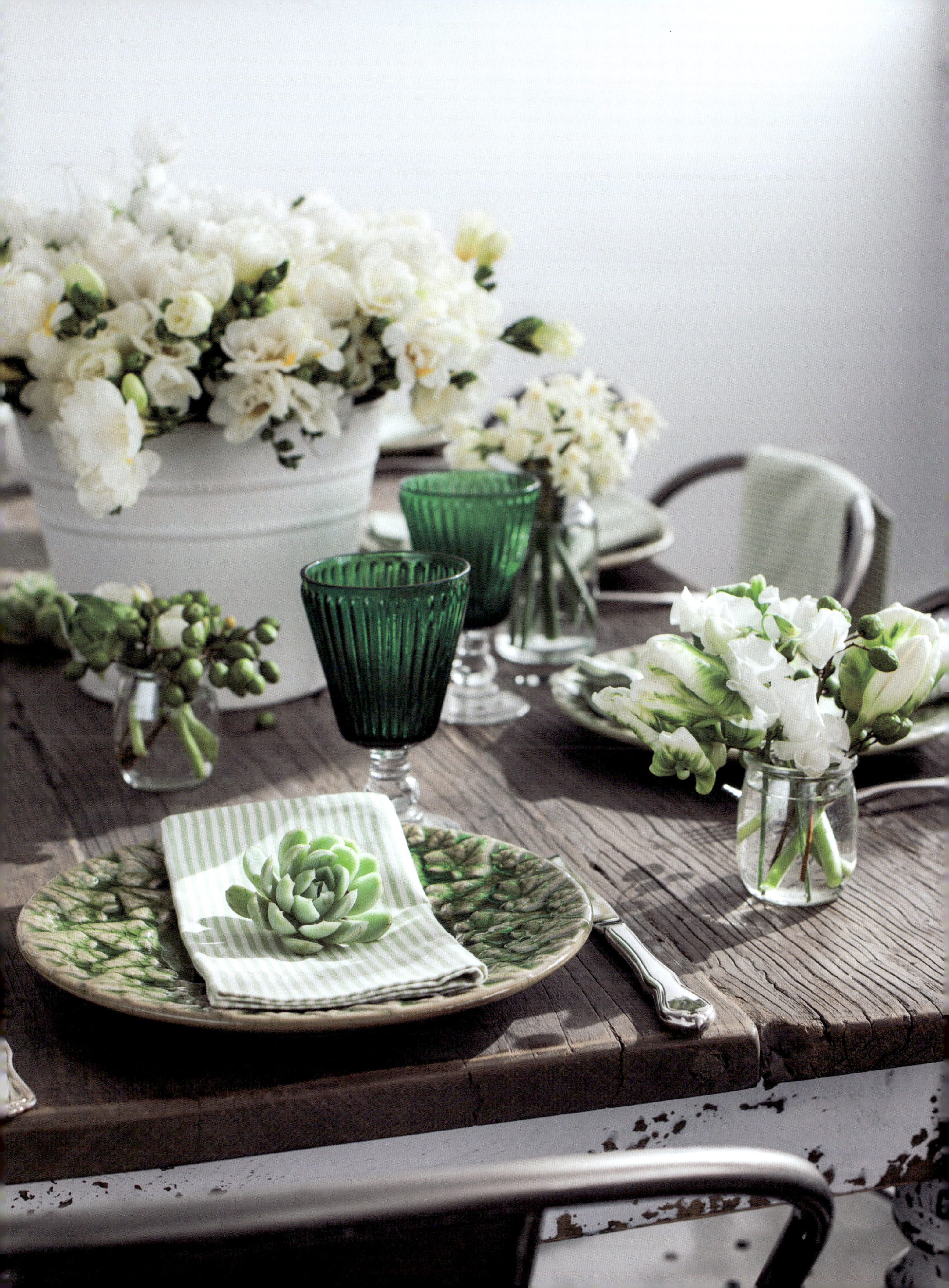

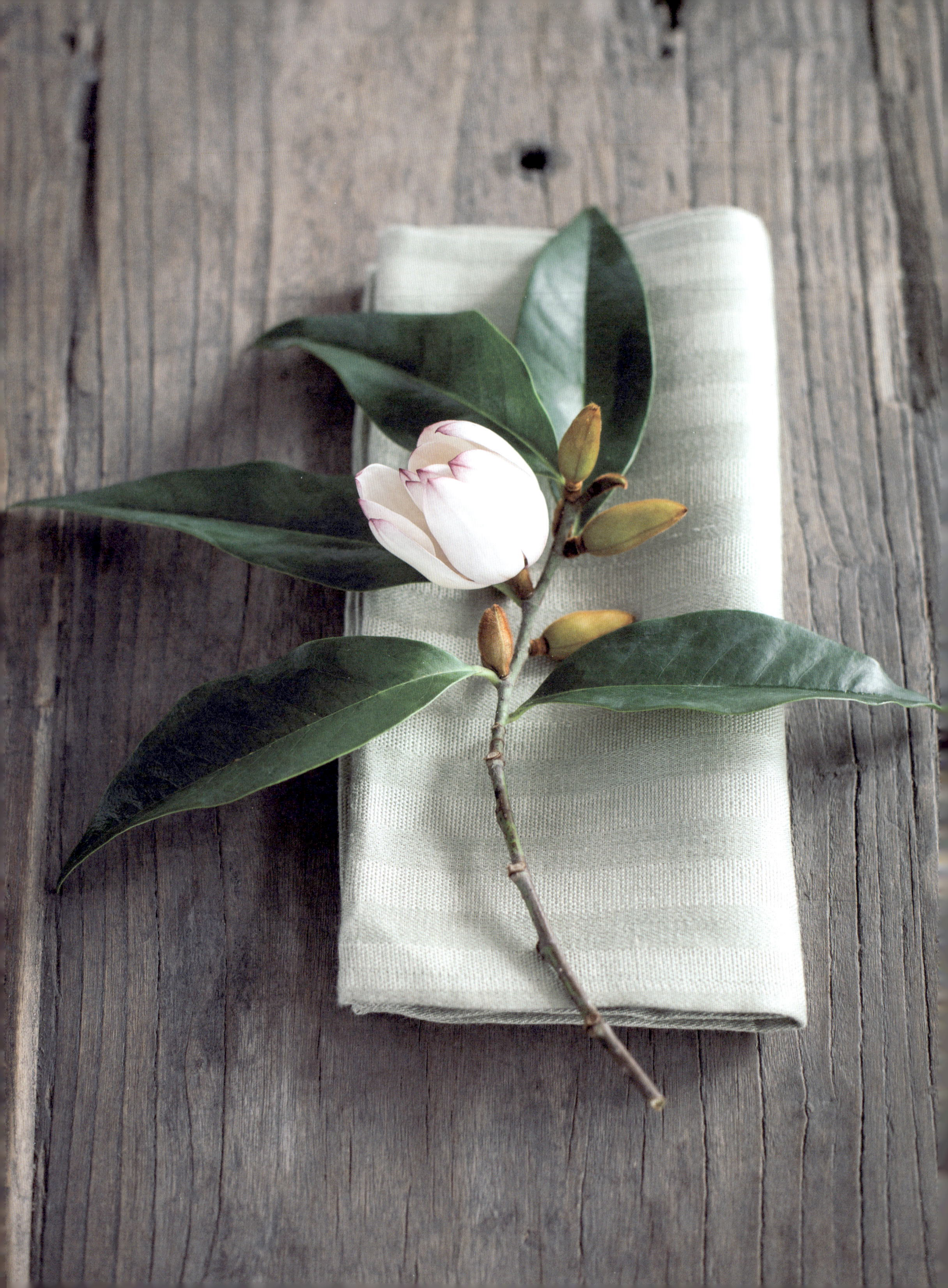

The magnificence of a single magnolia bloom makes a bold statement as shown on the left. And bright minty shades of green are enhanced by a perfect piece of citrus (above right) and a small collection of individually contained carnations (right).

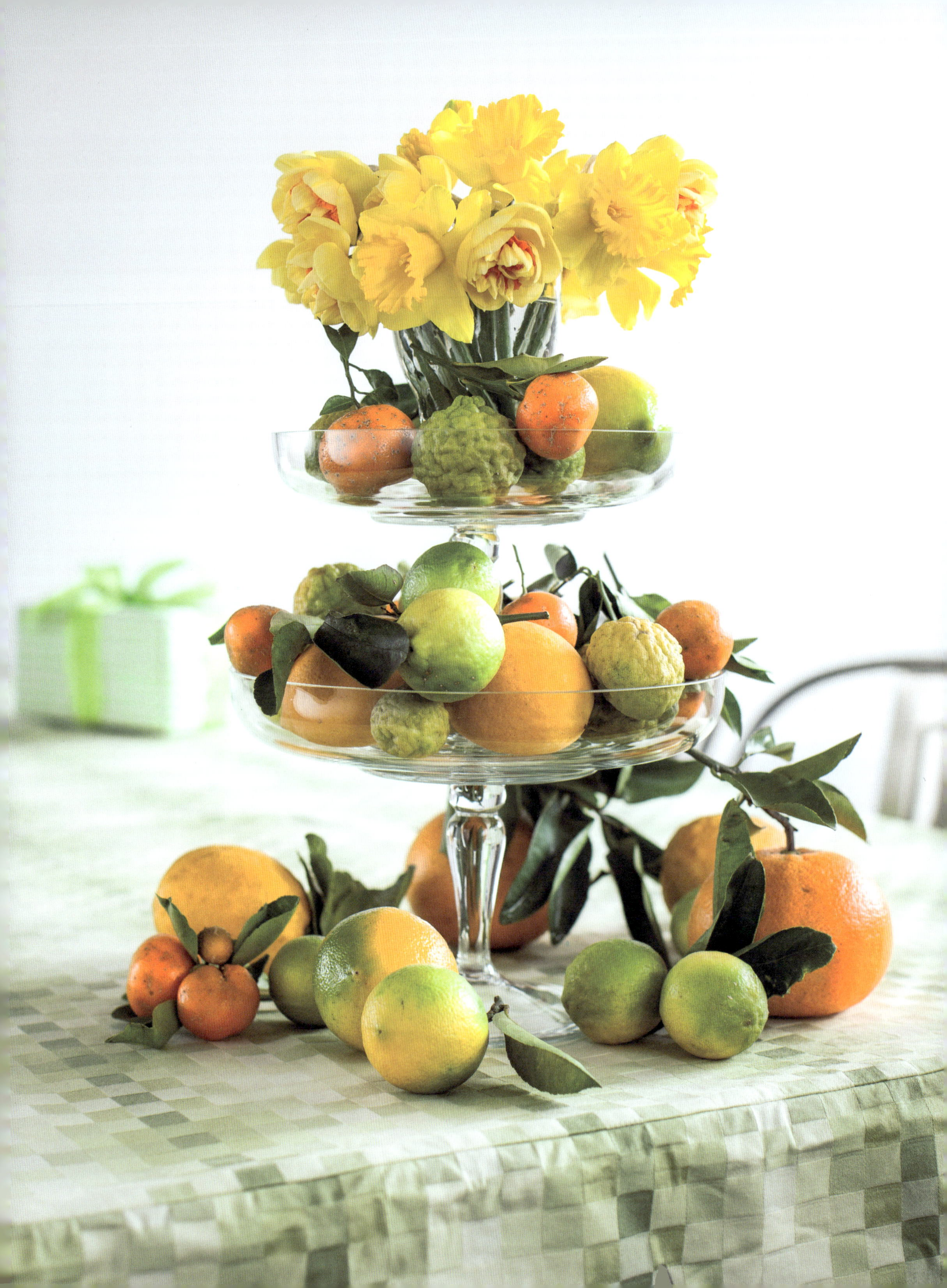

The jewel-like hues of these assorted citrus fruits exquisitely partner the exuberance of late winter daffodils.

Overleaf a casual table setting is enhanced by an equally informal arrangement of chrysanthemums, citrus, freesias, orchids and stock.

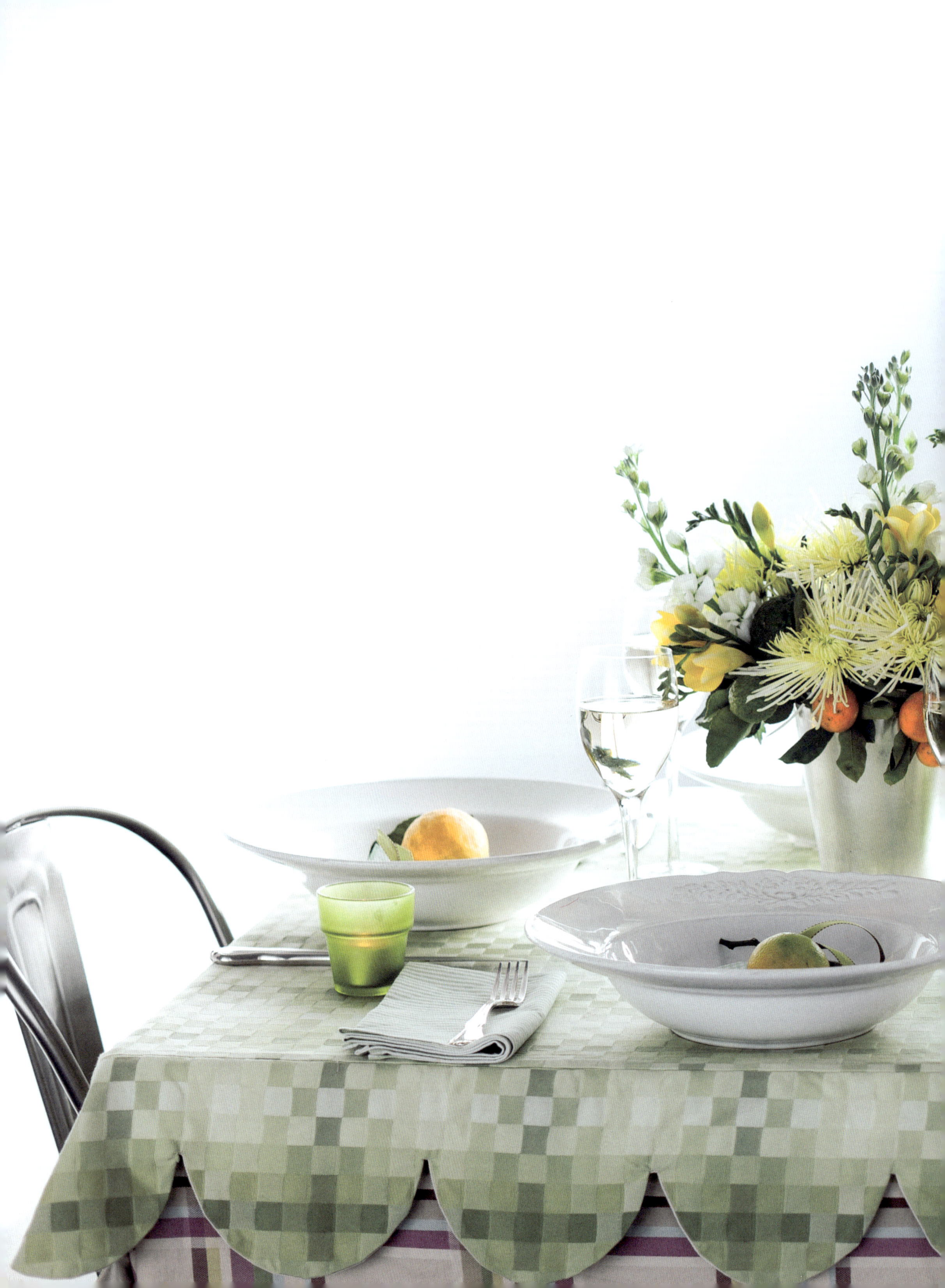

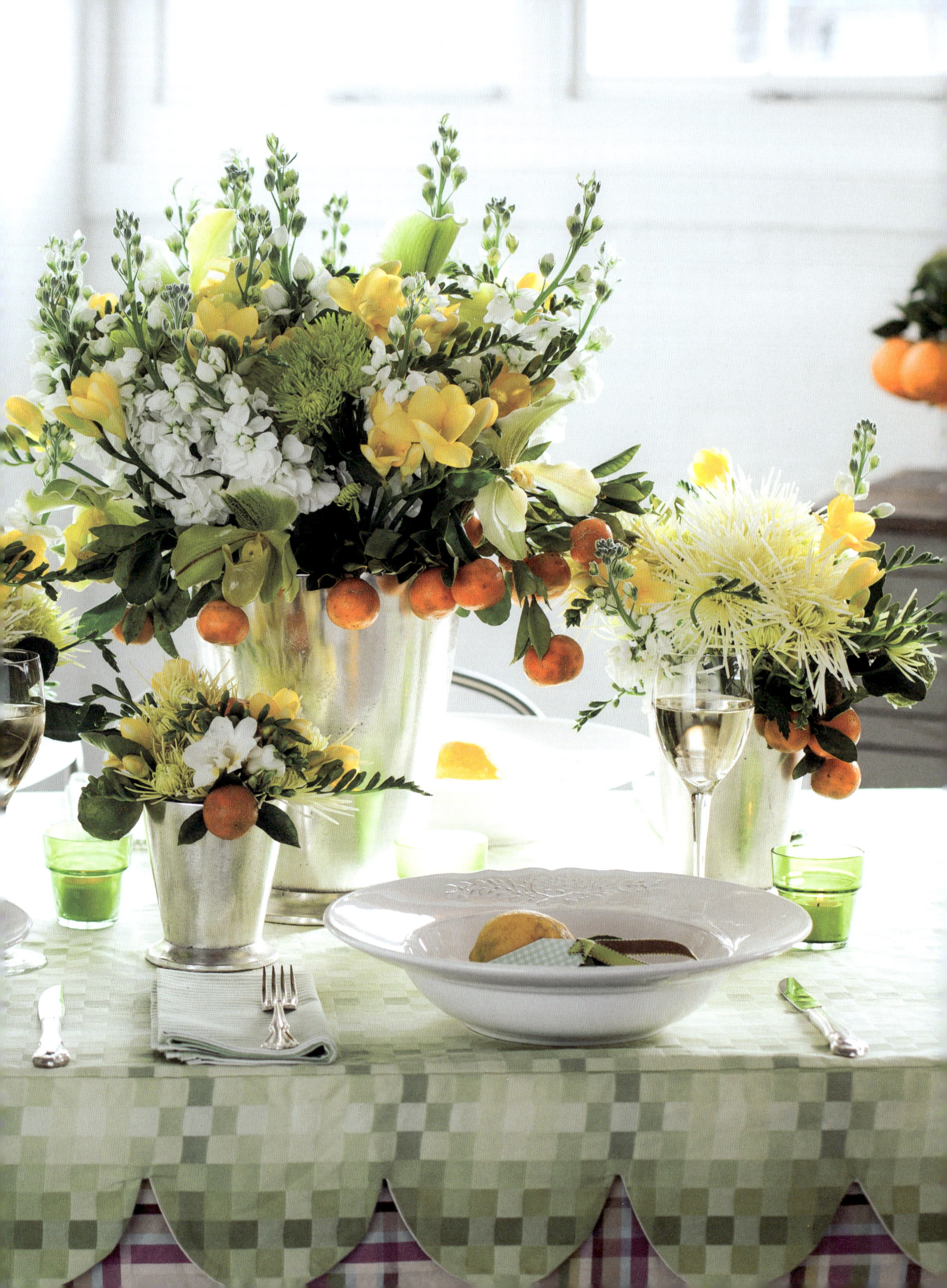

If the occasion calls for champagne, then make it even more celebratory by topping up the ice bucket or container of your choice with massed chrysanthemums, carnations and miniature roses as seen on the previous pages. A bowl or two of sugared citrus, including leaves, will add to the festive ambience.

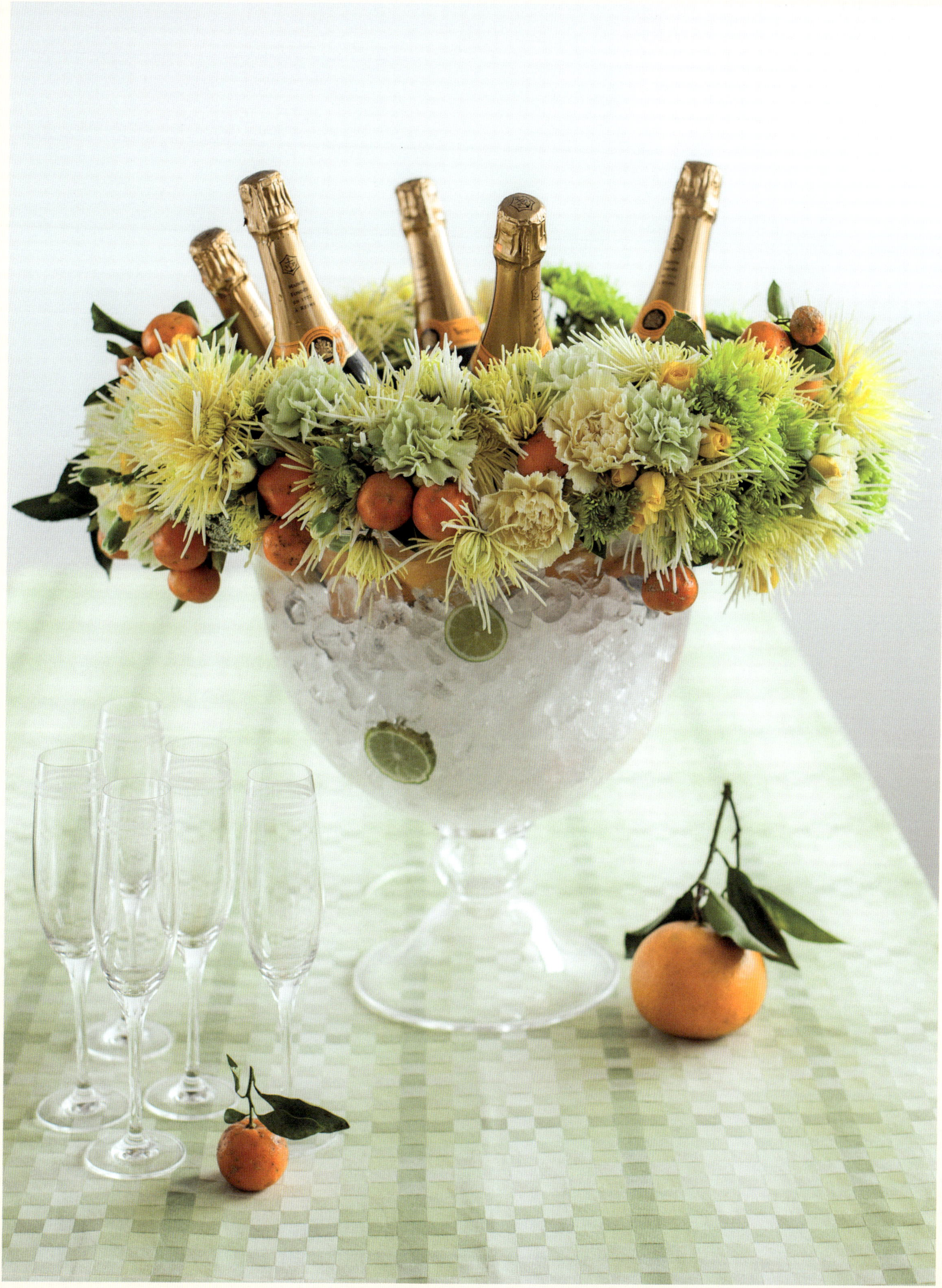

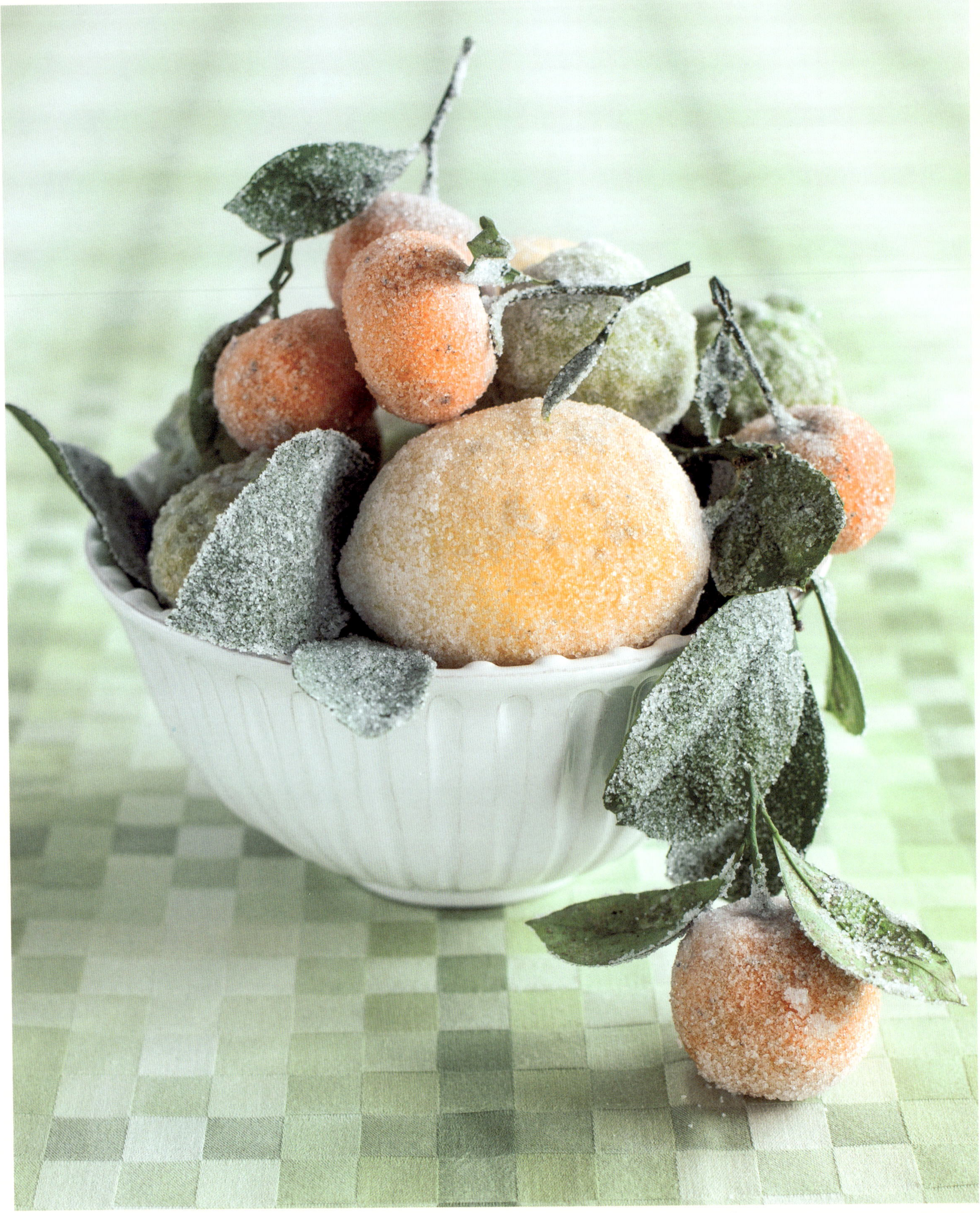

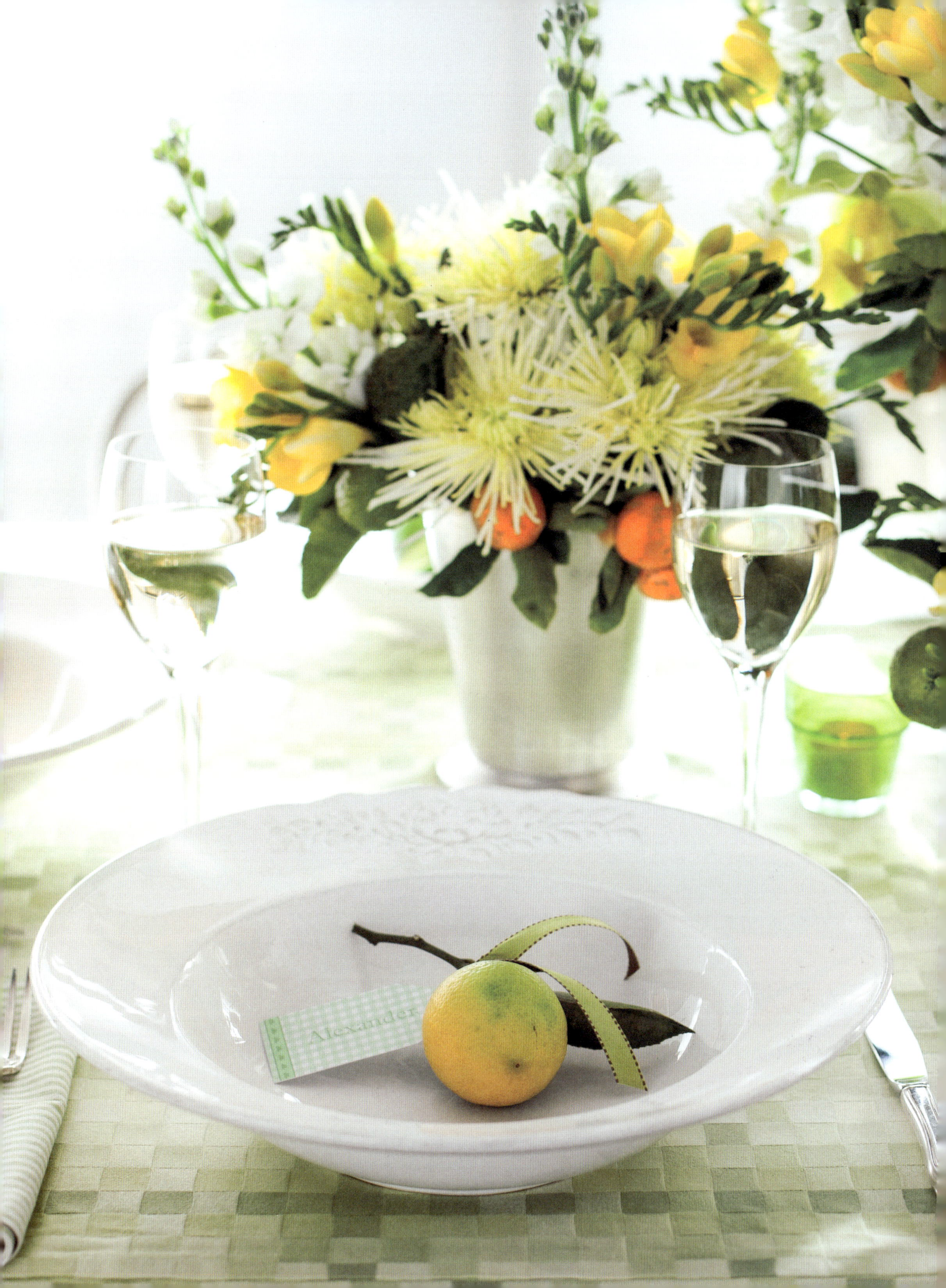
Alexander

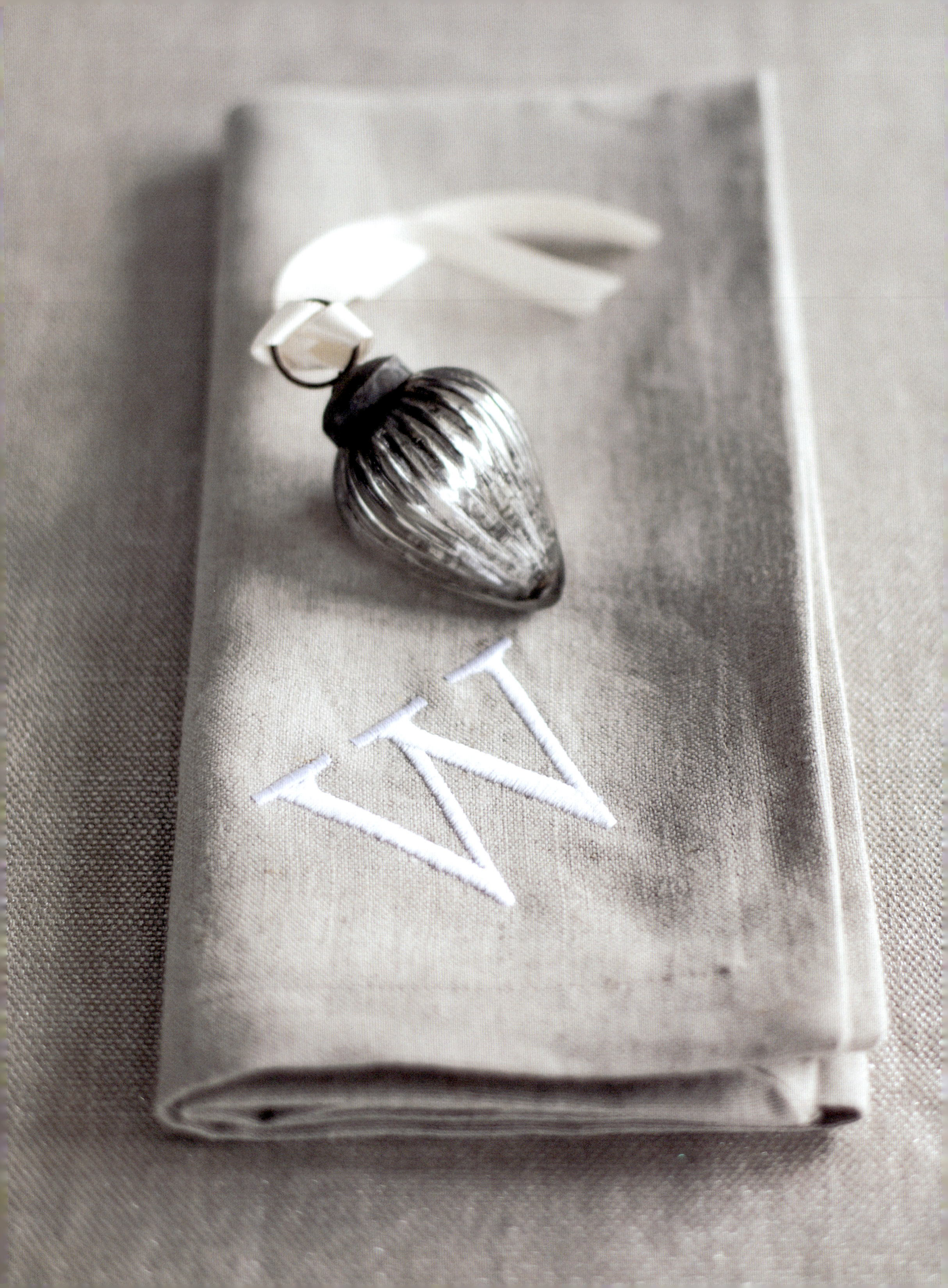

HOLIDAYS

Flowers seem
intended for the
solace of ordinary
humanity.

John Ruskin

Although the majority of the themes throughout this chapter celebrate Christmas, most if not all of them – with just a few minor adaptations – can be used to mark a variety of occasions at any time of year. Having said that, Christmas remains my very favourite celebration; it's a magical time, not least because it provides so many opportunities for me to come up with new ideas, especially ones that are based on creating a wonderfully sparkly ambience.

Take your cue from the colours around you. In some parts of the world Christmas is experienced in the middle of summer while in Europe and North America in particular it's a time of year when winter's frosty breath is ever present. So wherever you are and whatever you are celebrating, when it comes to choosing flowers base your choice on the colours most predominant in your home.

That said, you don't need to slavishly copy them; it's as much a matter of enhancing what is already in place through subtle colour differences and textures. Much of this effect can be created by utilising interesting accessories such as mirrors and richly textured fabrics as seen here and overleaf in these arrangements of stock, tulips, roses and peonies.

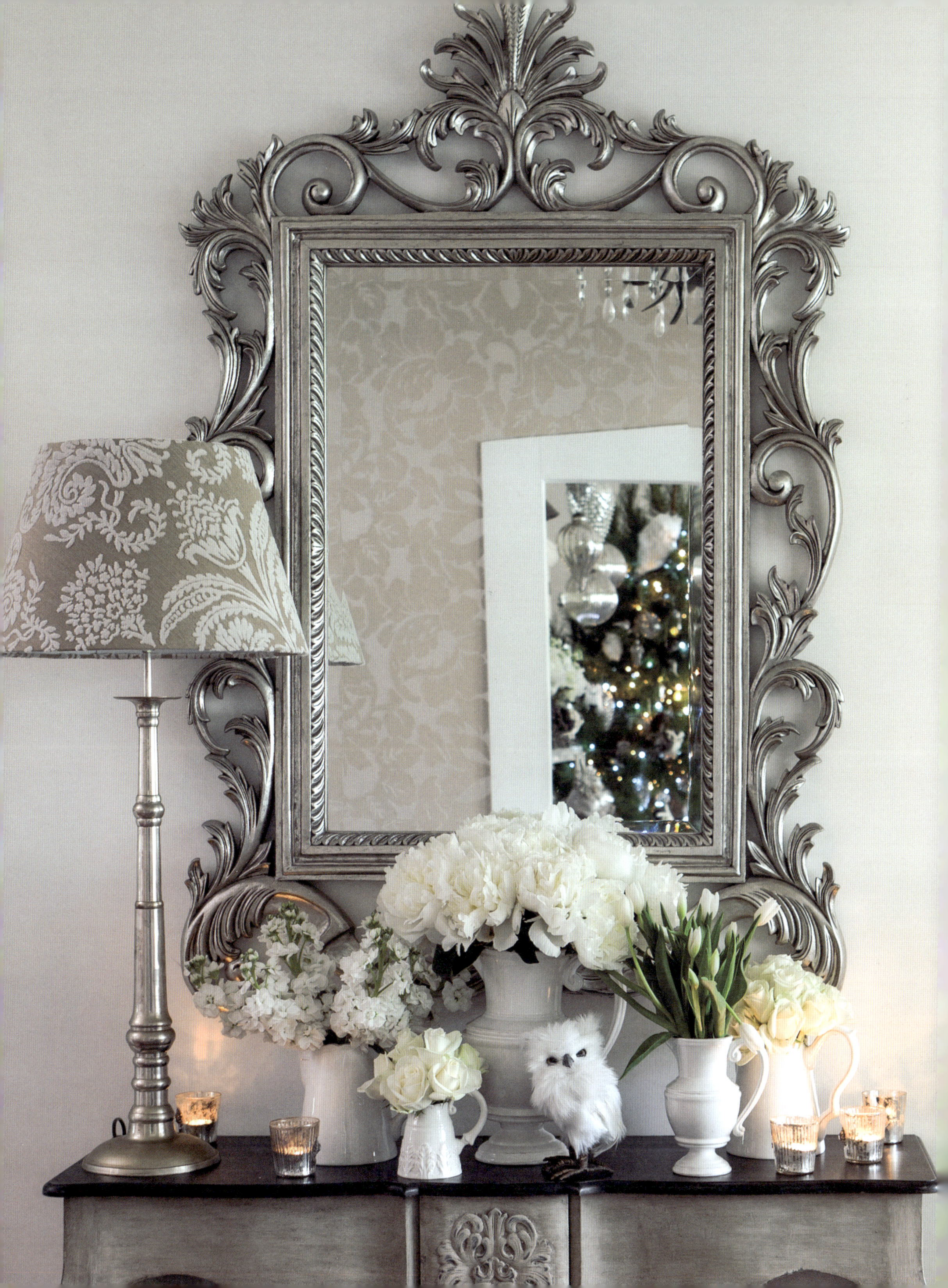

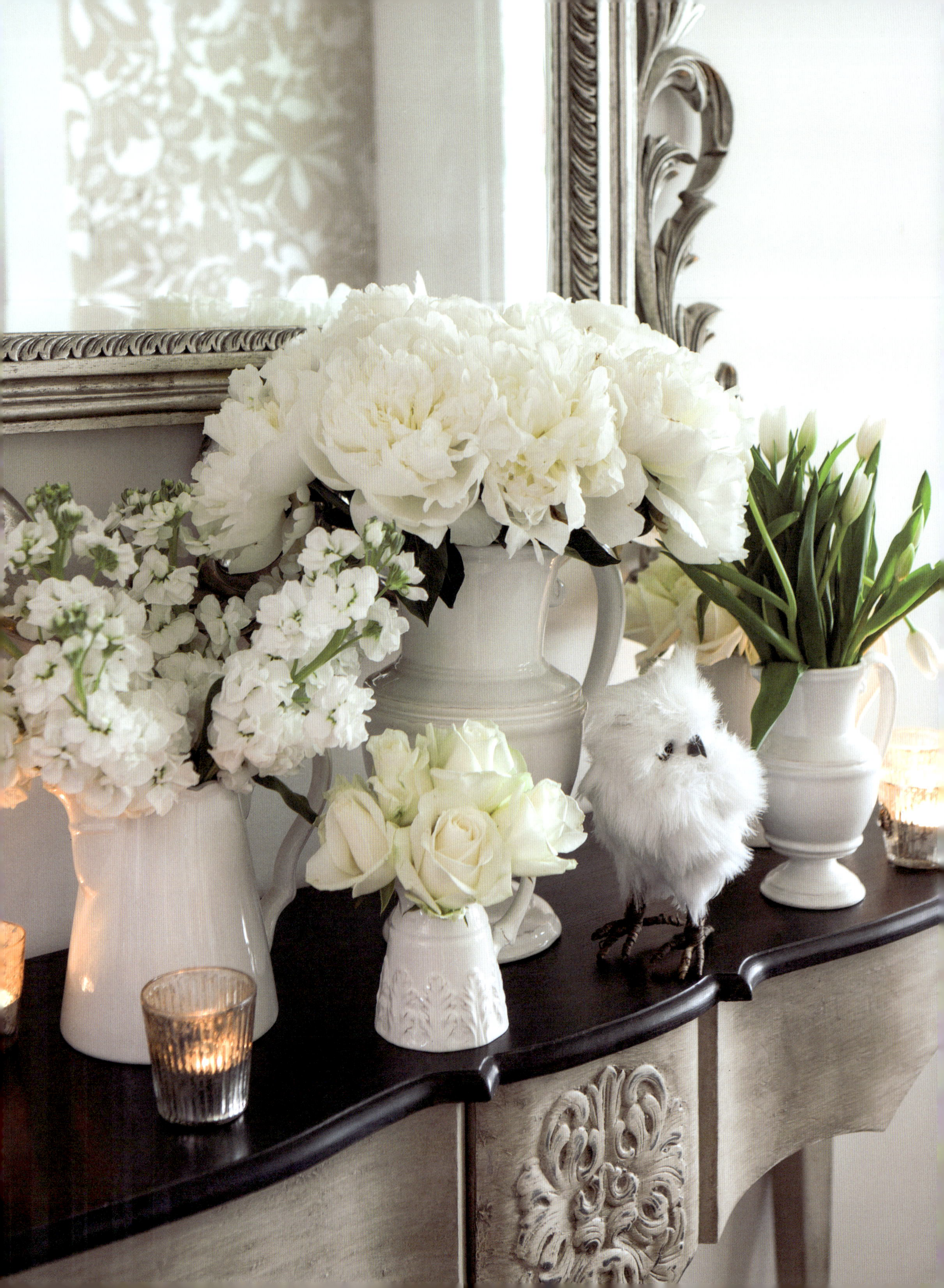

Feel free to add a meaningful touch to your arrangements. While this might be in the form of a special souvenir or perhaps a collectible of some sort, remember the 'less is more' rule. The idea of adding objects is to complement your floral arrangements, not overwhelm them so that the blooms take second place.

Any arrangement of massed flowers in front of a mirror will immediately double the effect; not a bad thing when you want them to go as far as possible. And placing a few tea light candles in between the containers will add to the festive look, whatever the occasion.

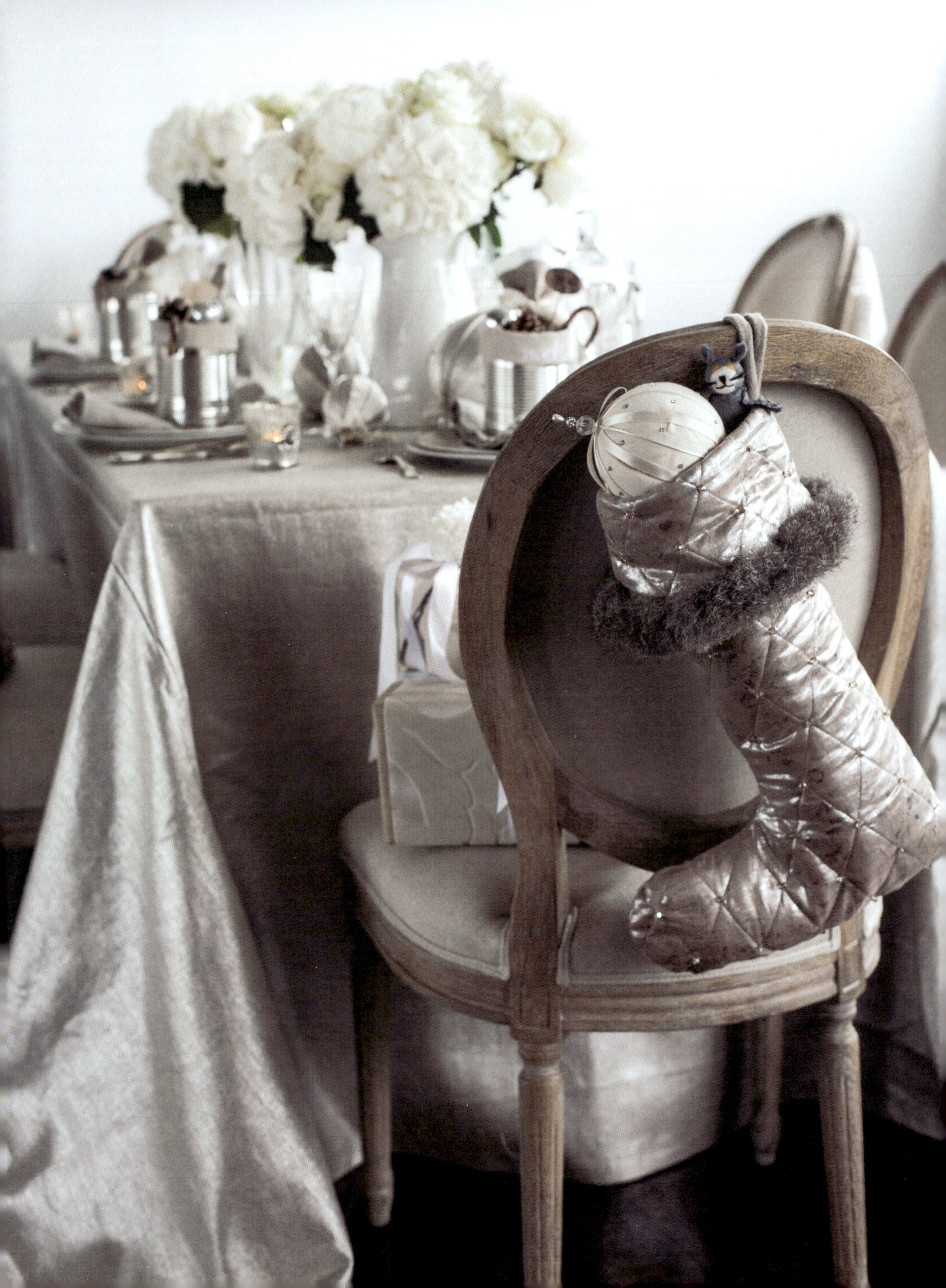

If you cannot do great things,
do small things in a great way.

Napoleon Hill

Subtlety is the keynote in the setting featured here and in the next few pages. Peonies, hydrangeas and roses stand tall on the table while the metallic sheen on many of the neutral-coloured accessories projects a quiet elegance.

As for the embellishments overleaf, they range from place settings fashioned from simple tin cans and tiny pillows stuffed with scented dried herbs through to cushions studded with Swarovski crystals.

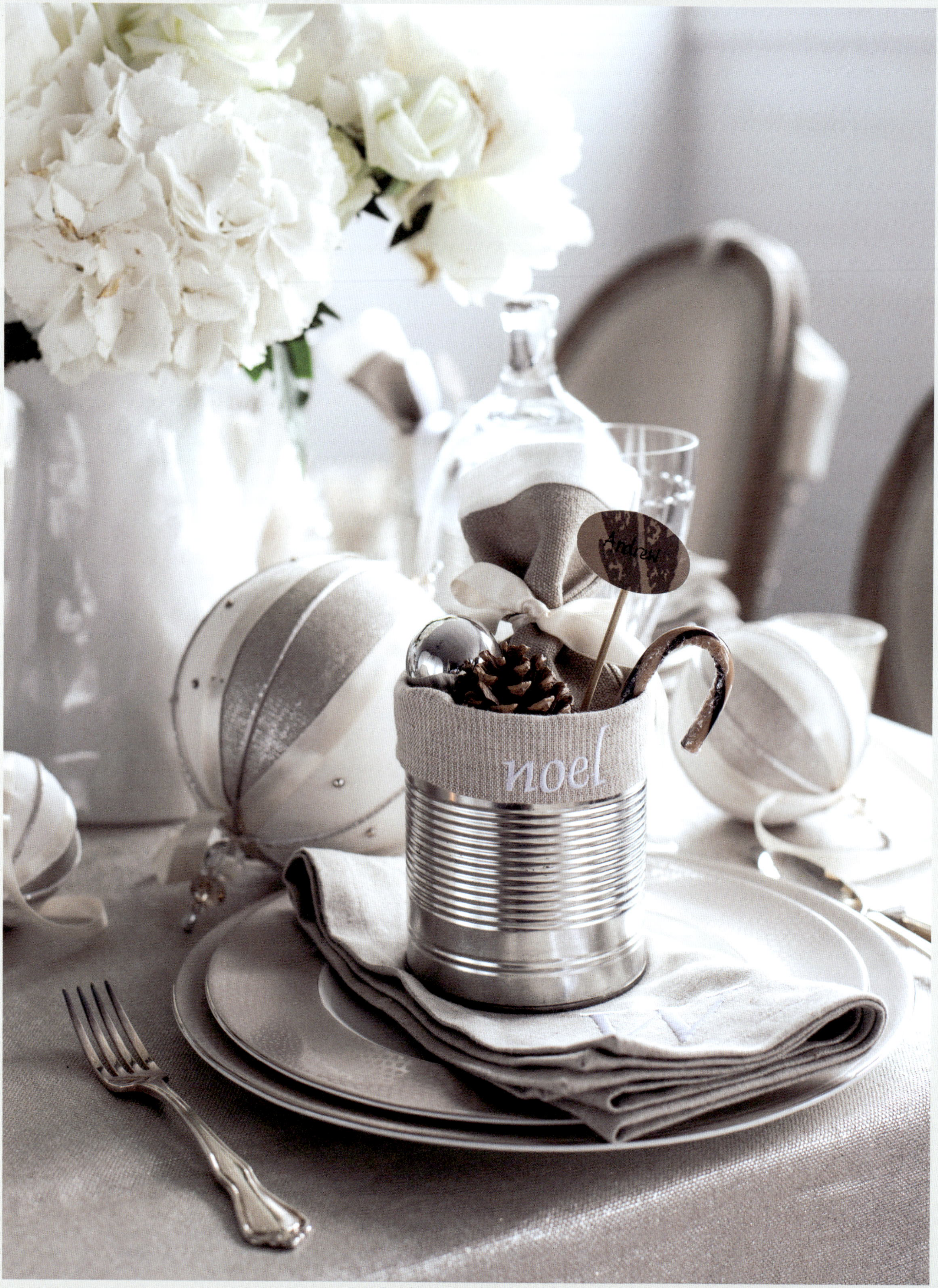
Andrew
noel

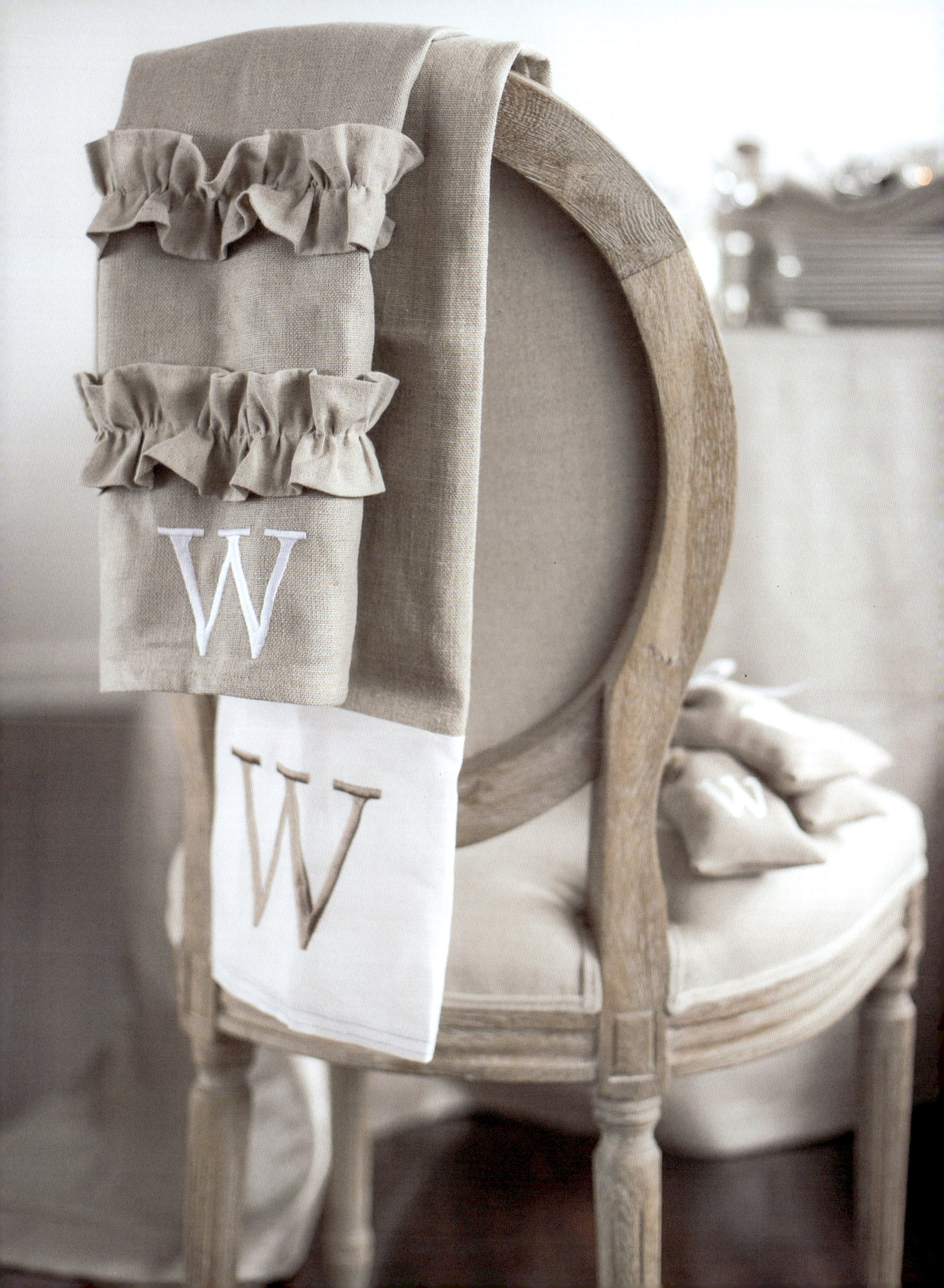
W
W

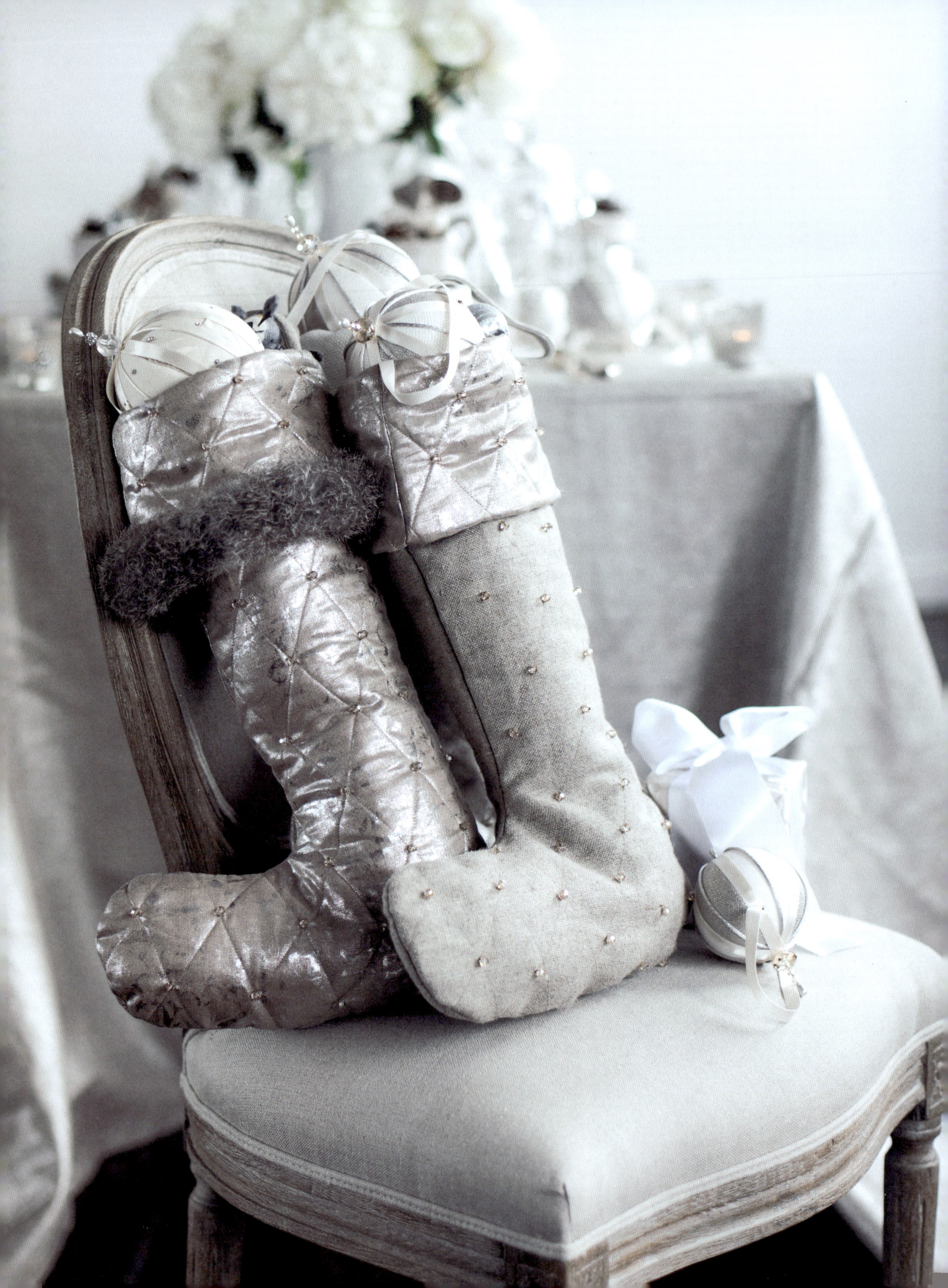

Overleaf this large ice bucket, transformed by its covering of lisianthus, chrysanthemums, roses, bay leaves and buxus inserted into a swag of Oasis foam (right), presides over the classic simplicity of white roses highlighted by tiny tea light candles. As the light sparkles on the champagne glasses arrayed to one side a sense of anticipation starts to build.

Holidays 273

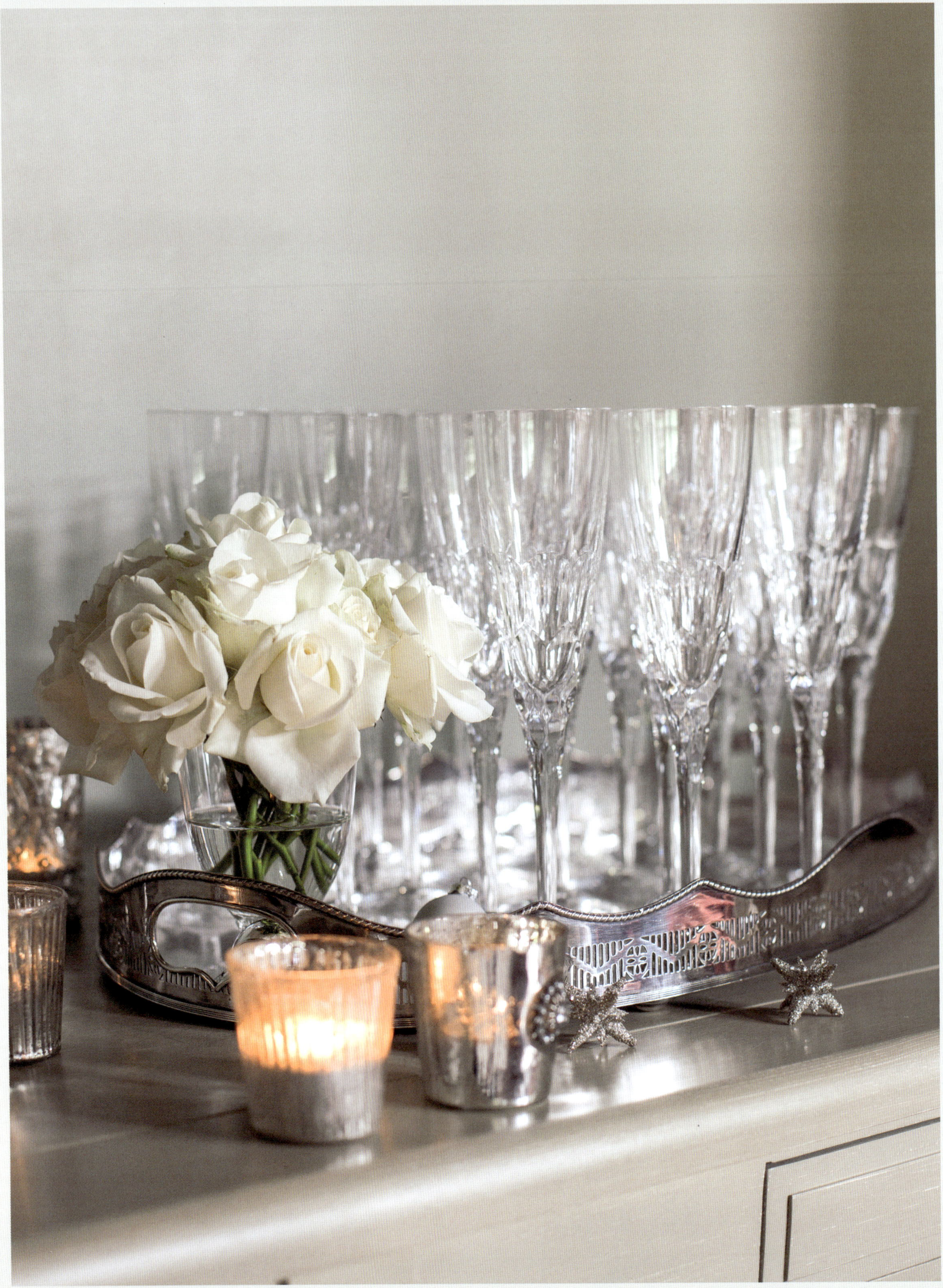

May flowers always line your path and sunshine light your day.

May songbirds serenade you every step along the way.

May a rainbow run beside you in a sky that's always blue.

And may happiness fill your heart each day your whole life through.

Irish saying

Peonies, lisianthus and hydrangeas look stunning in white (above) and provide a serene backdrop to the plump cushions (right) decorated with tiny Swarovski crystals.

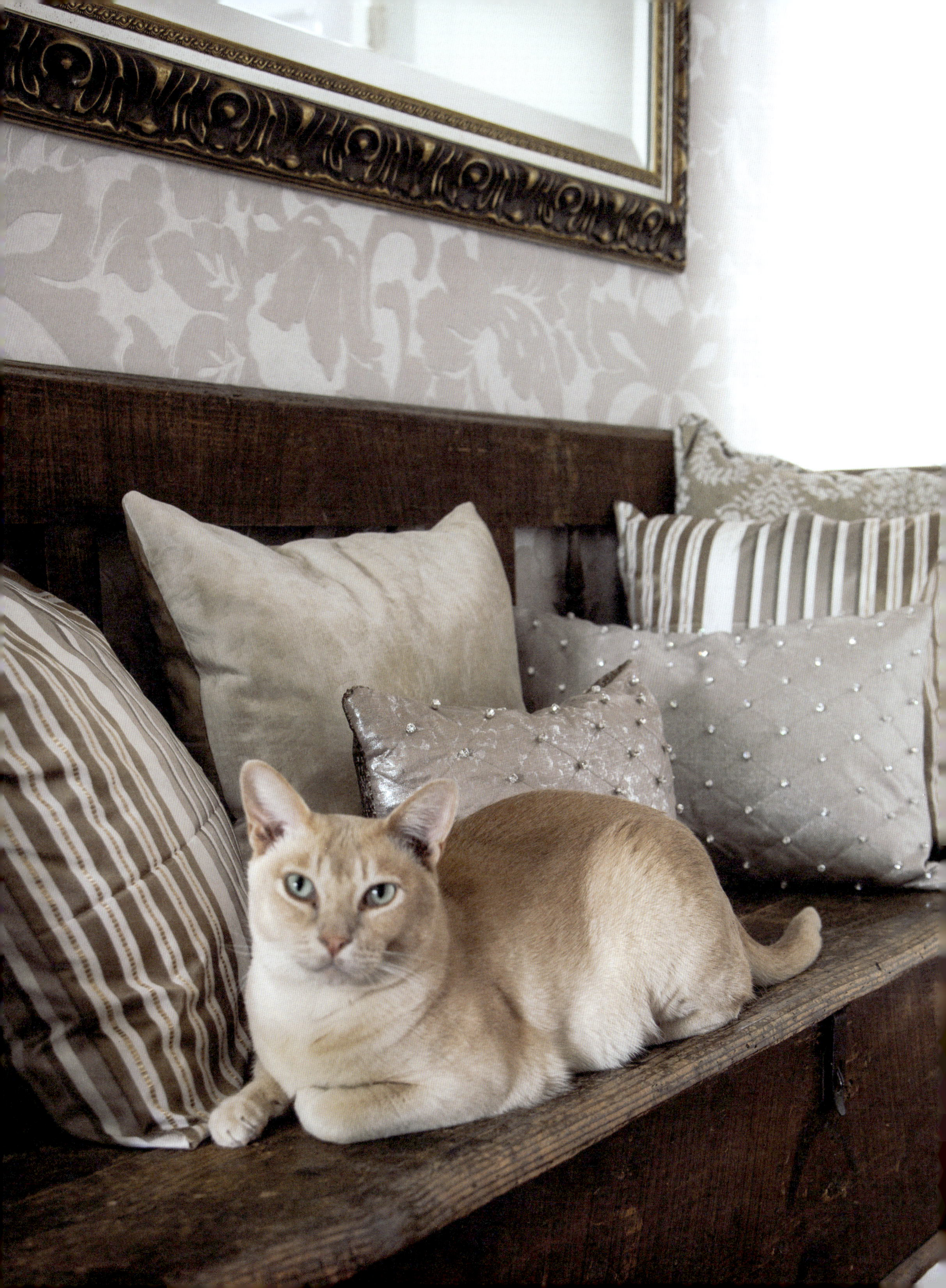

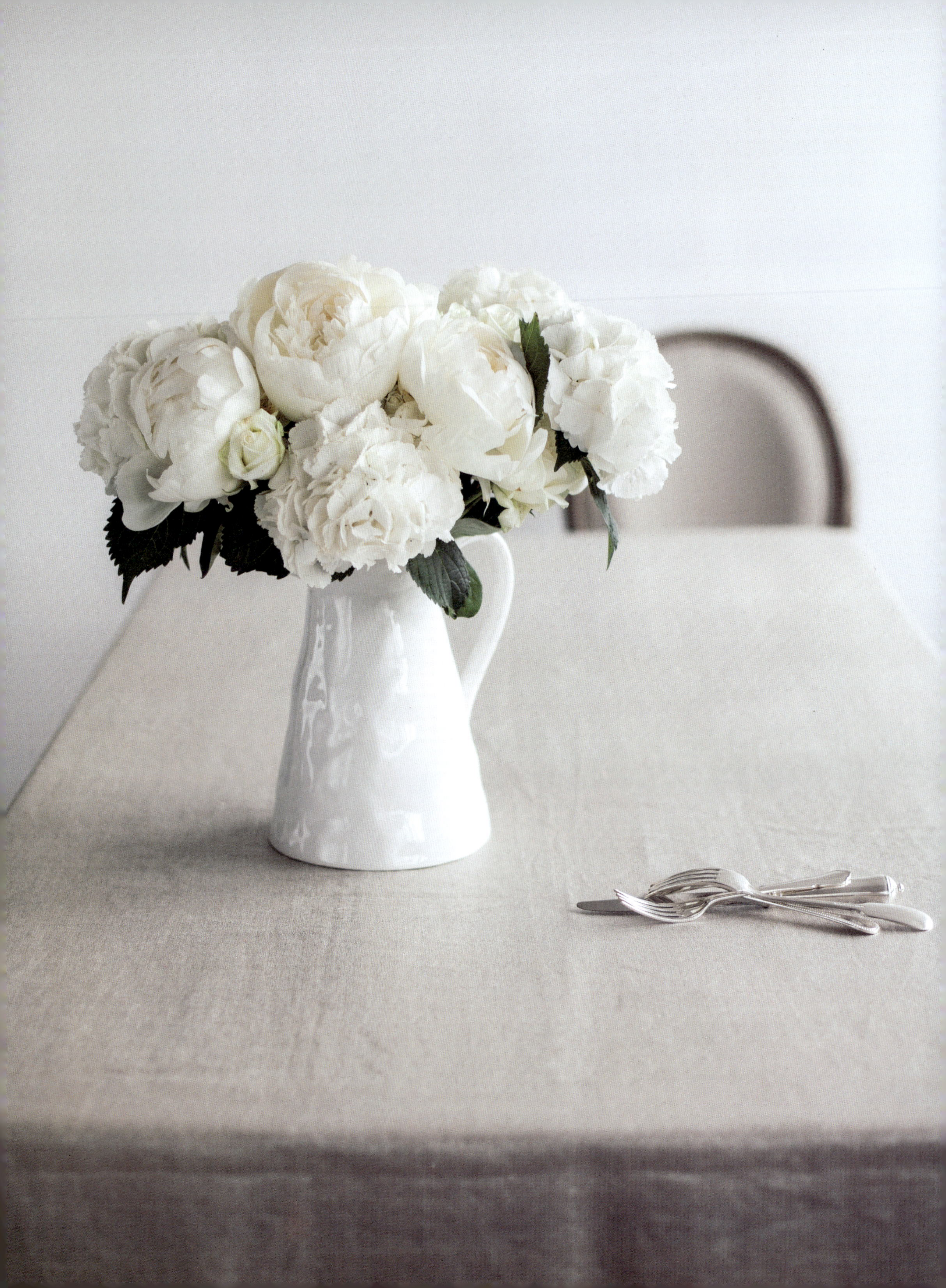

Bunched peonies, hydrangeas and roses in shades of creamy white spill out of this classical white jug (left).

There will always be occasions when a bit of ostentation can go a long way. Christmas is a great example of such a time and is illustrated here and overleaf by an arrangement of peonies, stock and roses enhanced on all sides – front and back and even the top – by a selection of glass kugels (spheres and other shapes), hanging gift stockings and, of course, a magnificently decorated tree.

Nothing beats the pleasantly sharp tang of fresh pine needles so reminiscent of Christmas. Although you might be tempted by the amazingly lifelike foldaway faux Christmas trees now so prevalent, your family and friends will thank you for the extra effort required in sourcing and decorating the real thing. Just remember to water it every day.

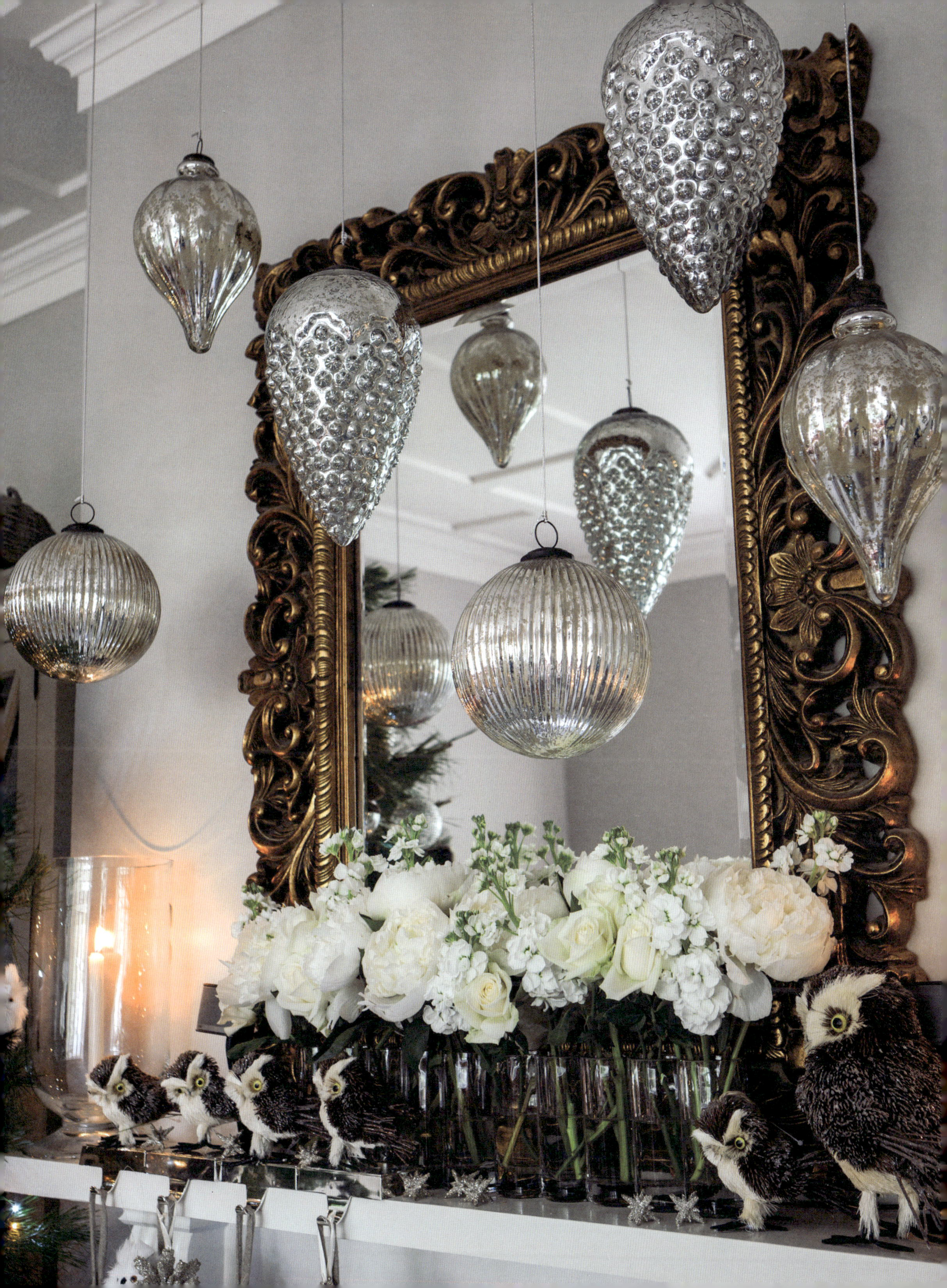

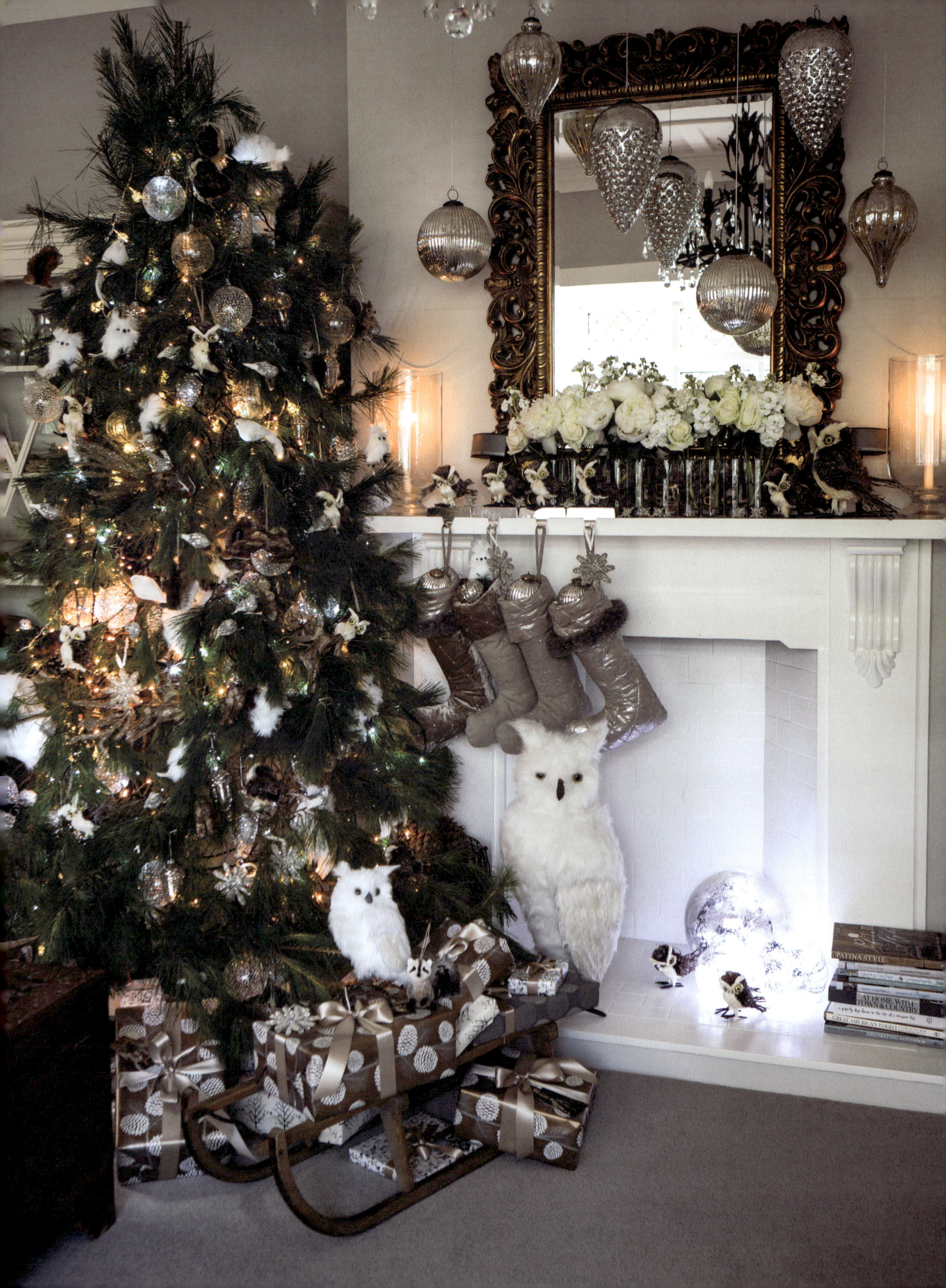

The perfect Christmas tree?
All Christmas trees are
perfect!

Charles N. Barnard

Soft pinks highlight this Christmas table setting, which like most others in this chapter could just as easily be used to mark another celebratory occasion. Think birthday, anniversary – maybe even a promotion. After all, how much of an excuse do you really need to create such a gorgeous ambience?

As always, the flowers are the stars of this setting. The profusion of peonies, roses, freesias, stock and camellia leaves – which have been brushed with PVA glue and then dusted with sugar – has been designed to spill out and draw the eye to the centre of the table.

joyeux noël

noël

Too much of a good thing can be wonderful.

Mae West

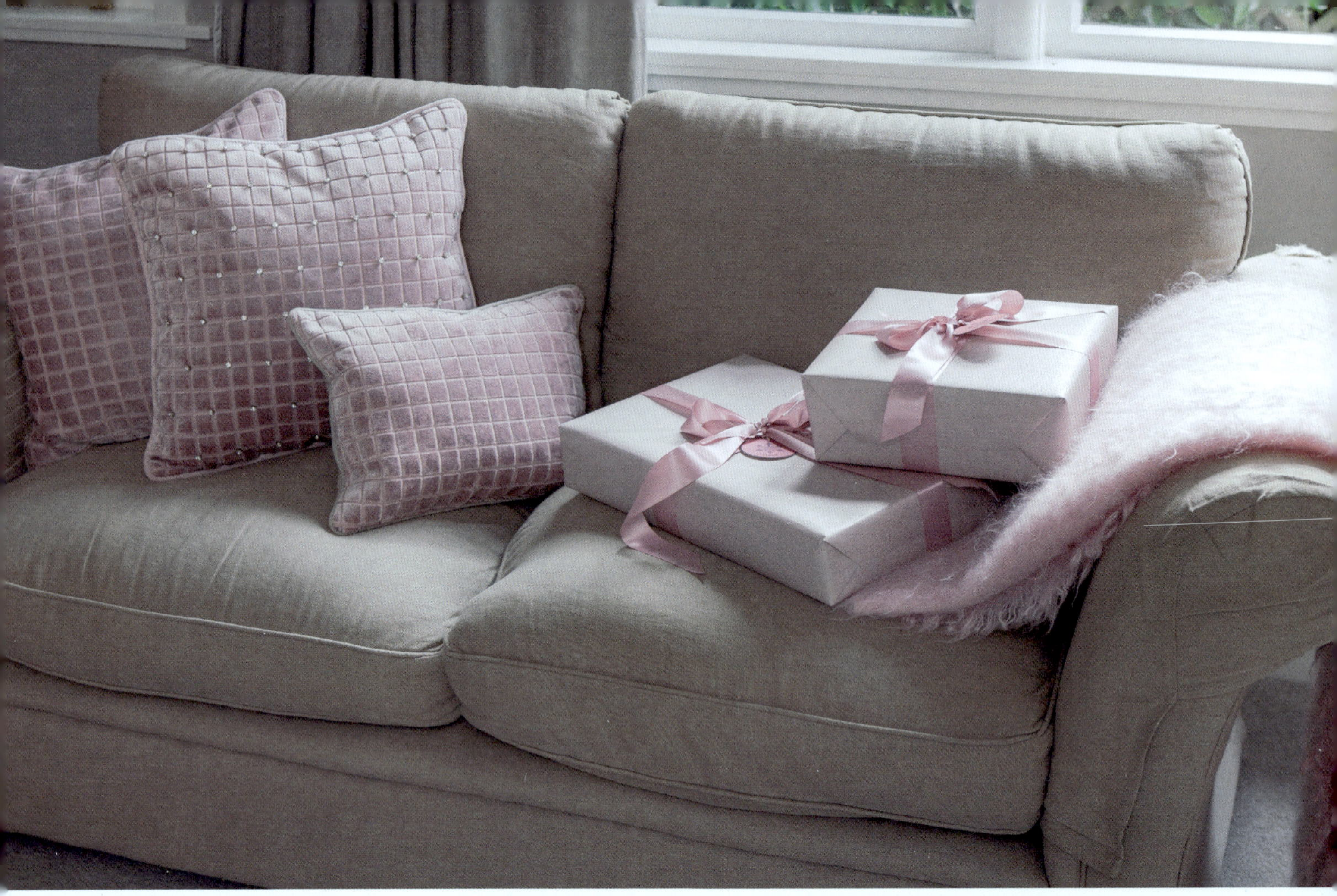

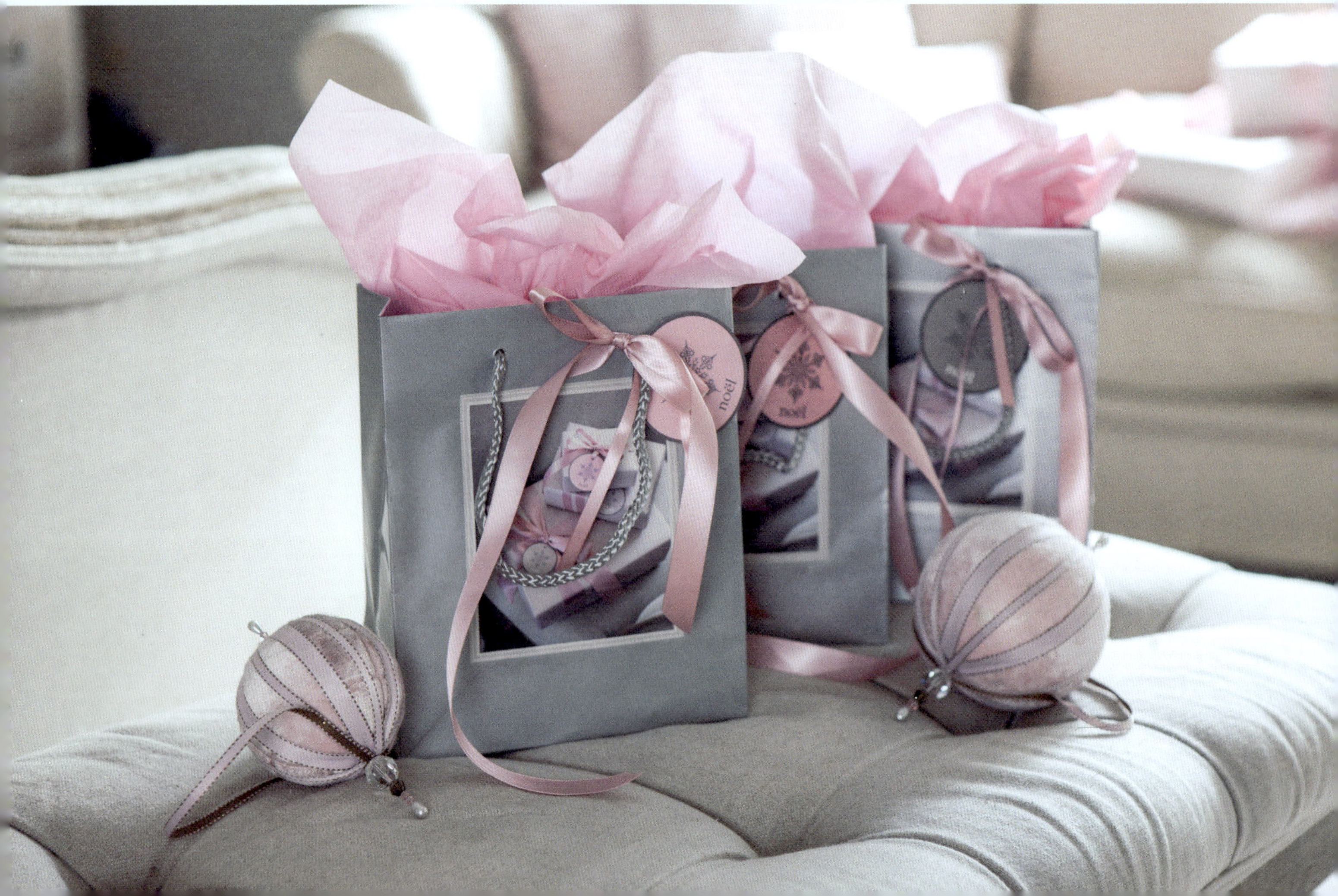
noël
noël

Holidays 289

Flowers and other decorative touches will always enhance any part of the house: a bedroom, an informal office or perhaps just a quiet corner that invites you to curl up with a book …

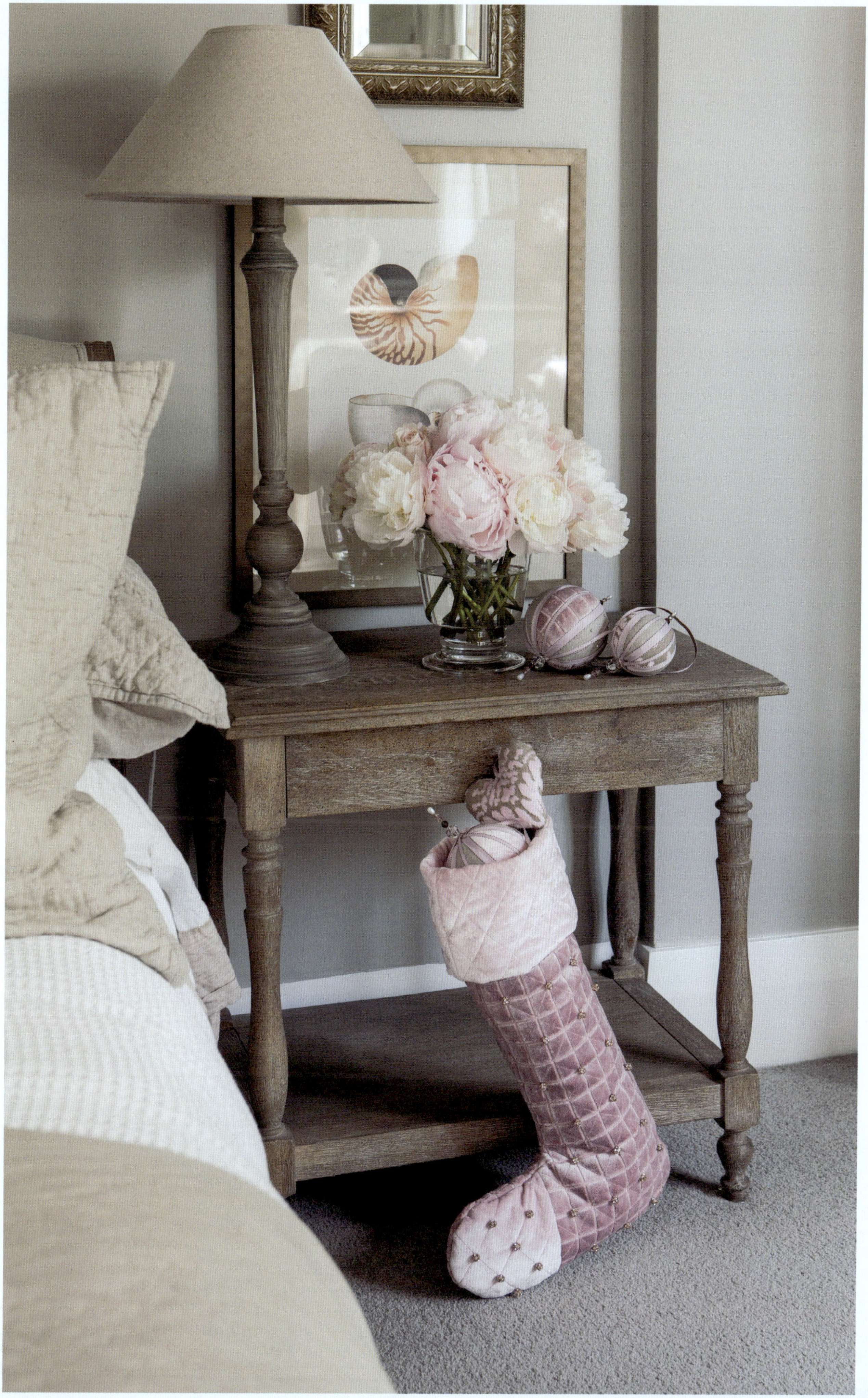

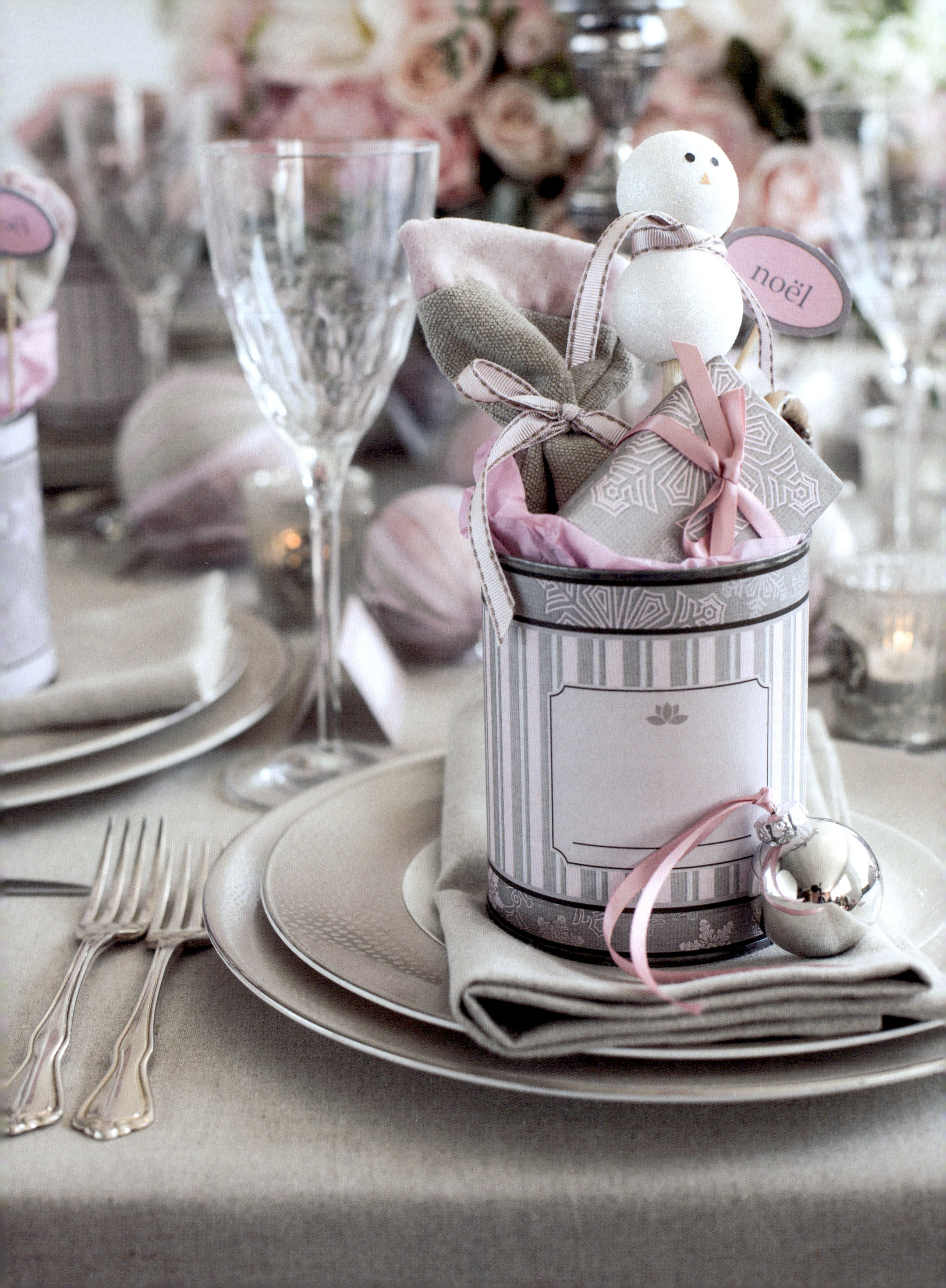
noël

Although this table setting is quite busy, the soft colour scheme allows extra touches that could look cluttered if a stronger palette were used.

The festive-looking container at each place setting could just as easily feature a posy, but in any event it's all about the overall look rather than expensive gifts.

It's not how much we give, but how much love we put into giving.

Mother Teresa

When you have a mass of softly coloured flowers to play with, a classic arrangement such as the one shown on the right and overleaf is hard to beat. Place the flowers in their receptacle as close to each other as possible, then check for any gaps. Lastly, ensure the arrangement looks good from all visible angles.

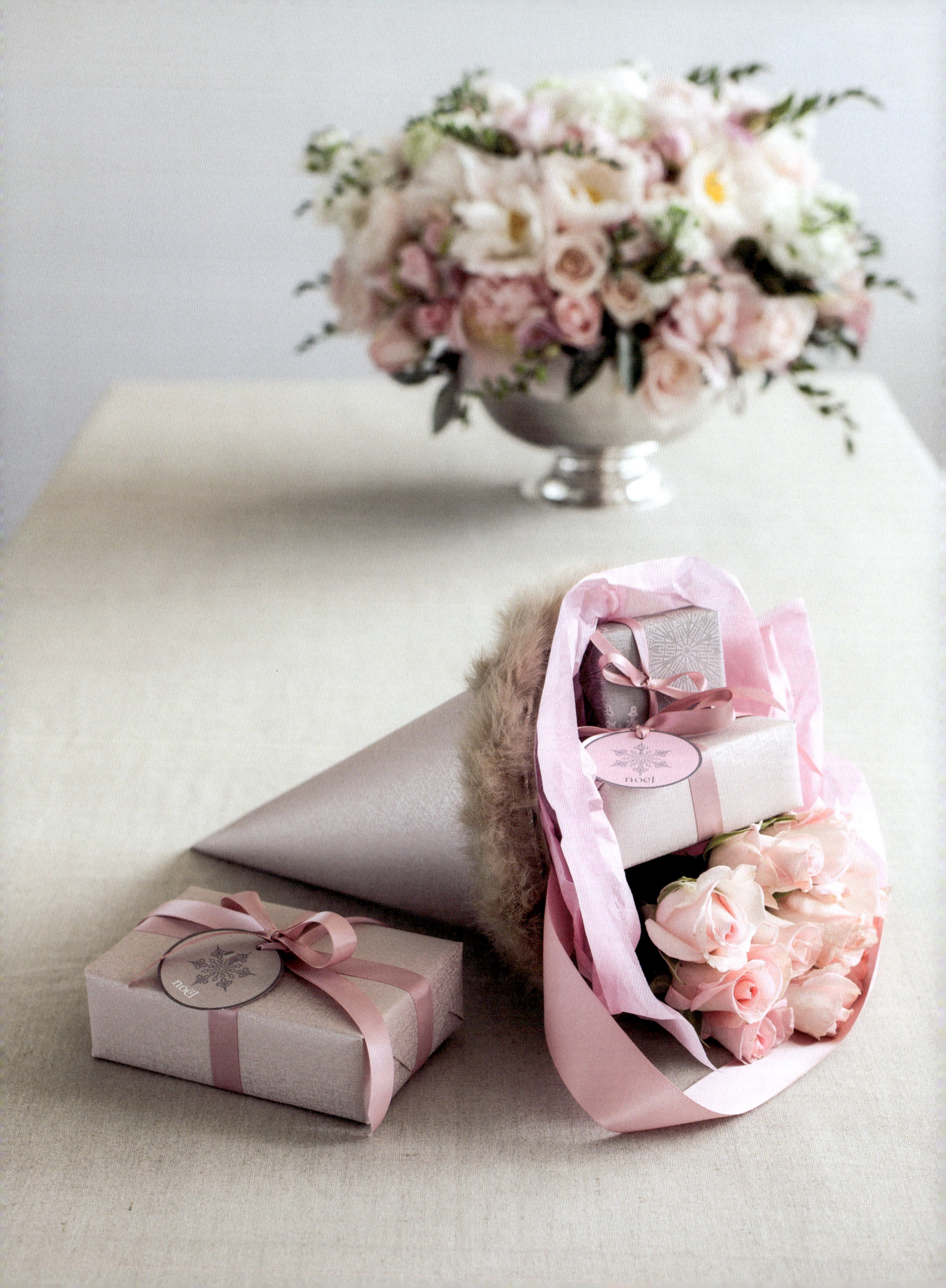
noël
noël

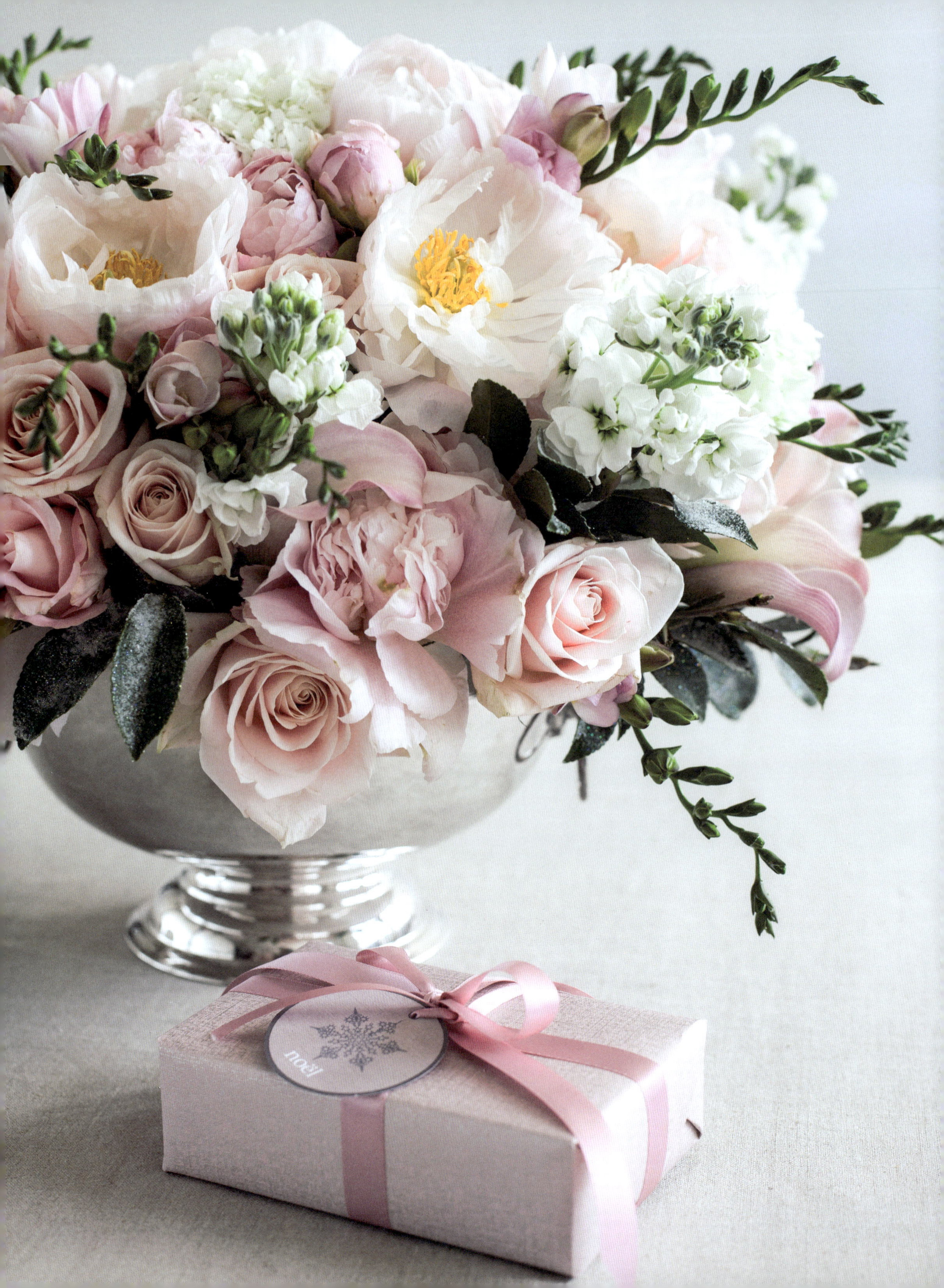
noel

I am as curious about colour as one would be visiting a new country, because I have never concentrated so closely on colour expression. Up to now I have waited at the gates of the temple.

Henri Matisse

Some special occasions call for more than just tasty treats; a feast for the eyes is just as satisfying and can be achieved quite easily using pre-soaked pieces of round Oasis foam by firmly wrapping them in leaves and securing with pins. Flowers of your choice can then be pushed down into the foam from the top. Display your exquisite floral handiwork on pastel-coloured cake stands.

For these – and the other floral cakes illustrated in this book – choose the most tender young buds to decorate the top and sides and keep the colour palette simple. If fragrant blooms are available, then you'll have a creation that is not just a visual treat, but also an exquisite olfactory experience.

Gâteaux rose

Noël macarons

noël

300 Holidays

This bud of love, by summer's ripening breath, May prove a beauteous flower when next we meet.

William Shakespeare

Recycled cans, decorated simply and effectively as shown above, make perfect receptacles for small posies that you can choose to give to your guests on their departure, while a plain glass jar filled with fragrant party favours (right) makes an attractive accessory.

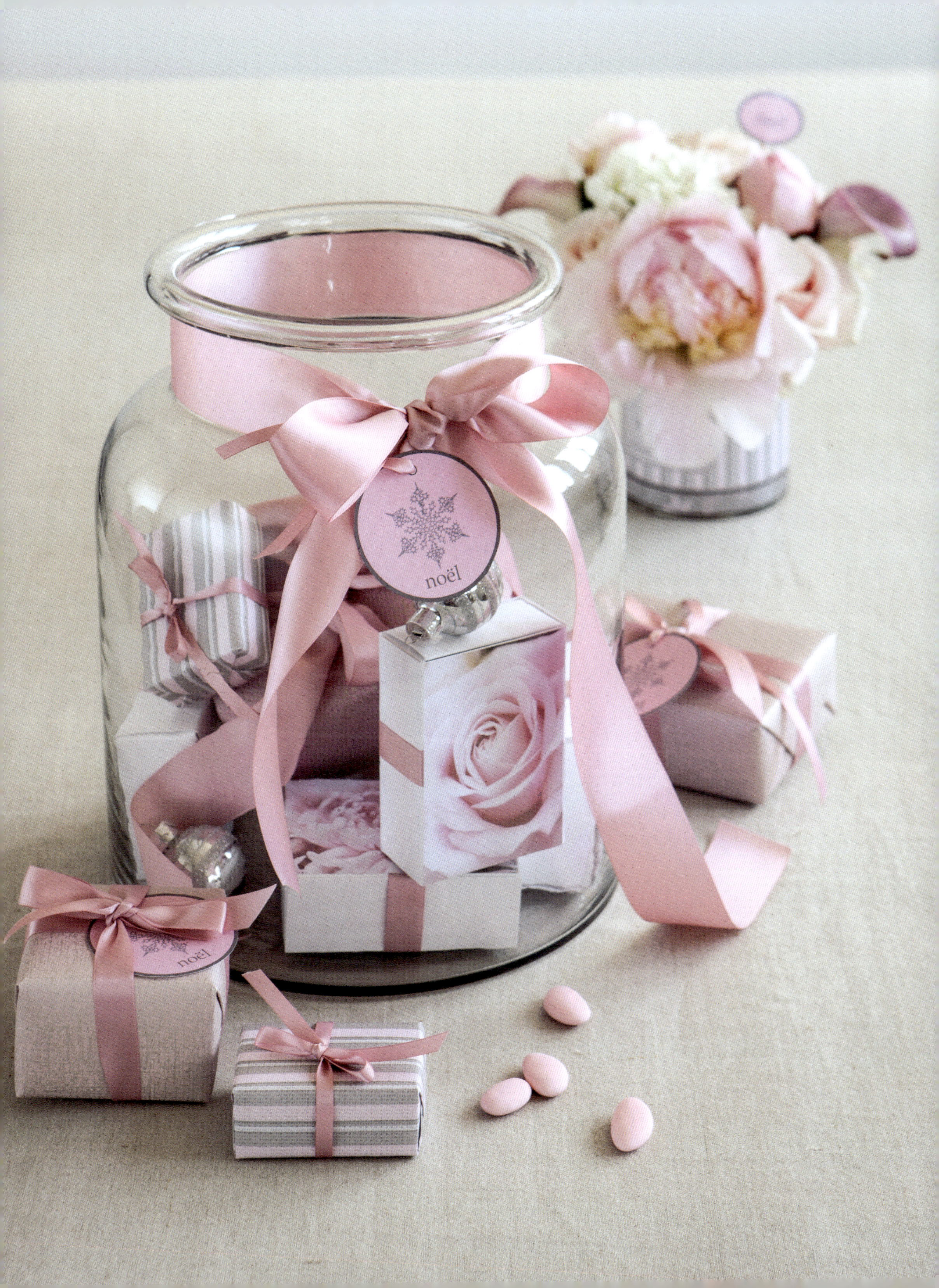
noël
noël

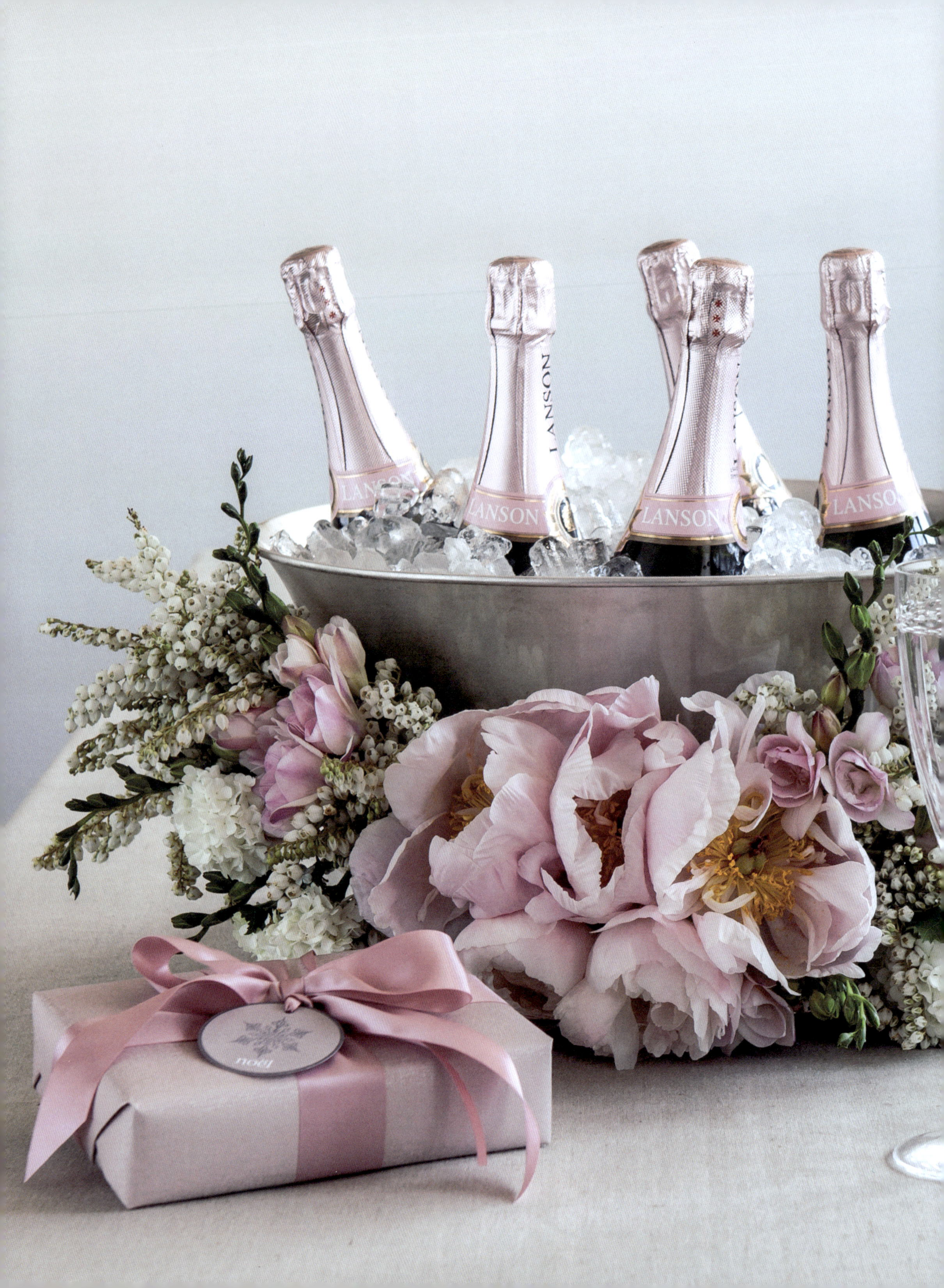
LANSON

Whichever container you utilise to chill your party bubbles, lend it an extra festive air by using a garland of Oasis foam to attach to the party bucket and then adding the stems of an assortment of flowers such as the peonies, freesias and New Zealand lily of the valley seen here.

Flowers are the music of the ground, from earth's lips spoken without sound.

Edwin Curran

When you want to use colour for dramatic effect, especially for a traditional Christmas, it's hard to go past these short-stemmed rich deep red peonies perfectly complemented by creamy white roses on these pages.

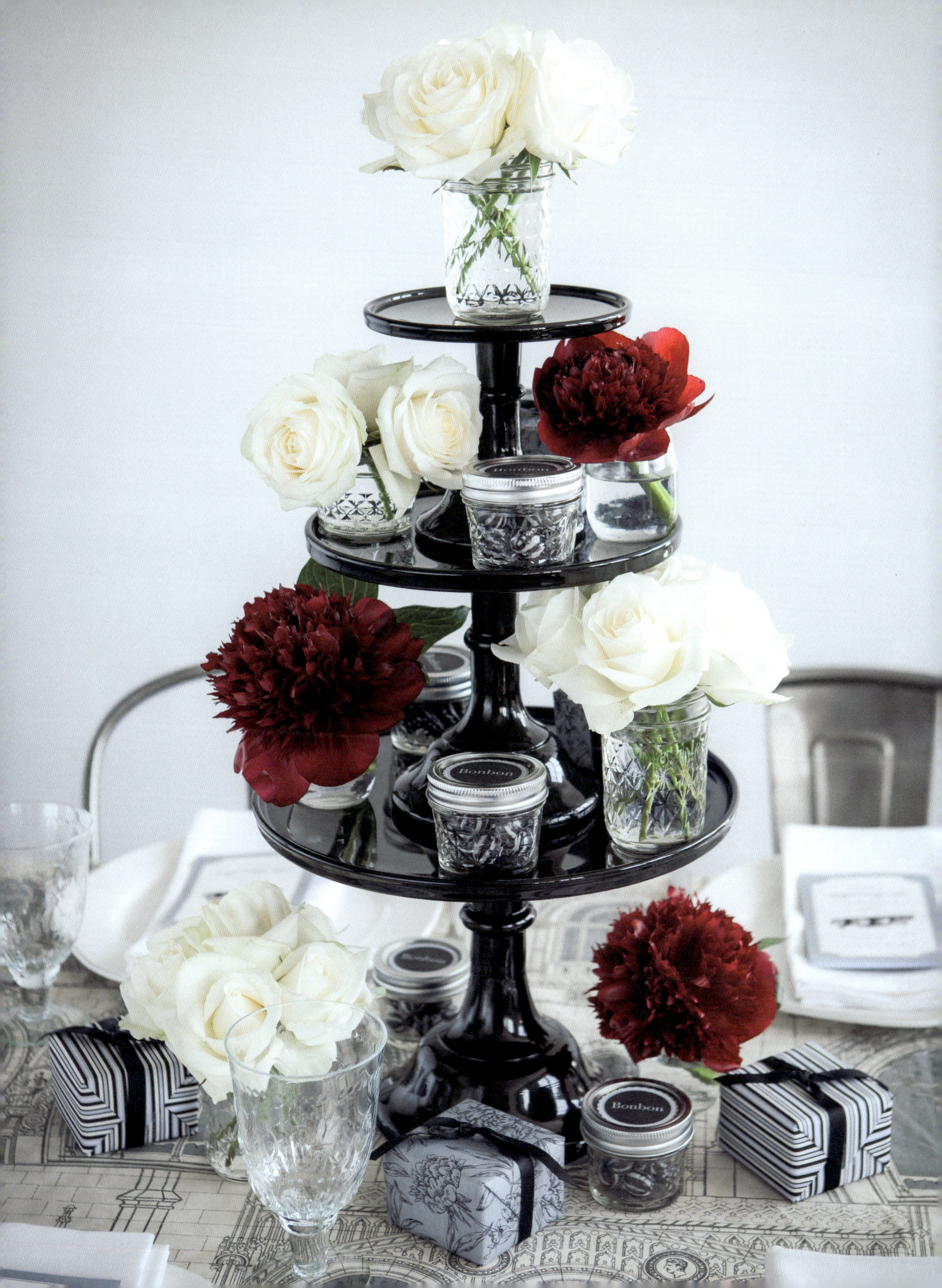
Bonbon
Bonbon

Smaller posies of roses, tulips and anemones and delicate little tea light candles support the dramatic effect of the massed deep-red peonies in the centre of the table. The velvet Christmas stockings that decorate each setting can later be filled with a selection of small treats for guests to take home.

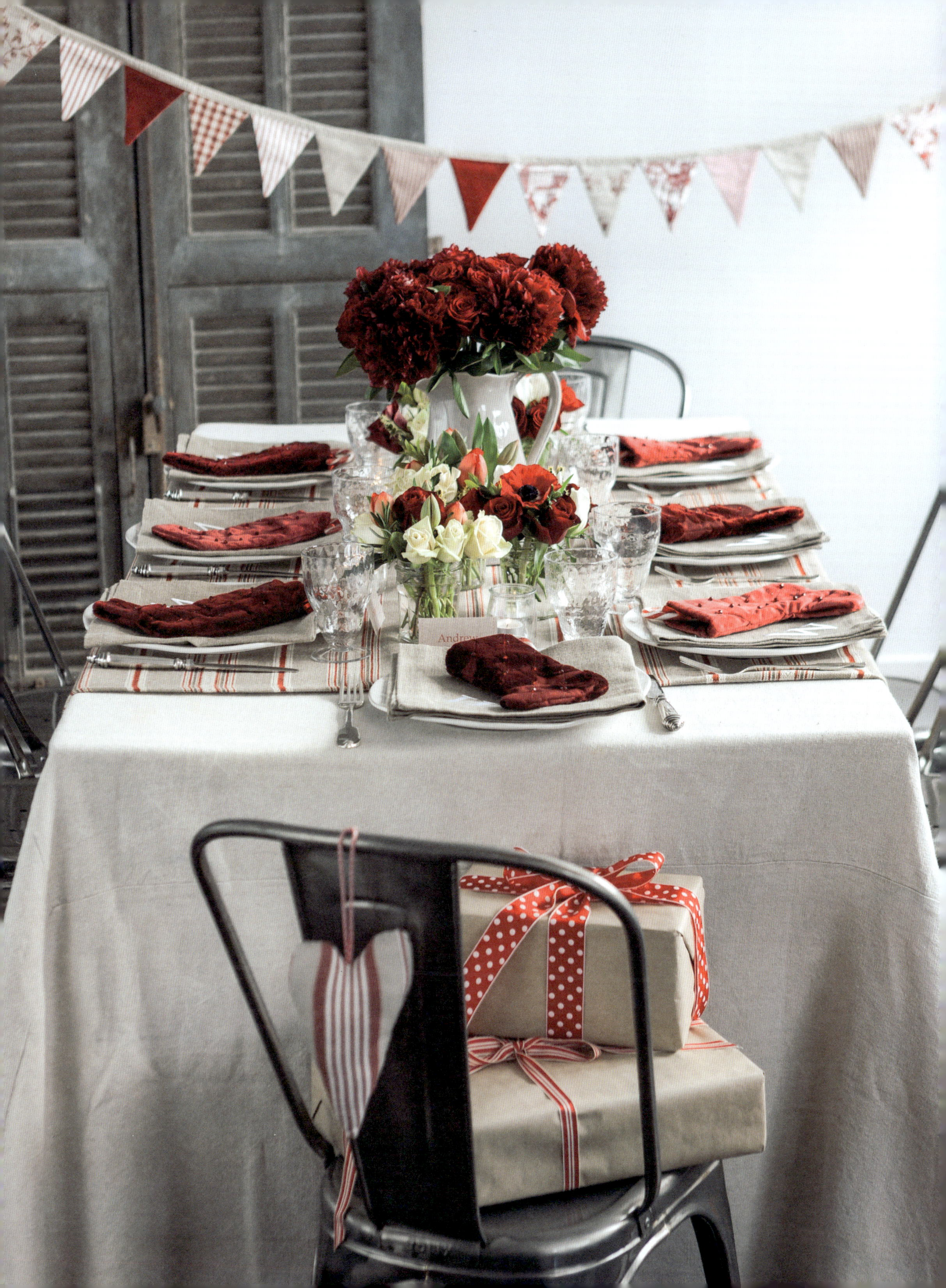

Christmas is a great time for expressing your creativity in many different ways; will your theme be modern, traditional, rustic or perhaps a combination?

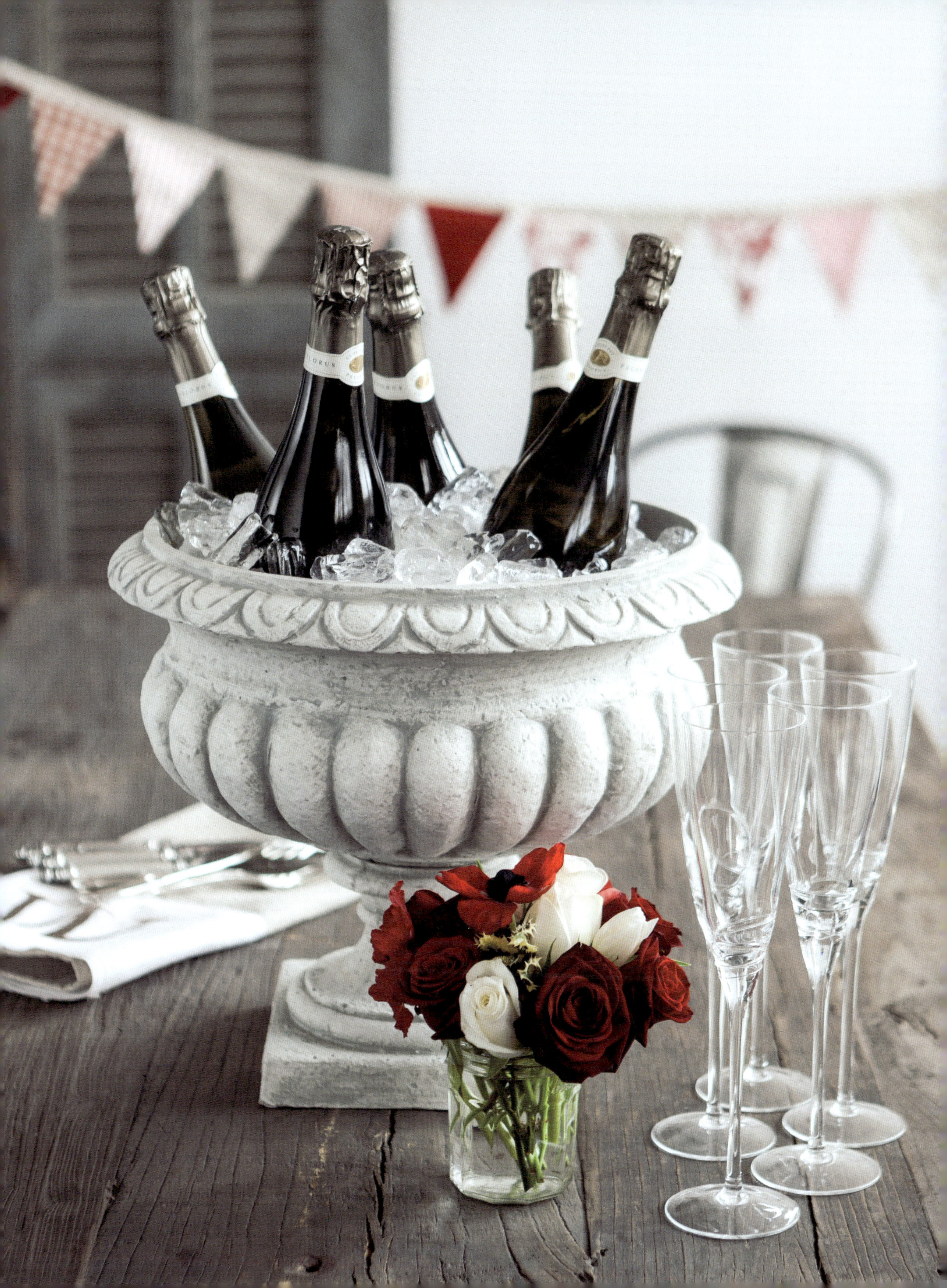
PELORUS

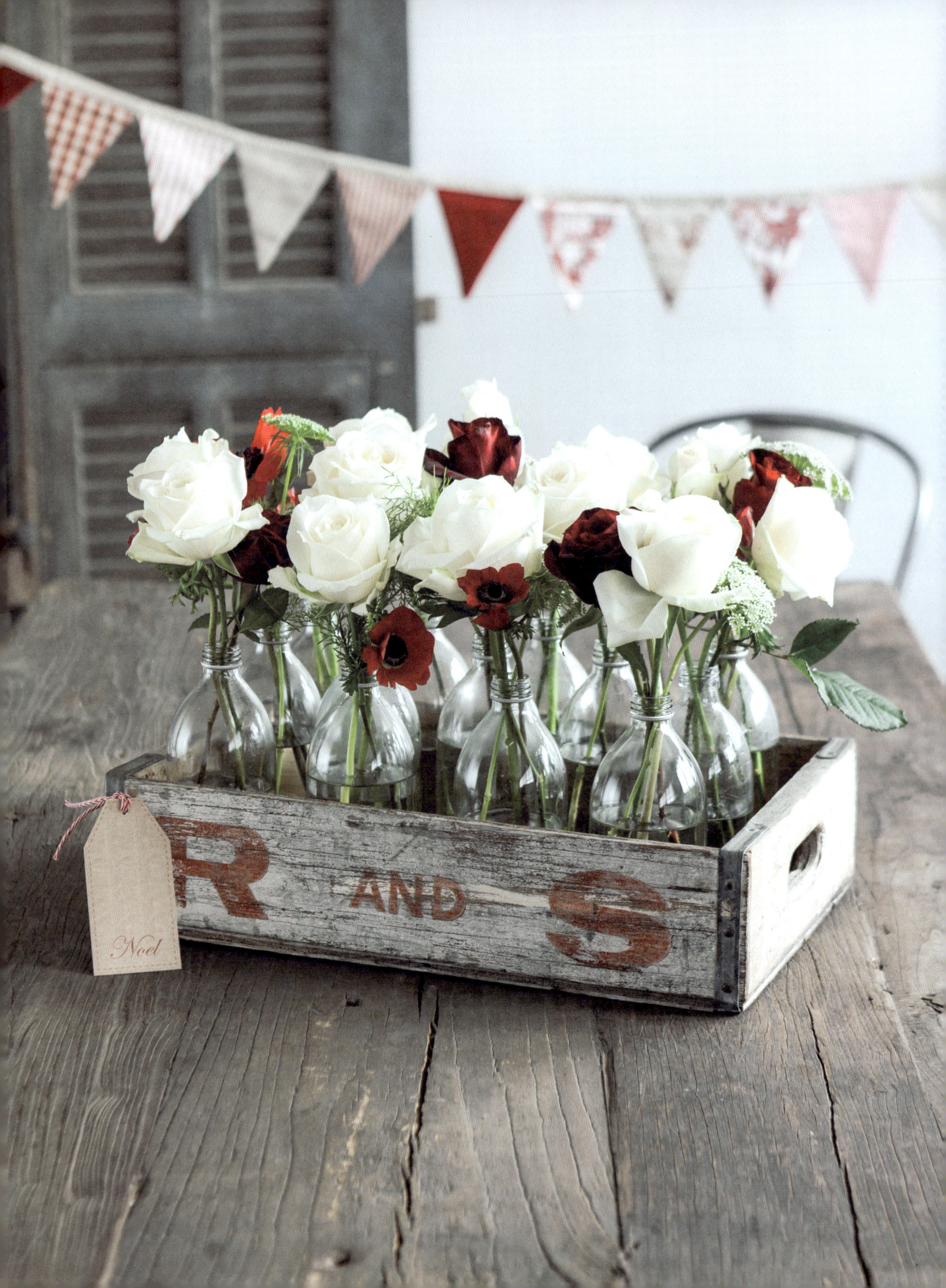
R AND S
Noel

Colours speak all languages.

Joseph Addison

Add colour and personality to your home during the festive season by using a variety of receptacles to hold your favourite blooms.

Be bold with red – it's a strong enough colour to mix in many different ways. Here red table accessories and assorted floral and check patterns stand out against a plain red background. The floral centrepiece includes lilies, stock, chrysanthemums, roses and bay leaves.

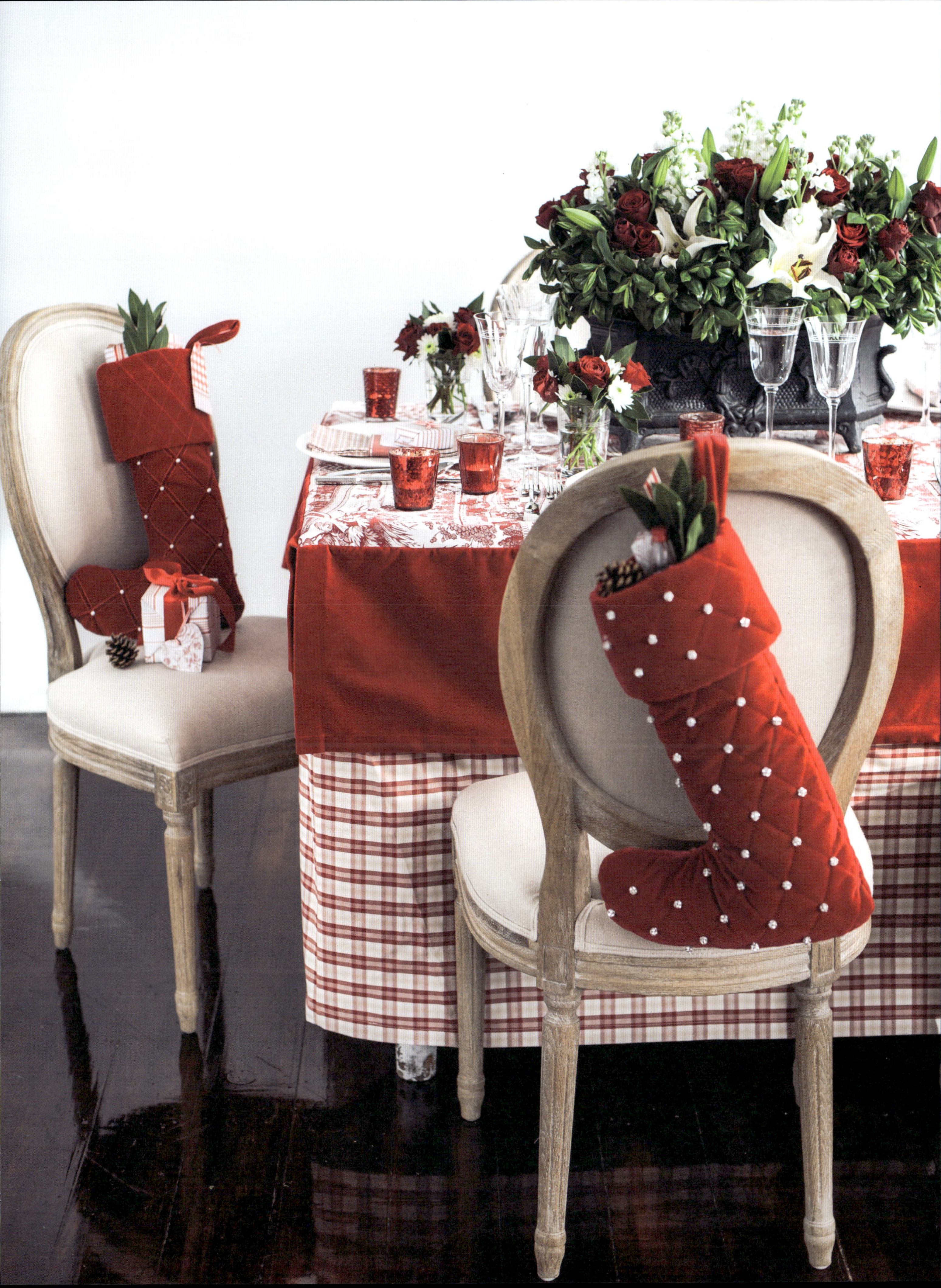

Serene arrangements of white roses (lower left) and a mass of deep-red roses as well as peonies (right) complement quiet corners.

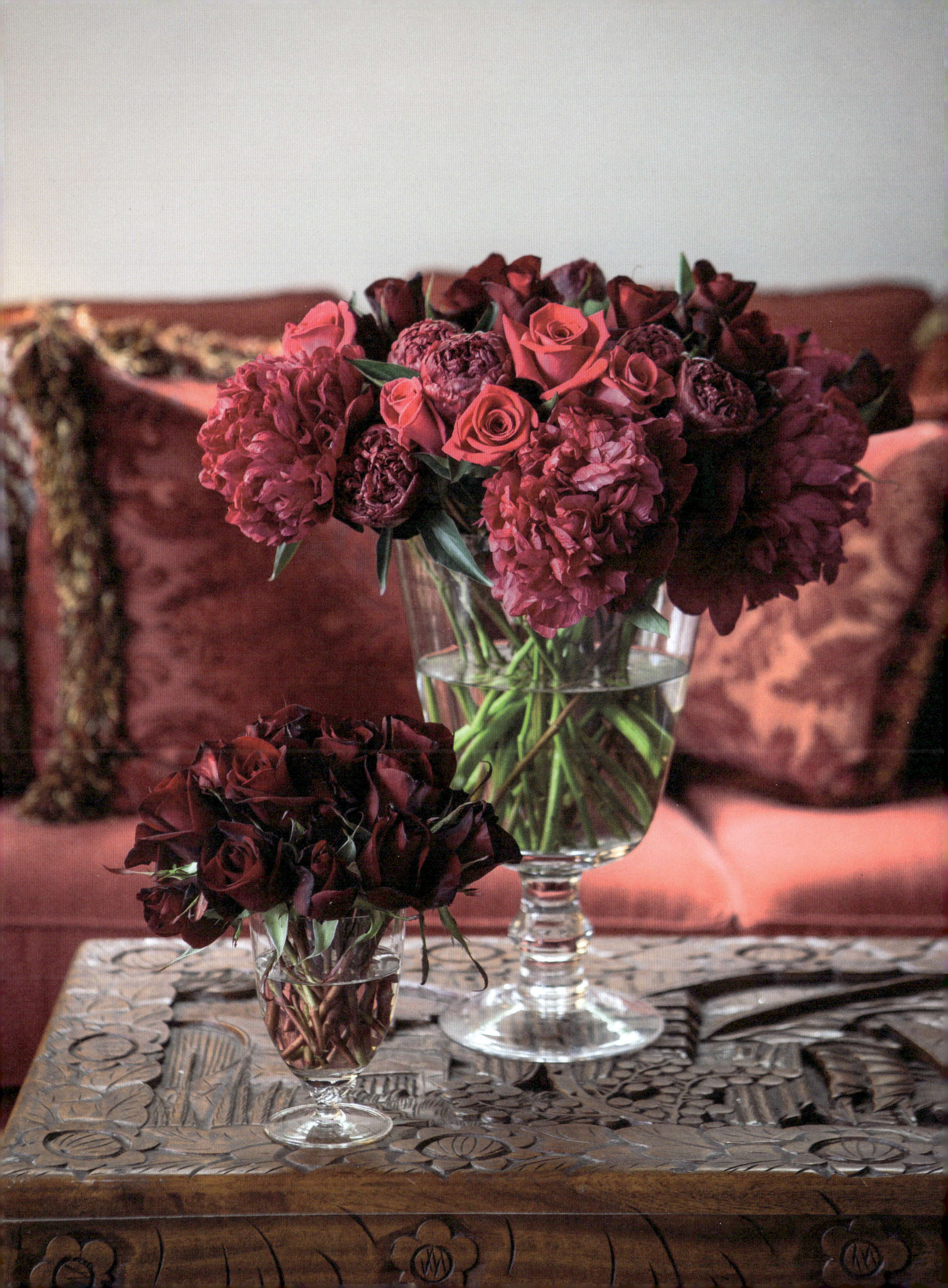

Plain paper wrapping looks especially effective when highlighted (above) by a soft ribbon topped with a seasonal spray. And a powdering of icing sugar drifted over these posies of freesias, roses, tulips and bay leaves creates an impression of the lightest of snowdrifts.

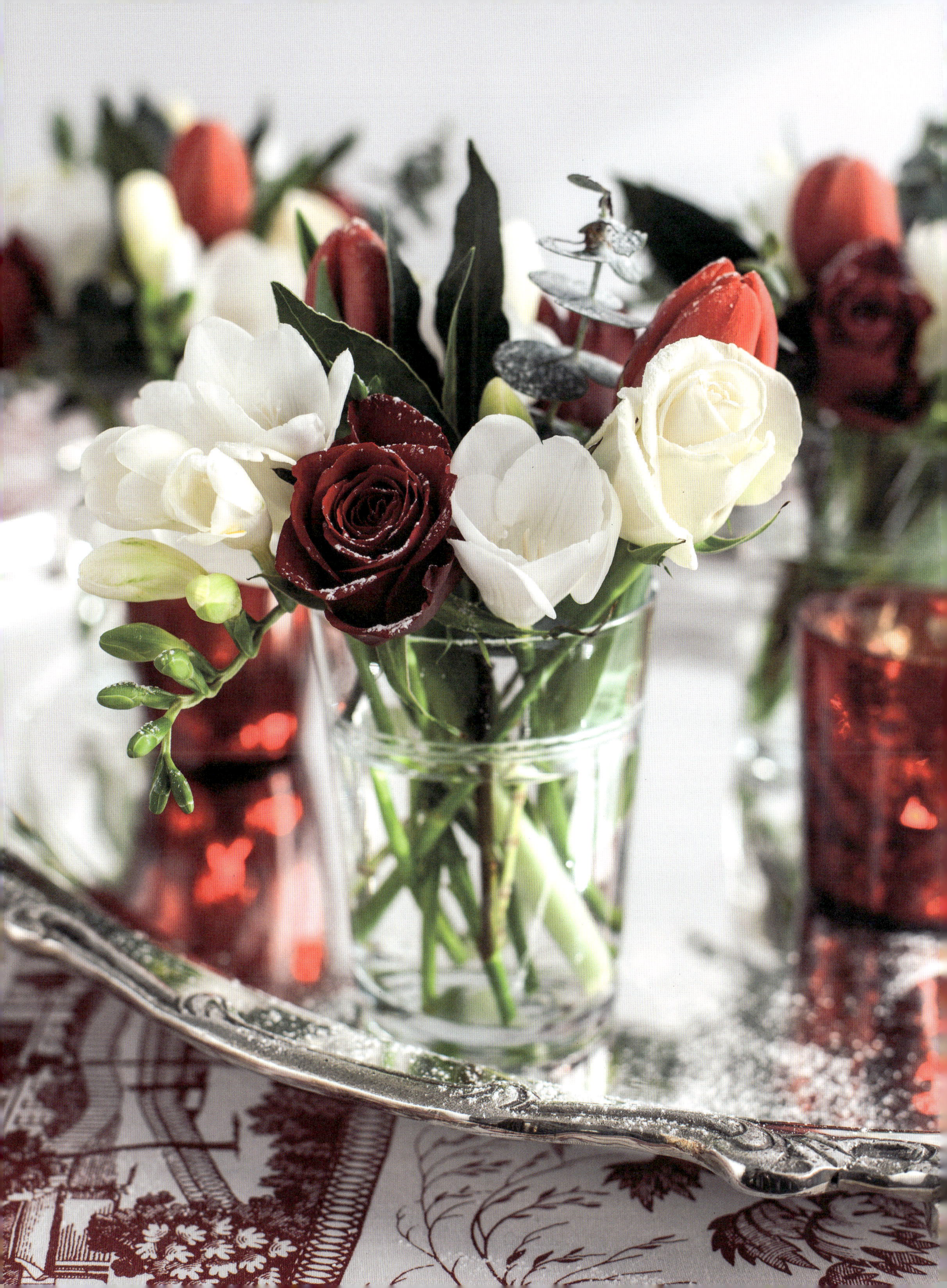

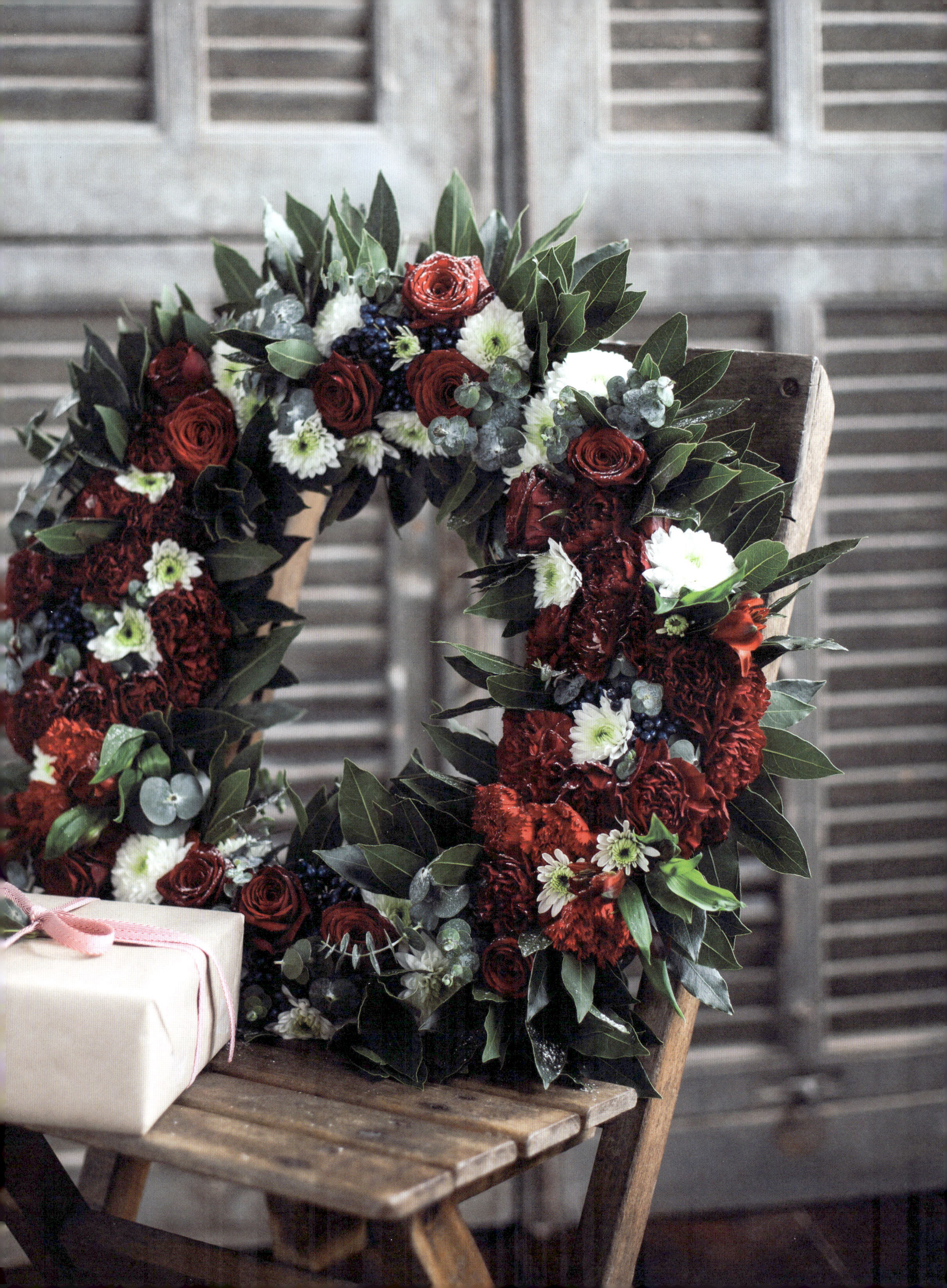

A festive wreath in traditional colours (left) made up of eucalyptus, roses, bay leaves, chrysanthemums and carnations will look good anywhere in your home.

Make family and friends feel extra special with these personalised Christmas crackers.

The actual flower is the plant's highest fulfilment, and are not here exclusively for herbaria, county floras and plant geography: they are here first of all for delight.

John Ruskin

Your house guests will thank you for adding these special co-ordinated fragrant floral touches to their room.

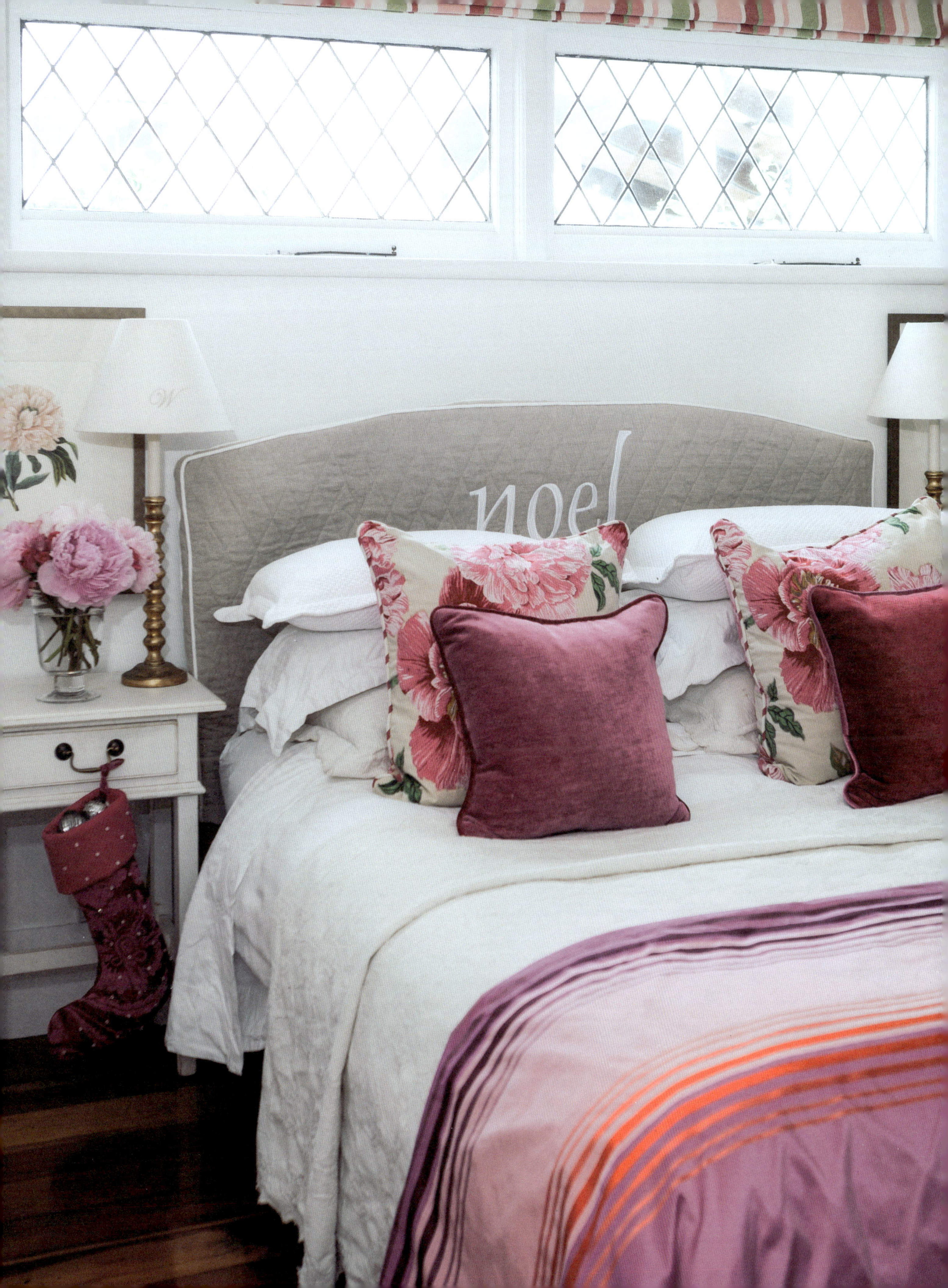
noel

With its long history reaching back to pagan times Easter is another time of year that lends itself to a colourful and celebratory décor, with or without special guests such as the rabbit and his small friends as seen here.

Use brightly coloured paper plates and other containers to make it an Easter that any children in the house will never forget. As for creating the decorative centrepieces, simply layer Oasis floral foam in trays, top with fresh wheat grass, then use your finger to drill holes through the layers in which you can then 'plant' cut tulips.

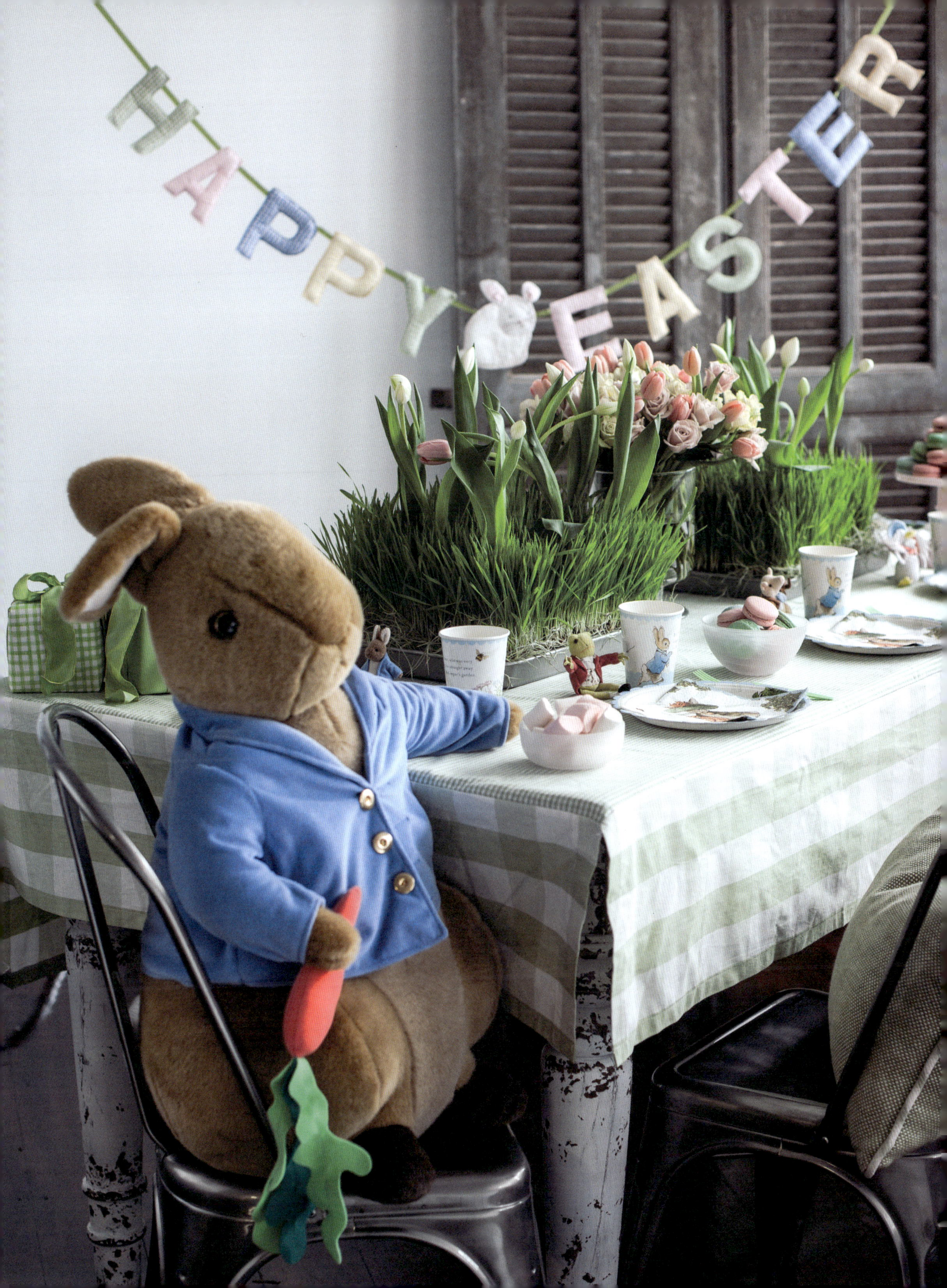
HAPPY EASTER

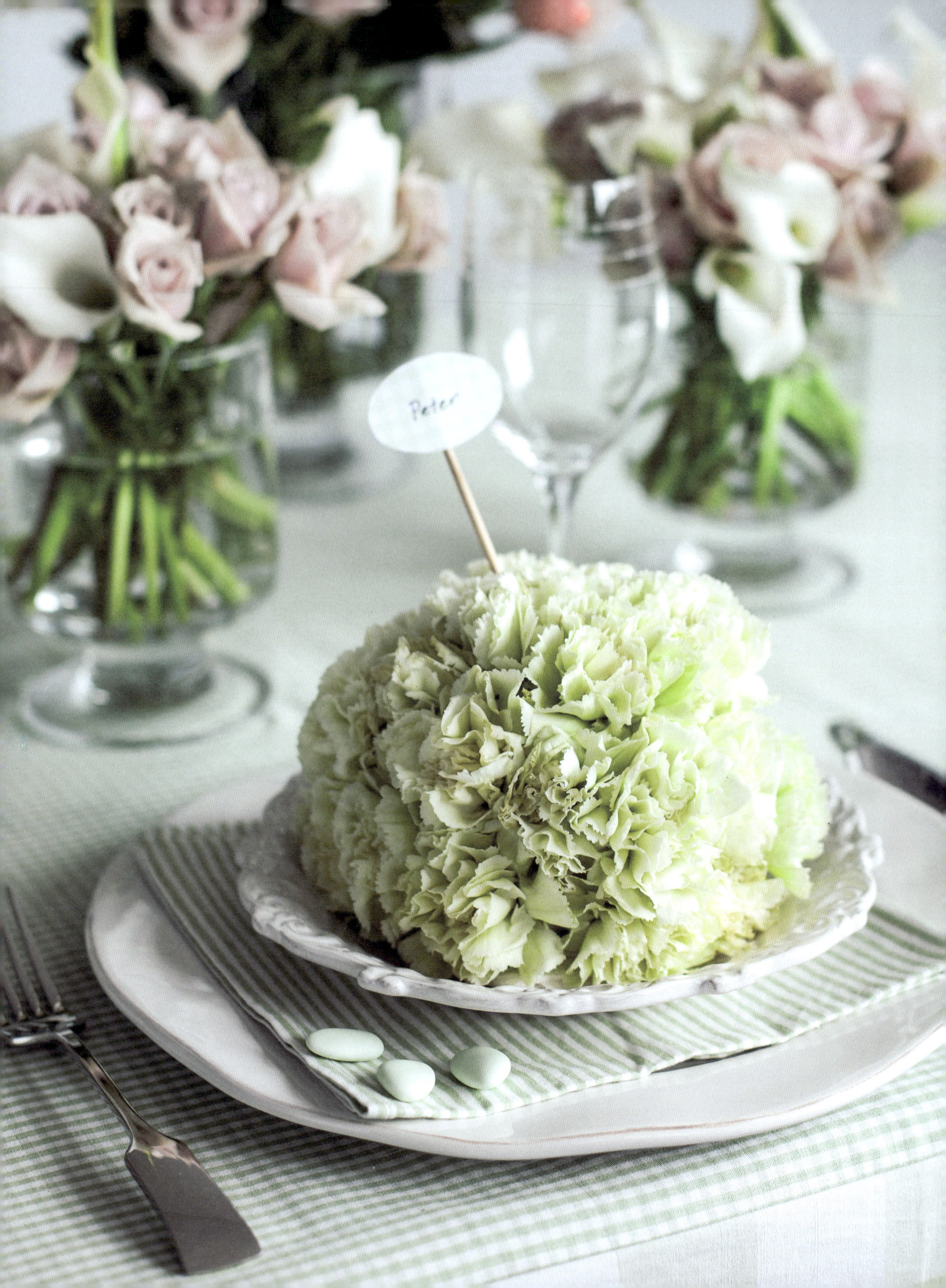
Peter

Although I've included this exquisite setting (left) featuring calla lilies, roses, tulips and carnations (the latter 'flowerball' effect was created using Oasis floral foam), as the basis for Easter décor, you could use it any time an occasion calls for a fresh look with delicate colours and textures.

Real eggshells star in this pretty garland (right). However, a light touch is required to blow each one before painting them and threading the fragile shells onto thin ribbon or twine and then adding dainty flowers such as erlicheer.

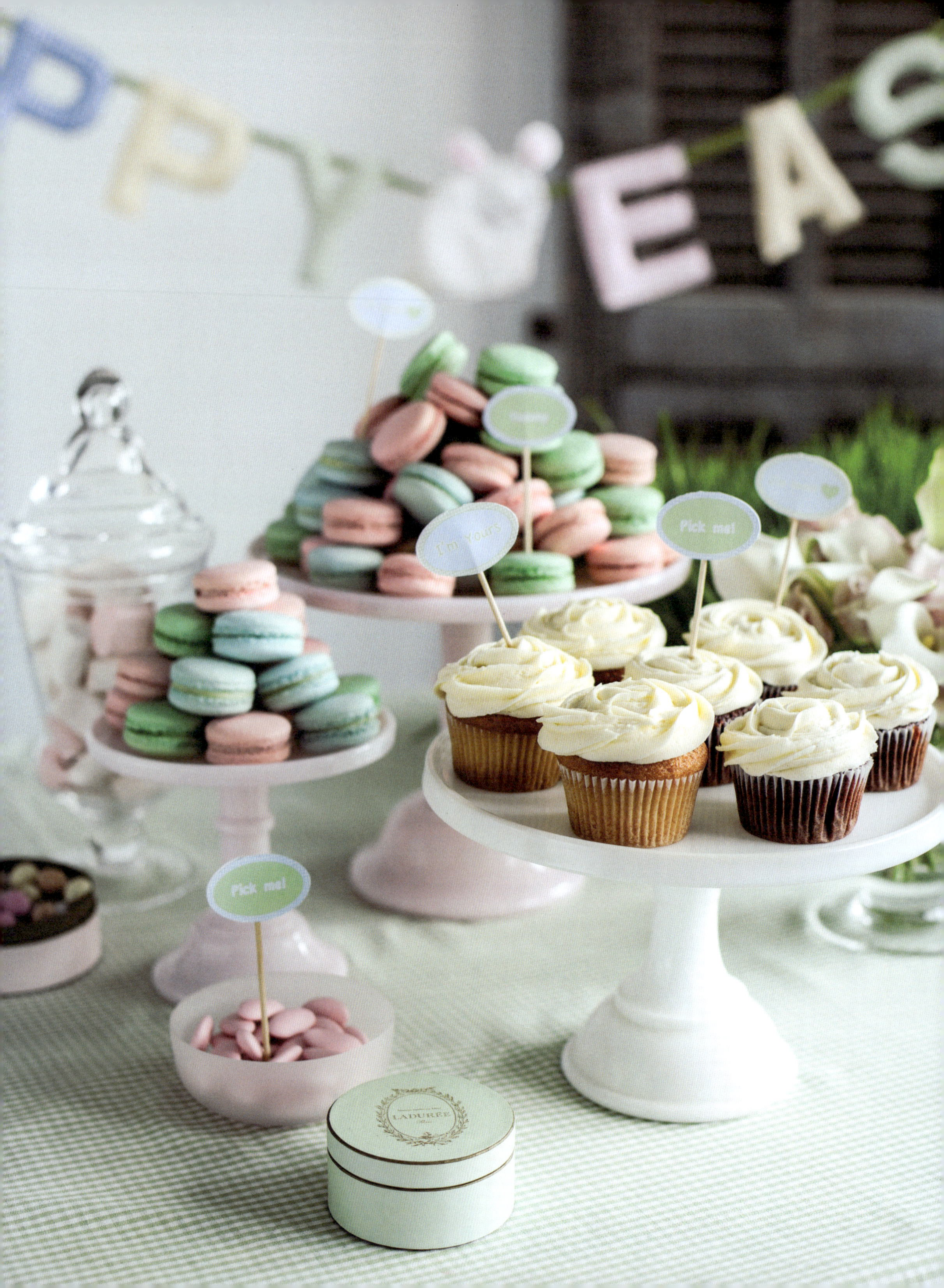

I'm Yours
Pick me!
Pick me!
LADURÉE

All these delicious edible treats – cupcakes and macarons – have been colour co-ordinated to match the Easter theme. The candy pink of the macarons sitting on the fresh green napkin (right) reflects the colours of the floral centrepieces. An arrangement of scented stock and chrysanthemums (top right) completes the setting.

CARING FOR FRESH CUT FLOWERS

Nothing makes a home look or feel more welcoming than a beautiful arrangement of fresh cut flowers. Here are a few tips to make sure your fresh flowers look lovelier and last longer.

- Buy your flowers from a reputable outlet and choose blooms with firm petals and buds that show a hint of colour to ensure the flowers will fully develop and open.

- Ensure the flowers are well wrapped for protection – and if they'll be out of water for a while, ask that the stems be wrapped with damp paper.

- Use thoroughly clean vases and containers – bacteria kills flowers.

- Use cut flower food – this contains the correct ingredients to feed the flowers properly, keeps bacteria at bay, encourages buds to open and lengthens the life of the flowers.

- Cut stems at an angle. This gives the stem a bigger area from which to draw water and prevents it from resting flat on the bottom of the vase and sealing itself.

- Don't smash the stems or use blunt scissors as this inhibits water uptake and causes bacteria to multiply more quickly and over a larger area. It also causes the flower undue stress, which will shorten its life.

- Use lukewarm water – there's less oxygen in it which helps prevent air bubbles in the stem that will block water uptake. Lukewarm water can also encourage some flowers to open up. The only exceptions are certain spring flowers such as daffodils and tulips, which prefer cold water.

- Don't place flowers in a draught as it will chill the flowers. Direct sunlight or over-warm central heating should also be avoided as this encourages bacteria to breed.

- Don't mix daffodils or narcissi with other cut flowers. When cut they emit latex from their stems, which shortens the life of other flowers. Arrange daffodils alone in vases or add special bulb cut flower food that makes them safe to mix with other flowers. You can also place them in a bucket of water for at least 12 hours on their own, and then arrange with other flowers, making sure you don't cut the stem again.

- Don't place arrangements near a bowl of fruit. Ripening fruit releases tiny amounts of ethylene gas, which prematurely ages flowers. Dying flowers do the same so always remove them from the vase.

- Top up the water and add fresh flower food in the right proportion every few days.

- Forget putting copper coins, lemonade, bleach or aspirin in the water. These popular tricks don't actually work nor do they feed your flowers adequately.

Instructions for making a floral ice bucket, and also flower swags using Oasis foam, along with templates for the labels, gift tags and related personalised stationery that appear throughout this book, can be downloaded at www.sandrakaminski.com

THANKS A BUNCH!

We are spoilt for choice in New Zealand with the wonderful variety and superb quality of fresh flowers available from our local florists and flower sellers. We take for granted that many varieties of our favourite blooms are available all year round and often arrive at the auctions and flower wholesalers within hours of being picked. There are hundreds of growers throughout the country who are committed to producing fresh flowers for our local and export market.

Thanks to their passion, expertise and commitment, together with New Zealand's perfect flower-growing climate, we have a bountiful supply of a wide range of beautiful fresh cut flowers available throughout the year.

The companies listed opposite provided fresh flowers and foliage for the arrangements in this book.

BOSCH FLOWERS
787 Waitakere Road,
Kumeu
AUCKLAND 0891
Tel 64 9 412 6282
uitdebosch@xtra.co.nz

B & P KAY
40 Maxted Road,
Drury
AUCKLAND 2579
Tel 64 27 276 2844
www.bokay.co.nz

EUREKA NURSERIES
148 Appleby Road RD1,
Drury
AUCKLAND 2577
Tel 64 21 438 735
eurqual@callplus.net.nz

KJ FLOWERS LTD
305 Fitzgerald Road RD1,
Drury
AUCKLAND 2577
Tel 64 27 270 4182
kjflowers@slingshot.co.nz

LILIES BY BLEWDEN
54 Pukerimu Lane RD3
CAMBRIDGE 3495
Tel 64 274 712 156
www.lilies.co.nz

NORANA LILIES
530 Oruarangi Road,
Mangere
AUCKLAND 2022
Tel 64 274 366 544
southernflora@xnet.co.nz

OAKMEADOWS
Karaka North Road, RD1,
Papakura
AUCKLAND 2580
Tel 64 21 994 269
oakmeadows@clear.net.nz

PRIMAVERA FLOWERS
51 Sommerville Road RD1,
Waiuku
AUCKLAND 2681
Tel 64 21 030 3629
mollie.obrien@hotmail.com

PUGH'S CLOVERLEA
FLOWERS
33 Cloverlea Road
PALMERSTON NORTH
4475
Tel 64 27 446 3870

RIVERLAND NURSERIES
38A Waimarie Road,
Whenuapai
AUCKLAND 0618
Tel 64 274 769 761
riverland@xnet.co.nz

SHIPHERD NURSERIES
Shipherd Road, RD3,
Pukekohe
AUCKLAND 2678
Tel 64 21 750 302
www.shipherdnurseries.co.nz

T & R ROBB
319 Parker Lane RD2,
Pukekohe
AUCKLAND 2677
Tel 64 9 239 0501
robbtcra@xtra.co.nz

VAN BERLO LIMITED
465 Fitzgerald Road RD1,
Drury
AUCKLAND 2577
Tel 64 274 952 114
berlo@xtra.co.nz

VAN LIER NURSERIES
241 Riverhead Road RD2,
Kumeu
AUCKLAND 0892
Tel 64 275 485 951
www.vanlier.co.nz

WILFLORA
20 Boness Road, RD9
PALMERSTON NORTH 4479
Tel 64 274 683 019
www.wilflora.com

SUPPLIERS

Please note that the following list of suppliers are mostly wholesalers, rather than retailers. However, they will be happy to advise where you can buy their products.

CC Interiors
www.ccinteriors.co.nz
Tel 64 9 5891950

French Country Collections
www.frenchcountrycollections.co.nz
Tel 64 9 376 6440

Icon Textiles
www.icontextiles.co.nz
Tel 64 9 302 1652

Le Forge
www.leforge.co.nz
Tel 64 9 815 5909

Martha's Furnishing Fabric
www.marthas.co.nz
Tel 64 9 523 3655

Mt Gabriel Christmas Trees
www.christmastrees.co.nz
Tel 64 9 294 6177

Old Mill Road
www.oldmillroad.co
Tel 64 9 360 0234

Potterybarn
www.potterybarn.com

Scarlet Ribbons
Tel 64 7 574 8446

The Remarkable Sweet Shop
www.remarkablesweetshop.co.nz
Tel 64 3 409 8656

ACKNOWLEDGEMENTS

The wonderful variety, quality and availability of fresh flowers is testament indeed to the skills of our local flower growers.

This book has been strongly supported by the team from the National Flower Promotion Group, who sourced and provided the best of each season's blooms grown by local flower growers. Thanks so much to them and United Flower Growers Limited for their generosity. NFPG's slogan is a simple statement, *Feel good with flowers* – I couldn't agree more!

Thank you to my publisher Renée Lang for her faith and determination. And special thanks to photographer Geoff Hedley for helping to create the most beautiful images I could ever hope for; you captured the dream I saw in my head. To publicist Deborah Delaney, I could not have done this without your ongoing belief in this book, your support and your sense of humour. To Trevor Newman, a wonderful, talented designer, thank you for all your patience, understanding and incredible attention to detail.

Many thanks to Liz Emtage; your sewing is stunning. And to pastry chef Emi Hosokawa, your macarons not only are a visual delight, they are even better to taste.

Thank you to my parents, Joan and Graeme Brown, for allowing their property to become a pumpkin farm so I could have all the varieties I needed for the autumn shoots, and allowing me to borrow their beautiful silver collection whenever I needed to enhance and embellish the flowers. Sadly, my mother passed away just as we completed this book, but I have only to look at the images here to recall all her love and support.

Lastly to my children, Zachary and Alexander, thank you for all the love and kisses . . .

First published in 2013 by Renaissance Publishing, Auckland
PO Box 56 716, Dominion Road, Auckland 1446,
New Zealand
www.renaissancepublishing.co.nz

1 3 5 7 9 10 8 6 4 2

Copyright in text: © 2013 Sandra Kaminski
Copyright in photogrphy: © 2013 Geoff Hedley
Copyright: © 2013 Renaissance Publishing

The right of Sandra Kaminski to be identified as the author of this work in terms of section 96 of the Copyright Act 1994 is hereby asserted.

ISBN: 978-0-9864521-7-8

A catalogue record for this book is available from the National Library of New Zealand

Design: Newman Design
www.trevornewman.co.nz

This book is copyright. Except for the purpose of fair reviewing, no part of this publication may be reproduced, stored in a retrieval system, or transmitted in any form or by any means, electronic, mechanical, photocopying, recording or otherwise, without the prior permission of the publishers and copyright holders. Infringers of copyright render themselves liable to prosecution.

Printed in China through Asia Pacific Offset Limited

I once had a rose named after me and I was very flattered. But I was not pleased to read the description in the catalogue: no good in a bed, but fine up against a wall

Eleanor Roosevelt

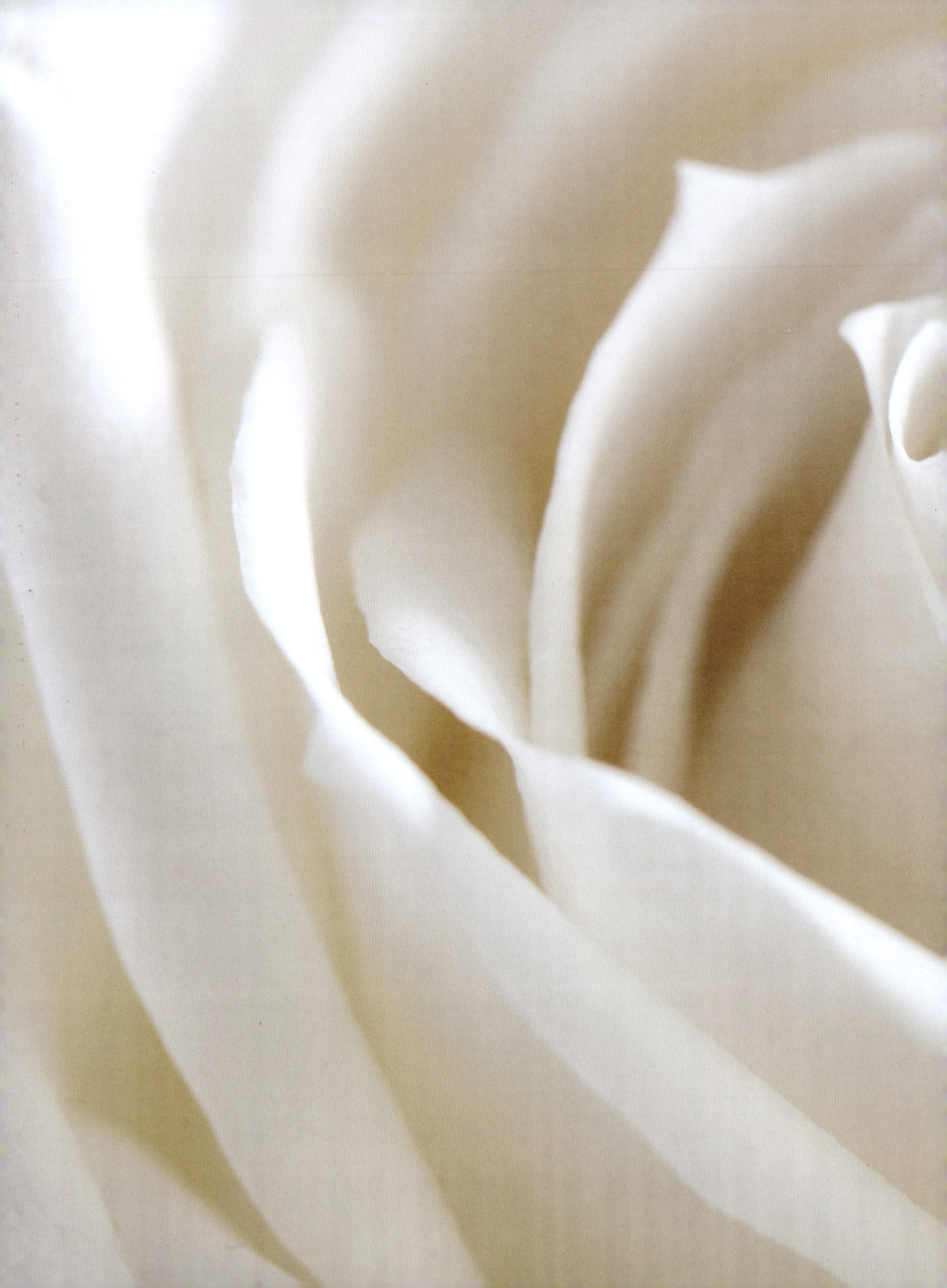